Among the Lilies

A COOKBOOK SEASONED WITH SPIRITUAL TRUTH

First Baptist Church of Atlanta World Missions Ministry

Women in Missions
Atlanta, Georgia

Among the Lilies
Women in Missions
First Baptist Church of Atlanta
754 Peachtree Street, NE
Atlanta, Georgia 30365

"Consider the lilies of the field..."
Matthew 6:28

First Printing   20,000 Copies   October 1992

Library of Congress Catalog Card Number 91-067281
ISBN 0-9631412-0-1

*Scripture quotations are from the New American Standard
Bible. © The Lockman Foundation, 1960, 1962, 1963, 1968,
1971, 1972, 1973, 1975, 1977.*

Printed in Mexico for
WIMMER BROTHERS
A Wimmer Company
Memphis • Dallas

TABLE OF CONTENTS

Among the Lilies

Every journey begins with a single step and the first step was taken for *Among the Lilies* when Julia Chamblee proposed that Women in Missions produce a cookbook.

THE COOKBOOK COMMITTEE

Sandy Hutchinson, Chairman

Leslie Brautigam

Julia Chamblee

Jeanette Morgan

Karen Rogeberg

FBA ADMINISTRATOR AND WORLD MISSIONS ADVISOR

George Morgan

CO-DIRECTORS OF WOMEN IN MISSIONS

Jeanette Morgan

Jere Leavell

PHOTOGRAPHY

Dr. Charles F. Stanley

Tim Olive

PHOTOGRAPHIC CONCEPT AND DESIGN

Tim Olive

INTRODUCTION

Among the Lilies, the title of our cookbook, originates from Scripture. As we read the Word, it appears that of all the flowers created by God, the lily was most favored.

Lilies are intriguing not only for their magnificent appearance, but also for how uniquely they are formed. Each flower has an underground bulb that stores nourishment and supplies the plant with food even through severe dry seasons. Amazingly, lilies reproduce themselves, multiplying and increasing in number. Being perennial, they live for many years bringing beauty and fragrance to the world around them. The cherished quality admired by the Lord as evidenced in the lily was that of total rest. The lilies of the field rested fully in the splendor provided for them. Interestingly, these are inherent qualities of the church.

In both the Old and New Testaments, lilies hold special places of high esteem representing loveliness and spiritual truth. In the Old Testament, their fragrance enhanced Solomon's garden. Among the thorn-covered flowers, the lily nestled and yet its beauty outshone them all. God's promise to Israel, if she were to return to Him, was that she would blossom like a lily. (Hosea 14:5)

Jesus used the unique beauty of the lily to illustrate the importance of resting in Him. The Lord pointed to the lilies and said, "…observe how the lilies of the field grow, they do not toil nor do they spin." (Matthew 6:28) In Philippians 4:6 the Lord told us not to be anxious for anything. The lily rested completely in the Creator's provision; so should we.

As you use this cookbook, it is our prayer that the photographs and scripture will remind you to experience the reality of this wonderful promise—as we rest in Him, He supplies our needs. May each promise nourish your spirit as the words of Jesus encouraged those hungering as He walked among the lilies.

"And Jesus said unto them, I am the Bread of Life; he that cometh to me shall never hunger, and he that believeth on me shall never thirst." (John 6:33-35)

It is our heartfelt desire that those of you reading this cookbook have already tasted of the Bread of Life and know the joy of never being spiritually hungry or thirsty.

If you are indeed hungry and thirsty, we invite you to enter into the fulfillment of the promise.

PURPOSE

When you do your daily tasks, do you have God's ultimate vision and purpose on your heart? The ladies at First Baptist Atlanta (FBA) certainly do. As *Among the Lilies* has been created, its purpose has been much larger than merely adding variety to our menus. These ladies have carefully designed this cookbook to be used to reach the world for Jesus Christ!

Among the Lilies has been developed for financing world missions. All proceeds will be used to support the Faith Promise missions program at FBA. Faith Promise missions was founded at FBA in 1980 with a small budget and one supported missionary. God has truly blessed our church's commitment to world evangelization over the years. We have seen tremendous growth in our church locally, and we have seen our missionary force expanded as well. Currently we are supporting over 100 missionary families in 35 different countries. Faith Promise resources make it possible for FBA to put its loving arms around people all over the globe.

You can make a greater impact in the world for Christ by asking God to stretch your vision to match His and asking Him to show you how to develop your routine activities into earth changing activities. Perhaps each time you use one of these recipes you could pray for a missionary or an unreached people group. See how simple it is to change a daily activity into an eternally impacting event!

You thought you were only buying a cookbook; instead God is using you through this purchase to reach Hindus in India and Muslims in Jordan. It is our prayer at FBA that you, through your activities, will become a light enabling others to see Christ. I hope *Among the Lilies* will be a blessing to you and your family. Remember that we are blessed to be a blessing.

Minister of World Missions,

Larry Ragan

FOREWORD

The beauty of the photographs, the wisdom of the scriptures, and the nourishment of the recipes make *Among the Lilies* more than a cookbook. It is a treasure to enrich one's life, a tool to expand one's culinary skills, and a gift to share with friends.

This book is the fulfillment of a vision, a labor of love, and the product of many months of diligent searching, cooking, testing, and I am sure "tasting" the favorite recipes of hundreds which were received from interested contributors.

Among the Lilies represents a generous investment of time on the part of the committee to produce such a beautiful and practical tool for the homemaker. I want to personally express my appreciation to these women for their disciplined determination to hold up their standard of excellence. This cookbook will be a delightful addition to any woman's kitchen.

Charles F. Stanley

WHAT MAN IS THERE AMONG YOU,

WHEN HIS SON SHALL ASK HIM

FOR A LOAF, WILL GIVE HIM A STONE?...

HOW MUCH MORE SHALL YOUR FATHER WHO

IS IN HEAVEN GIVE WHAT IS GOOD

TO THOSE WHO ASK HIM!!

Matt. 7:9 & 7:11

Passion Play Finale

Chocolate Mint Mousse Cake

Fresh Coconut Cake with
Lemon-Orange Filling

Fresh Fruit Tart

Praline Pecan Cheesecake

Raspberry Bombe

Heavenly Trifle

Nancy's Pound Cake

Lemon Tassies

Salted Nuts

Party Punch

Coffee

Since the original performance of the Atlanta Passion Play in 1977, the number of people attending has grown to more than 38,000 per year, including visitors from as far away as California. It is the highlight of the Easter season for members of First Baptist Church Atlanta and the many who come annually from neighboring states. The perfect ending to this event is the gathering together of friends to celebrate our Lord's resurrection.

Spring Bridal Luncheon

Hot Chicken Salad

Raspberry Romaine

Dijon Carrots

Zucchini Muffins with
Molded Strawberry Butter

Pineapple Mint Sherbet

Chocolate-Tipped Butter Cookies

Fruited Iced Tea

The Spring Bridal Luncheon is filled with gaiety and excitement as special friends and family share in the joy and gladness of a new beginning. Honor the bride-to-be with this elegant ladies' luncheon.

Christmas Dinner Party

Hot Spiced Tea

Breast of Turkey Supreme

Grilled Pork Tenderloin

Rice Dressing

Green Vegetables with Herb Butter

Cranberry Salad Ring

Savory Stuffed Onions

Heavenly Yeast Rolls

Pumpkin Cheesecake

Experience the true spirit of Christmas, honoring God's gift to the world, Jesus Christ, the Messiah. We invite you to enjoy all the blessings of this holiday season with the better than ever Christmas dinner.

Fourth of July Block Party

Gazpacho

Deep Fried Turkey

Potato Salad

Broccoli-Bacon Salad

Apple Curried Beans

Perky Pickles

Herb Bread

Mustard Mousse

Assorted Fresh Fruit Tray

Raspberry Swirl Cookies

Buttermilk Pecan Pie

Keeping in touch with our friends and neighbors throughout the community is becoming more difficult in our fast paced life. A special occasion such as a Fourth of July Block Party affords us the opportunity to come together socially, as well as lending importance to the privilege of walking in freedom in America.

Holiday Brunch

Grapefruit Ice

Cheese Blintz Casserole

Kiwi Strawberry Salad

Bacon Wrapped Water Chestnuts

Liza's Biscuits

with Country Ham

Balsamic Green Beans

Cranberry Apple Bake with Almond
Flavored Whipped Cream

Orange Blossom Punch

Enjoy time-out with good friends during the holidays for a mid-morning brunch. This festive menu will add zest to your holiday celebration.

Get Acquainted Coffee

Hot Ham and Cheese Party Sandwiches

Cheesy Date Pastries

Strawberries Dipped in White or Dark
Chocolate

Spiced Pecans

Puff Pastry with Chicken Salad

Almond Skillet Cake

White Chocolate Cake

Coffee Bar with Assorted Toppings

Host a get acquainted coffee to welcome new neighbors. This time-honored tradition will introduce them into the community and encourage new friendships.

International Soup & Salad Luncheon

MANDARIN SALAD

ROMAN EGG AND SPINACH SOUP

PARAGUAYAN CORNBREAD

PAPER BAG APPLE PIE WITH
PRALINE SAUCE

VANILLA ICE CREAM

*Gracious living is enhanced by international friendships
and cuisine, adding new flavors and interests to menus.
New friendships inspire and delight our hearts.*

Siesta Fiesta

CHICKEN FAJITAS

STEAK FAJITAS

SEASONED TACO MEAT

FLOUR TORTILLAS

TACO SHELLS

SHREDDED LETTUCE AND CHEESE

SLICED BLACK OLIVES AND JALAPEÑO PEPPERS

REFRIED BEANS

CHOPPED SPRING ONIONS AND TOMATOES

SOUR CREAM

EASY GUACAMOLE

ICE CREAM SUNDAE BAR

*Gatherings for young people provide opportunities for
relief from the daily pressures of school and work, as well as
an occasion to develop friendships. Siesta Fiesta is designed
to allow each guest the freedom to create an original entree
and, at the same time, offers effortless social interaction.*

Men's Retreat Feast

SPINACH DIP IN PUMPERNICKEL BREAD

MEXICAN ROLL-UPS WITH SALSA

ICEBERG LETTUCE WEDGES WITH FAVORITE
DRESSING

BARBECUE BRISKET

BLEU CHEESE AND WALNUT GREEN BEANS

POTATOES PARMESAN

SOUR DOUGH ROLLS

SOUTH GEORGIA PEACH ICE CREAM

MISSISSIPPI MUD CAKE

$250 COOKIES

Men's retreats usually include sporting events which generate hearty appetites. This feast promises to satisfy the golfer, tennis player, or the armchair quarterback.

Seafood Medley

WHITE GRAPE SPARKLE

CRABMEAT MOUSSE WITH
ASSORTED CRACKERS

SWEET AND SOUR SLAW

GRILLED SALMON TERIYAKI

PASTA WITH SHELLFISH

VEGETABLE JUBILEE

BLACK BEANS AND RICE

CHEESE DILL DROP BISCUITS

FRESH ORANGE SECTIONS WITH GOLDEN
FRUIT SAUCE

Make way for the catch of the day! Savor the gifts of the sea feasting on a bountiful buffet. The seafood medley is sure to please.

Evening with Friends

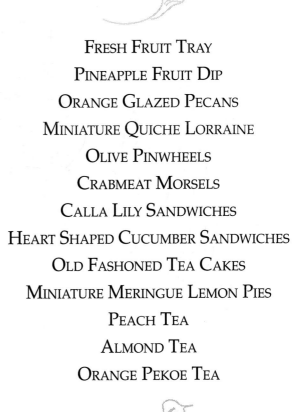

Hot Tomato Cocktail

Pickled Shrimp

Bleu Cheese Apple Salad

Eye of Round Roast

Creamy Stuffed Potatoes

Marinated Bean Bundles

Party Bread

Sugar Plum Cake with Hard Sauce

Take time to relax and enjoy your evening. Few things are more refreshing than fellowship with good friends. A warm casual atmosphere provides the perfect setting for this intimate dinner.

Fun and Fancy Tea

Fresh Fruit Tray

Pineapple Fruit Dip

Orange Glazed Pecans

Miniature Quiche Lorraine

Olive Pinwheels

Crabmeat Morsels

Calla Lily Sandwiches

Heart Shaped Cucumber Sandwiches

Old Fashoned Tea Cakes

Miniature Meringue Lemon Pies

Peach Tea

Almond Tea

Orange Pekoe Tea

It has become a much anticipated tradition for the ladies in the Love Sunday School Class to have high tea at midnight on their annual retreat. Dressed in their pajamas, the ladies don their fancy hats, fox tail stoles and dainty gloves. Carrying their favorite tea cups, they gather around the silver tea set to have proper tea at midnight.

OOK AT THE BIRDS OF THE AIR,

THAT THEY DO NOT SOW, NEITHER

DO THEY REAP, NOR GATHER INTO BARNS,

AND YET YOUR HEAVENLY FATHER FEEDS

THEM. ARE YOU NOT WORTH MUCH MORE

THAN THEY?

Matt. 6:26

Bacon-Wrapped Water Chestnuts

1	(16 ounce) package bacon
3	(8 ounce) cans whole water chestnuts, drained
	Soy sauce

Cut bacon slices in thirds. Wrap a slice around each chestnut and secure with wooden pick. Place in single layer in 13x9x2-inch baking dish. Sprinkle liberally with soy sauce. Chill in refrigerator for up to 1 hour. Bake, uncovered, at 350 degrees for 40 minutes. Drain on paper towel and remove picks before serving. Serve warm.

Yield: 4 dozen

Chicken-Bacon Nuggets

4	chicken breast halves
¼	cup orange marmalade
2	tablespoons soy sauce
½	teaspoon salt
½	teaspoon ginger
⅛	teaspoon garlic powder
½	(16 ounce) package sliced bacon

Remove skin and bone from chicken. Cut into bite-sized pieces and place in shallow pan. Combine marmalade, soy sauce and seasonings. Pour over chicken pieces to marinate. Broil bacon slices until partially cooked but not crisp. Cut each slice in half. Wrap a bacon slice around each piece of chicken and secure with wooden pick. Broil for 5 minutes or until chicken is tender, turning nuggets once and brushing with remaining marinade. Remove picks before serving.

Yield: 2 dozen

Oriental Chicken Wings

20 to 25	chicken wings
	Vegetable oil
1	cup soy sauce
1	cup firmly-packed brown sugar

Blot wings with paper towel to absorb excess moisture. Simmer wings in oil in large skillet over low heat until golden brown and tender. Drain to remove excess grease. Combine soy sauce and brown sugar; pour over wings. Simmer for 15 to 20 minutes or until chicken is caramelized. Serve as appetizers or with sauce over rice for entree.

Yield: 20 to 25

Swedish Meatballs

1	pound ground beef
1	cup breadcrumbs
1½	teaspoons salt
¼	teaspoon nutmeg
3	tablespoons grated onion
1	(5 ounce) can evaporated milk
1	(5 ounce) can water
1	egg
	Vegetable oil
1	(12 ounce) can chili sauce
1	(10 ounce) jar grape jelly
	Juice of ½ lemon

Combine beef, breadcrumbs, seasonings, onion, milk, water and egg. Mix thoroughly and shape into 1-inch balls. Sauté meatballs in hot oil until browned. Combine chili sauce, jelly and lemon juice; add to meatballs and simmer for 20 to 30 minutes. Serve hot.

Yield: 2 dozen

HAM-ALMOND PINWHEELS

1	(8 ounce) package cream cheese, softened
3	tablespoons finely chopped almonds
2	tablespoons mayonnaise
1	teaspoon Worcestershire sauce
½	teaspoon mustard
¼	teaspoon paprika
	Dash of salt
4	thin slices boiled ham
4	dozen round buttery crackers

Beat cream cheese until smooth. Stir in almonds, mayonnaise, Worcestershire sauce, mustard, paprika and salt; mix thoroughly. Spread mixture evenly on ham slices and roll up, jelly roll fashion. Chill overnight. Cut each roll into 12 slices and place each on a cracker to serve.

Yield: 4 dozen

OLIVE PINWHEELS

1	(8 ounce) package cream cheese, softened
½	teaspoon onion salt
	Milk
14	slices fresh white bread
1	(3 ounce) package smoked sliced beef
1	(7 ounce) jar pimiento-stuffed green olives

Combine cream cheese and onion salt; add milk, a small amount at a time, until consistency to spread. Trim crusts from bread slices. Place 2 slices side by side; moisten adjacent edges with small amount of water on fingertips and press to form a rectangle. Repeat with remaining bread to form 7 pieces. Using rolling pin, roll bread rectangles to flatten and lengthen; do not increase width. Spread 1 side of each bread piece with thin layer of cream cheese mixture. Cover with 2 slices beef, pressing lightly to stick to cheese spread. Turn bread over and spread with cheese; do not add beef slices. Along 1 short edge, place olives end to end, just touching. Roll tightly, jelly roll fashion. Place on plastic wrap and roll to enclose securely. Chill for at least 4 hours. Cut each roll into ¼-inch slices.

Pinwheels may be prepared 2 to 3 days in advance and stored in refrigerator before slicing and serving.

Yield: 8 dozen

HAM AND CHEESE PARTY SANDWICHES

1	cup butter or margarine, softened
3	tablespoons prepared mustard
3	tablespoons poppy seed
1	teaspoon Worcestershire sauce
1	medium-sized onion, minced (optional)
1	pound boneless cooked ham, minced
1	(12 ounce) package Swiss cheese, grated
5	dozen small party rolls

Preheat oven to 400 degrees. Combine butter and seasonings, blending thoroughly. Add onion, ham and cheese; mix well. Slice each roll in half lengthwise. Spread ham mixture on lower half of each roll, cover with upper half of roll and press edges to seal. Bake, covered with aluminum foil, for 10 to 15 minutes.

Sandwiches may be assembled and frozen. Let stand, covered with plastic wrap, at room temperature to thaw before baking.

Yield: 5 dozen

CALLA LILY SANDWICHES

1	(2 ounce) package slivered almonds
2 to 3	drops yellow food coloring
54	slices fresh white sandwich bread
1	(8 ounce) package cream cheese, softened
2	tablespoons orange marmalade

Combine almonds and food coloring in a jar, cover with lid and shake vigorously until almonds are evenly tinted. Using rolling pin, roll each bread slice to ⅛-inch thickness. Using 2½-inch biscuit cutter, cut circles from bread slices. Combine cheese and marmalade, mixing until smooth. Spread about 1 teaspoon cheese mixture on each bread round. Pinch edges of portion of circle together to form a calla lily shape. Press an almond into the pinched portion to represent a flower stamen.

Yield: 4½ dozen

CUCUMBER SANDWICHES

1	tablespoon Worcestershire sauce
2	tablespoons minced fresh dill
1	drop hot pepper sauce
5	tablespoons lemon juice
2	scallions, minced
1	small clove garlic, minced
⅛	teaspoon salt
1	(8 ounce) package cream cheese, softened
24	slices fresh white bread
3 or 4	cucumbers, unpared and thinly sliced
1	bunch dill for garnish

Combine Worcestershire sauce, dill, hot pepper sauce, lemon juice, scallions, garlic and salt in food processor bowl. Add cream cheese in small chunks, processing until blended. Chill for 20 minutes or until spreading consistency. Cut bread into shapes (use canapé cutters or cut with knife into triangles). Spread each with thin layer of seasoned cream cheese, top with cucumber slice and garnish with dill sprig.

Yield: 4 to 6 dozen

VEGGIE BARS

2	(8 ounce) packages refrigerated crescent rolls
1	egg, beaten
2	(8 ounce) packages cream cheese, softened
1	cup mayonnaise
1	envelope ranch salad dressing mix
6	slices bacon, cooked and crumbled
½ to ⅔	cup chopped broccoli
½ to ⅔	cup chopped cauliflower
½ to ⅔	cup sliced mushrooms
½ to ⅔	cup diced green pepper
½ to ⅔	cup diced tomatoes
½ to ⅔	cup sliced carrots
½ to ⅔	cup diced celery
¾	cup (3 ounces) shredded Cheddar cheese

Preheat oven according to roll package directions. Unroll dough without separating into triangles and place in 15x10x1-inch jelly roll pan, lightly pressing seams and perforations together. Brush egg on dough. Bake according to package directions. Set aside to cool. Blend cream cheese, mayonnaise and salad dressing mix. Spread cheese mixture on crust. Sprinkle bacon, vegetables and Cheddar cheese on cream cheese layer. Chill for at least 2 hours. Cut into bars.

Yield: 4 dozen

MEXICAN ROLLUPS

1 (8 ounce) package cream cheese, softened
1 (4 ounce) can mild green chilies
⅛ teaspoon garlic powder
10 large flour tortillas

The day before serving, combine cream cheese, chilies and garlic powder in food processor container; process until smooth. Thinly spread mixture on each tortilla. Roll up each tortilla and wrap individually in plastic wrap or store together in air-tight container. Chill overnight. Cut each roll into 4 slices. Serve with medium salsa.

If mild chilies are used, serve with medium salsa; if medium hot chilies are used, serve with mild salsa.

Yield: 3¼ dozen

CRABMEAT MORSELS

1 (8 ounce) jar pasteurized process cheese spread
1 (6½ ounce) can flaked crabmeat, drained
Dash of garlic powder
¼ cup butter, softened
1½ tablespoons mayonnaise
6 English muffins, split

Preheat oven to 400 degrees. Combine cheese spread, crabmeat, garlic powder, butter and mayonnaise; mix thoroughly. Spread mixture evenly on muffin halves. Cut each half into quarters and place on baking sheet. Bake for 5 to 8 minutes or until lightly browned.

Morsels may be assembled in advance and frozen. Place frozen pieces on baking sheet and bake for 10 minutes.

Yield: 2 dozen

CRAB STUFFED SNOW PEAS

½ pound fresh snow peas, washed and trimmed
Salt
2 (6 ounce) packages frozen crabmeat, thawed and well drained
2 hard cooked eggs, finely chopped
¼ cup mayonnaise
1 tablespoon lemon juice
1 teaspoon capers
3 tablespoons minced celery
3 dashes hot pepper sauce

Split snow peas along upper edge. Blanch in lightly salted boiling water for 10 seconds, submerge in cold water, remove and drain. Let stand to cool. Chill, covered, up to 24 hours. Combine crab, eggs, mayonnaise, lemon juice, capers, celery and hot pepper sauce; mix gently to avoid breaking up crab chunks. Spoon rounded teaspoon of filling into each snow pea. Chill up to 6 hours.

Yield: 5 to 6 dozen

CHEESY DATE PASTRIES

2	cups (8 ounces) grated sharp Cheddar cheese
½	cup butter
1¼	cups all-purpose flour
1	teaspoon salt
	Dash of red pepper
1	(8 ounce) package dates, chopped
½	cup firmly-packed brown sugar
¼	cup water
¾	cup finely chopped nuts

Combine cheese, butter, flour, salt and red pepper, using pastry blender to mix until dough forms. Roll dough on lightly-floured surface. Cut circles with medium-sized biscuit cutter. Combine dates, brown sugar and water in saucepan; cook over medium heat until thickened and most of moisture has evaporated. Cool. Stir nuts into date mixture. Spoon small amount of filling on half of each pastry circle, fold to form half circle and press edges to seal. Pierce with fork tines to vent steam. Bake on baking sheet at 350 degrees for 15 to 20 minutes.

Yield: 4 to 5 dozen

SPINACH BALLS

2	(10 ounce) packages frozen chopped spinach
6	eggs, well beaten
3	cups herb seasoned stuffing mix
1	large onion, chopped
¾	cup butter, melted
¼	cup grated Parmesan cheese
1	tablespoon black pepper
1½	teaspoons garlic salt
½	teaspoon thyme

Prepare spinach according to package directions, drain well and press to remove excess moisture. Combine spinach with eggs, stuffing mix, onion, butter, cheese and seasonings. Shape mixture into ¾-inch balls and place on lightly greased baking sheet. Bake at 325 degrees for 15 to 20 minutes.
Unbaked spinach balls can be frozen. Thaw slightly and bake at 325 degrees for 20 to 25 minutes.

Yield: 11 dozen

ARTICHOKE DIP

2	(15 ounce) cans artichoke hearts, drained and chopped
1	cup grated Parmesan cheese
1	cup mayonnaise
	Onion flakes to taste

Combine artichokes, cheese and mayonnaise, mixing well. Stir in onion to taste. Spoon into 8-inch square baking dish. Bake at 350 degrees until bubbly and lightly browned. Serve hot with assorted crackers.

Yield: 3 cups

Avocado Dip

1	ripe avocado, peeled and mashed
2	(3 ounce) packages cream cheese, softened
2	tablespoons milk
1	tablespoon lemon juice
1	tablespoon grated onion
⅛	teaspoon salt
⅛	teaspoon garlic salt

Combine avocado, cream cheese and milk; beat until smooth. Stir in lemon juice, onion and seasonings, blending well. Serve with chips or fresh vegetables.

Yield: 1¼ cups

Homemade Salsa

2	large tomatoes, seeded and chopped
2	jalapeño peppers, seeded and chopped
6	hot yellow peppers, seeded and chopped
8	cloves garlic, minced
1	(14½ ounce) can stewed tomatoes, chopped
¼	cup plus 2 tablespoons vegetable oil
1	tablespoon chopped cilantro
1	teaspoon dried oregano
½	teaspoon salt
½	teaspoon black pepper

Combine vegetables, stirring gently until mixed. Add oil, cilantro and seasonings; mix lightly. Serve with tortilla chips, fajitas or tacos.

Yield: 4 cups

Taco Bean Dip

1	(8 ounce) can refried beans
½	envelope taco seasoning mix
1	(6 ounce) jar hot red taco sauce
1	small onion, diced
1 or 2	tomatoes, diced
	Chili peppers to taste (optional)
½	cup sliced black olives (optional)
1	cup shredded lettuce (optional)
1	(16 ounce) carton sour cream
1	cup (8 ounces) shredded Monterey Jack or Cheddar cheese

Combine beans and taco seasoning, mixing thoroughly. Spread mixture in bottom of serving dish. Spoon taco sauce over bean layer. Sprinkle vegetables on taco sauce. Carefully spread sour cream over vegetables and sprinkle with cheese. Serve with nacho chips.

Yield: 5 to 6 cups

Cheese Ring

2	cups (16 ounces) grated sharp Cheddar cheese
1	cup mayonnaise
1	cup chopped pecans
1	small onion, grated
¼ to ½	teaspoon black pepper
	Dash of cayenne pepper
1	(8 ounce) jar strawberry jam

Combine cheese, mayonnaise, pecans, onion and seasonings, blending well. Shape into a ring on serving plate. Spoon jam into center of ring. Chill for 2 to 3 hours. Serve with round buttery crackers.

Yield: 4 cups

GAZPACHO

6	tomatoes, peeled
2	green onions
1	cucumber, unpeeled
½	stalk celery
1	zucchini squash (optional)
½	green bell pepper
	Juice of 1 lemon
1	teaspoon olive oil
½	teaspoon salt
¼	teaspoon black pepper
1	cup tomato or vegetable juice
1	teaspoon Worcestershire sauce
	Dash of hot pepper sauce
	Sour cream for garnish

Using food processor, chop each vegetable until fine. Combine vegetables, seasonings and juice. Stir in Worcestershire sauce and hot pepper sauce. Serve cold, garnishing each serving with a dollop of sour cream.

Yield: 4 to 6 servings

SPINACH DIP

2	(10 ounce) packages frozen chopped spinach
1	(8 ounce) can water chestnuts, drained and chopped
1	cup mayonnaise
1	(8 ounce) carton sour cream
1	envelope vegetable soup mix

The day before serving, prepare spinach according to package directions. Drain and squeeze to remove moisture. Combine spinach, water chestnuts, mayonnaise, sour cream and soup mix; mix thoroughly. Chill overnight. Serve with garlic, onion or plain round crackers.

Dip may be served from bread bowl. Cut 1-inch slice from top of round loaf of pumpernickel bread. Carefully cut or tear chunks of bread from center of loaf, leaving 1-inch thick walls. Spoon dip into bowl. Serve with bread chunks and pieces cut from top slice.

Yield: 5 cups

EASY GUACAMOLE

2	ripe avocadoes, peeled and mashed
1	tablespoon fresh lemon juice
½	teaspoon salt
¼	teaspoon onion powder
1	tablespoon green chili salsa or 2 diced green chilies
1	ripe tomato, seeded and finely chopped

Combine avocado, lemon juice, seasonings, salsa and tomato, blending thoroughly. Serve with nacho chips or nachos.

Yield: 1½ to 2 cups

CHUTNEY CHEESE BALL

1	(8 ounce) and 1 (3 ounce) package cream cheese, softened
½	pound bacon, cooked and crumbled
½	(8 ounce) jar chutney, chopped
¼	cup raisins
½	cup sliced green onion
1	cup cocktail peanuts
1	tablespoon curry powder

Combine cream cheese, bacon and chutney. Stir in raisins, onion, peanuts and curry powder, blending thoroughly. Shape into a ball. Chill before serving. Serve with crackers.

Yield: 3 cups

SALMON SPREAD

1	(16 ounce) can pink salmon, drained and boned
1	(8 ounce) package cream cheese, softened
⅛	teaspoon garlic salt
½	cup crushed walnuts

Combine cream cheese and salmon, blending well. Add garlic salt and mix well. Chill thoroughly. Shape salmon mixture into a ball, then roll in walnuts. Serve with snack crackers or spread on bread slices for open face sandwiches.

Yield: 2½ cups

CRABMEAT MOUSSE

2	tablespoons unflavored gelatin
½	cup water
1	(10½ ounce) can tomato soup, undiluted
1	(8 ounce) package cream cheese, cut in chunks
1	tablespoon lemon juice
1	cup mayonnaise
½	teaspoon Worcestershire sauce
¼	teaspoon hot pepper sauce
⅛	teaspoon dry mustard
1	(6½ ounce) can white crabmeat, flaked
1½	cups combination of chopped celery, parsley, onion and olives
	Pimiento-stuffed olives, sliced

Soften gelatin in water. Heat soup to boiling; stir in cheese and softened gelatin. Let stand until cool. Add lemon juice, mayonnaise, seasonings, crabmeat and chopped vegetables to cooled soup mixture; mix thoroughly. Line 6-cup mold with sliced olives. Pour crabmeat mixture into mold. Chill until firm. Serve with assorted crackers.

Yield: 6 to 8 servings

SEASONED OYSTER CRACKERS

¾	cup vegetable oil, warmed
1	envelope ranch style salad dressing mix
2	teaspoons dill weed
¼	teaspoon garlic powder (optional)
1	(16 ounce) package oyster crackers

Combine oil, salad dressing mix and seasonings, blending well. Pour seasoned oil over crackers, stirring until moisture is absorbed; do not cook. Store in tightly covered plastic container or tin.
Seasoned crackers will stay fresh for several weeks.

Yield: 8 to 10 cups

ORANGE-GLAZED PECANS

1	cup sugar
½	cup orange juice
1	teaspoon grated orange peel
2 to 3	tablespoons butter
½	teaspoon vanilla
3	cups toasted pecans

Combine sugar, orange juice and peel in small saucepan; cook until syrup reaches soft ball stage. Remove from heat. Add butter and vanilla, stirring until butter is melted. Add pecans and mix until all pieces are coated with glaze. Spread coated pecans on waxed paper or aluminum foil.
When dry and firm, separate into bite-sized pieces.
Glazed pecans should not be prepared in humid weather.

Yield: 3 cups

PINEAPPLE FRUIT DIP

1	large pineapple
¼	cup mayonnaise
1	banana
6	cherries
2	tablespoons honey
1½	tablespoons lemon juice, to taste
1	cup frozen whipped topping, thawed Assorted fresh fruit: strawberries, pineapple chunks, banana chunks, melon balls and other.

Cut pineapple in half crosswise. Core both sections, leaving lower half intact to form shell. Cut pineapple in chunks; set aside. Combine mayonnaise, banana, cherries, honey and lemon juice in blender; blend until smooth. Just before serving, stir whipped topping into fruit mixture and pour into pineapple shell. Place on serving tray and surround with assorted fruit for dipping.

Yield: 2 cups

GOUDA WITH PEPPER JELLY

1	large round Gouda cheese
1	(8 ounce) package refrigerated crescent rolls
1	(8 ounce) jar red pepper jelly

Remove wax from cheese. Wrap pastry around cheese, pressing to secure seams and tucking excess under ball. Place on baking sheet. Bake at 400 degrees for 10 minutes. Pour jelly over top of pastry. Serve with crackers.

Yield: 2 cups

SPICED PECANS

3	tablespoons butter, melted
3	tablespoons Worcestershire sauce
1	teaspoon salt
½	teaspoon ground cinnamon
¼	teaspoon garlic powder
¼	teaspoon ground red pepper
	Dash of hot pepper sauce
1	pound pecan halves

Combine butter, Worcestershire sauce and seasonings in large bowl; mix well. Add pecans, stirring gently until thoroughly coated. Spread pecans in a single layer in a 15x10x1-inch jelly roll pan. Bake at 300 degrees for 25 to 30 minutes, stirring frequently. Drain pecans on paper towels to absorb excess grease. Let cool. Store in an airtight container.

Yield: 5 cups

PERKY PICKLES

1	(46 ounce) jar Kosher dill pickles, drained and sliced
1½	cups sugar
1	small onion, sliced (optional)
½	cup vinegar
1	teaspoon celery salt
1	teaspoon mustard seed

Place pickle slices in original jar. Combine sugar, onion, vinegar and seasonings in a saucepan, blending well. Bring to a boil, remove from heat and let stand until cool. Pour mixture over pickles. Chill for at least 24 hours before serving. Store in refrigerator.

Yield: 1 quart

INFAMOUS PEPPER JELLY

8	green bell peppers
2 or 3	large hot chili peppers or 2 teaspoons crushed red pepper
7	cups sugar
1	cup vinegar
1	(6 ounce) package liquid fruit pectin
	Green food coloring

Separately grind green peppers and chili peppers, catching liquid. Drain pulp well, reserving liquid. Strain green pepper liquid. Measure chili pepper liquid (about ¼ cup) and add green pepper liquid to measure 2 cups. (If using pepper flakes, use all green pepper liquid). Mix liquid with sugar and vinegar in 8 to 10-quart Dutch oven. Bring to a full boil. Add pectin and boil vigorously for 1 minute. Remove from heat and let stand for 5 minutes. Skim foam from surface. Add a few drops food coloring, if desired. Pour into hot sterilized jelly jars, leaving ½ inch space. Wipe rims and seal with lids or paraffin. Let stand for at least 1 week before serving.

Yield: 7 or 8 half-pints

Appetizers

Green Tomato Refrigerator Pickles

3	large cloves garlic, quartered
3	small dried hot chili peppers, broken in halves
3	teaspoons pickling spice
10 to 12	green tomatoes
2	medium-sized onions, cut in 1-inch squares
1 or 2	red or green bell peppers, cut in 1-inch squares
3 or 4	large carrots
2 or 3	stalks celery
7½	cups water
2½	cups white vinegar
¼	cup salt

In 3 sterilized quart jars, place equal amounts of garlic, chili peppers and pickling spice. Cut each tomato into 6 wedges and divide among jars. Distribute onion and bell pepper among jars. Cut carrots and celery once lengthwise, then crosswise into squares; divide among jars. Combine water, vinegar and salt in saucepan; bring to a boil. Pour over vegetables, dividing liquid equally among jars. Cool, then seal with lid. Store in refrigerator for up to 3 months.

Yield: 3 quarts

Chicha Llanera

Venezuelan Rice-Cream Drink

1	cup cooked white rice
1½	cups milk
¼	cup sweetened condensed milk
1	tablespoon sugar
	Ground cinnamon

Combine rice, milk and sugar in blender container; blend for 3 minutes. Serve over ice cubes and sprinkle with cinnamon. May be served warm.
Chicha is a popular beverage in Venezuela. Because of its high carbohydrate level, it is often used in place of a meal.

Yield: 2 cups

Apple Shrub

1	cup chilled apple juice
½	cup orange sherbet

Pour juice over scoop of sherbet in individual glass. Serve with straw, spoon or both.

Yield: 1 serving

Party Punch

4	cups chilled cranberry juice
4	cups chilled pineapple juice
1	tablespoon almond extract
1	(2 liter) bottle chilled gingerale

Combine juices and almond extract. Just before serving, add gingerale.

Yield: 20 servings

ORANGE BLOSSOM PUNCH

- 3 (12 ounce) cans frozen orange juice concentrate, partially thawed
- 12 cups chilled apple juice
- 3 (1 quart) bottles chilled gingerale
  Fresh orange slices

Combine juices. Just before serving, add gingerale. Float orange slices on punch.

Yield: 50 servings

GRAPEFRUIT ICE

- ½ cup sugar
- 1 cup water
- 2½ cups pink grapefruit juice
- 2 tablespoons grenadine syrup

Combine sugar and water in small saucepan; bring to a boil, reduce heat and simmer for 5 minutes. Add syrup to grapefruit juice and grenadine syrup, mixing thoroughly. Freeze until firm. Place chunks in food processor or blender container and process until smooth. Serve immediately or store in freezer for up to 1 hour.

Yield: 3 or 4 servings

WHITE GRAPE SPARKLE

- 8 cups chilled white grape juice
- 1 (2 litre) bottle chilled lemon-lime carbonated soft drink

Combine grape juice and carbonated drink in large pitcher or serve from punch bowl with molded ice ring.

Yield: 25 to 30 servings

HOT TOMATO COCKTAIL

- 1 (46 ounce) can tomato juice
- 1 tablespoon Worcestershire sauce
  Few drops hot pepper sauce
  Juice of 1 lemon

Combine tomato juice, sauces and lemon juice in large saucepan. Heat thoroughly. Serve warm in mugs.

Yield: 6 to 8 servings

FRUITED ICED TEA

1	(6 ounce) can frozen lemonade concentrate, thawed
1	(6 ounce) can frozen orange juice concentrate, thawed
1½	cups sugar
7	tea bags
13 to 14	cups water
1	teaspoon almond extract

Combine juices and sugar in 1-gallon container. Place tea bags in saucepan filled with 4 to 5 cups water, bring to a boil and let steep for 5 minutes. Add tea liquid to juices. Using same tea bags, add 4 to 5 cups water to pan, bring to a boil, let steep for 5 minutes, add to juices; repeat process to measure 1 gallon tea. Stir in almond extract. Chill before serving. Tea may be prepared a day in advance.

Yield: 10 to 12 servings

HOT SPICED TEA

24	cups water
3	cups sugar
1	(46 ounce) can unsweetened orange juice
	Juice of 3 lemons
18	orange spice or orange pekoe tea bags
4 ½	teaspoons whole cloves
3	cinnamon sticks
1	(46 ounce) can pineapple juice, strained

Combine water and sugar in large stockpot; bring to a boil. Stir in orange and lemon juices and bring to a boil. Add tea bags, cloves and cinnamon sticks; cook at a low boil for 3 minutes. Remove from heat and let stand, covered, for 10 minutes. Strain to remove spices. Stir in pineapple juice.

Tea may be prepared 1 to 2 days in advance.

Yield: 39 servings

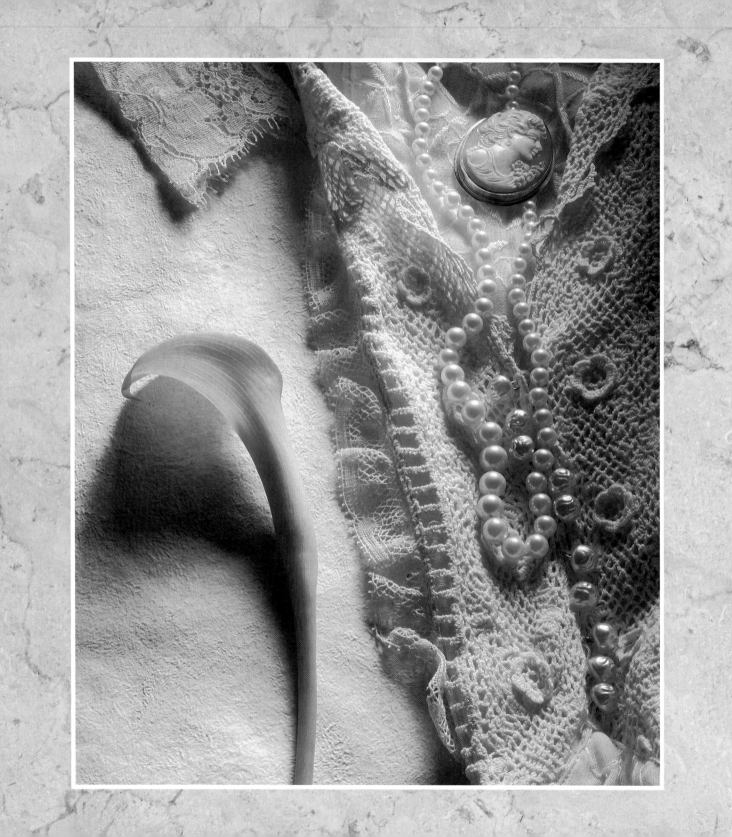

DO NOT BE ANXIOUS… FOR YOUR BODY, AS TO WHAT YOU SHALL PUT ON. SEEK FIRST HIS KINGDOM AND HIS RIGHTEOUSNESS; AND ALL THESE THINGS SHALL BE ADDED TO YOU.

Matt. 6:25, 33

GOLDEN SHRIMP PUFF

6	eggs
3	cups milk
2	tablespoons minced parsley
¾	teaspoon dry mustard
½	teaspoon salt
10	slices white bread, crusts trimmed and cubed
2	cups (8 ounces) shredded American cheese
2	cups cooked peeled shrimp

Beat eggs, milk and seasonings together. Stir in bread cubes, cheese and shrimp. Pour mixture into 11x7x 1½-inch baking dish. Bake, uncovered, at 325 degrees for 1 hour or until knife inserted near center comes out clean. Serve immediately.

Yield: 8 servings

CHEDDAR EGGS

9	eggs, beaten
1¾ to 2	cups half and half
⅛	teaspoon dry mustard
¼	teaspoon Worcestershire sauce
4	cups (16 ounces) grated Cheddar cheese
	Breadcrumbs
	Chopped parsley (optional)
	Chopped chives (optional)

Combine eggs and half and half; stir in seasonings. Pour egg mixture into greased 2-quart casserole or 8-inch square baking dish. Sprinkle cheese over egg mixture, then top with breadcrumbs, parsley and chives. Bake at 325 degrees for 20 to 30 minutes or until mixture is firm but not dry.

Yield: 6 servings

JOHN BUNYAN'S BREAKFAST

¼	pound bacon, diced
3	small potatoes, diced
1	cup onions, diced
5	eggs
2	tablespoons whipping cream
	Salt to taste
	Black pepper to taste
2	tablespoons chopped parsley
	Butter

Sauté bacon in large skillet until cooked. Add potatoes and onion; cook until potatoes are tender. Beat eggs and cream together; add with seasonings to bacon mixture. Stir to scramble while cooking just until eggs are firm, adding butter if necessary to prevent sticking.

Yield: 3 or 4 servings

DEVILED EGG CASSEROLE

12	hard-cooked eggs, deviled
2	cups medium white sauce
1	(3 ounce) jar dried beef, shredded
1	teaspoon grated onion
	Salt to taste
	Black pepper to taste
	Grated Parmesan cheese to taste

Place eggs, deviled according to own preferred method, in 9-inch square baking dish. Mix white sauce, beef, onion and seasonings; pour over eggs. Sprinkle with Parmesan cheese. Bake at 350 degrees for 20 minutes.

Yield: 6 servings

EGGS SUNRISE

8	hard-cooked eggs, sliced
1	cup onion, chopped
1	tablespoon butter or margarine
2	cups (8 ounces) grated Swiss cheese
1	(10¾ ounce) mushroom soup, undiluted
½	teaspoon seasoned salt
¼	teaspoon black pepper
1	teaspoon dill weed
1	teaspoon mustard
	Butter
20	slices party rye bread
	Paprika to taste

Arrange egg slices in bottom of buttered 10x8x2-inch baking dish. Sauté onion in butter until tender; spoon over eggs. Sprinkle cheese on eggs. Mix soup, salt, pepper, dill weed and mustard together; pour over cheese layer. Chill overnight. Place bread slices on sauce and sprinkle with paprika. Bake at 350 degrees for 35 to 40 minutes.

Yield: 4 to 6 servings

GREEN EGGS BENEDICT

1	(10¾ ounce) can cream of chicken soup, undiluted
¼	cup mayonnaise
⅓	cup milk
1	tablespoon lemon juice
⅛	teaspoon freshly ground nutmeg
6	slices cooked ham
3	English muffins, split and toasted
1	(10 ounce) package frozen leaf spinach, thawed and drained
6	eggs, poached
	Grated Parmesan cheese

Combine soup, mayonnaise, milk, lemon juice and nutmeg in saucepan; blend well and heat, stirring occasionally. Place ham slice on each muffin half, add spinach leaves and top with egg. Pour sauce over egg and sprinkle with cheese. Broil until lightly browned.

Yield: 6 servings

Scottish Eggs with Celery Sauce

1	pound bulk pork sausage
1	cup minced onion
1	cup breadcrumbs
2	eggs, divided and beaten
5	hard-cooked eggs, cooled, peeled and dried
1½	cups crushed corn flakes
1	cup chopped celery
¼	cup butter
¼	cup all-purpose flour
1	envelope dehydrated chicken broth or chicken bouillon cube
2	cups milk

Combine sausage, onion, breadcrumbs and 1 beaten egg. Mold 1/5 sausage mixture around each hard-cooked egg, completely covering egg. Dip coated egg in remaining beaten egg and roll in corn flakes. Place eggs in shallow baking dish or on broiler pan rack. Bake at 350 degrees for 35 to 40 minutes. Sauté celery in butter for 5 minutes or until tender. Blend in flour and bouillon; stir and cook for 30 seconds. Gradually add milk, stirring constantly, until sauce is bubbly. To serve, slice baked eggs in half lengthwise and spoon sauce over halves.

Yield: 5 servings

Welsh Rarebit

2	eggs, beaten
1	small onion, minced
¼	cup milk
2	cups (8 ounces) grated sharp Cheddar cheese
4	teaspoons margarine
¼	teaspoon salt
¼	teaspoon black pepper
2	English muffins, split and toasted
4	slices tomato
2	slices bacon, cooked and crumbled
	Chopped fresh basil to taste

Combine eggs, onion, milk, cheese, margarine and seasonings in heavy saucepan; cook over low to medium heat until cheese is melted and mixture is bubbly. Serve immediately over hot buttered English muffin halves. Top each serving with tomato slice, bacon and basil.

Yield: 4 servings

APPLE AND SAUSAGE QUICHE

1   cup chopped apple
2   tablespoons sugar
1   tablespoon lemon juice
      Dash of salt
      Dash of black pepper
1   small onion, chopped
3   tablespoons butter or margarine
6   links pork sausage or ½ pound bulk
      pork sausage, cooked
4   eggs
1   (8 ounce) carton sour cream
⅛   teaspoon nutmeg
      Dash of cayenne pepper
1   baked 9-inch pastry shell
½   cup (2 ounces) grated Cheddar cheese

Dredge apple in sugar, lemon juice, salt and pepper. Sauté apple with onion in butter until onion is just soft; remove from heat and cool for 20 minutes. Cut each sausage link in 3 pieces or crumble well-drained bulk sausage; add to cooled apple mixture. Beat eggs, sour cream, nutmeg, cayenne, salt and pepper together; add to sausage mixture. Pour into pastry shell. Bake at 350 degrees for 35 to 40 minutes or until knife tip inserted near center comes out clean. Sprinkle with cheese 10 minutes before completion of baking time. Let stand 5 minutes before serving.

Yield: 4 to 6 servings

BASIC QUICHE

1   small onion, diced
2   teaspoons butter
3   eggs, beaten
1   (8 ounce) package cream cheese,
      softened
1   cup milk
½   pound mushrooms, sliced (optional)
½   pound cubed baked or boiled ham
      (optional)
1   baked 9-inch deep dish pastry shell

Sauté onion in butter until transluscent; add to eggs. Melt cream cheese in milk in saucepan, stirring until smooth. Add eggs to cheese mixture. Arrange mushrooms, ham or other filler ingredients in pastry shell. Pour egg mixture into shell. Bake at 350 degrees for 35 to 40 minutes or until center is firm. Let stand 15 minutes before serving.

Yield: 4 to 6 servings

BREAKFAST QUICHE

1   pound mild bulk pork sausage, cooked and drained
1   pound hot bulk pork sausage, cooked and drained
2   baked 9-inch deep dish pastry shells
2   cups (8 ounces) shredded Cheddar cheese
2   cups (8 ounces) shredded mozzarella cheese
8   eggs, beaten
1½ cups milk
1   teaspoon salt
½   teaspoon black pepper

Place crumbled sausage in bottom and along sides of pastry shells. Sprinkle cheese on sausage. Combine eggs, milk and seasonings, mixing thoroughly. Pour over cheese and sausage. Bake at 375 degrees for 25 to 30 minutes or until center is firm.

Yield: 8 to 12 servings

QUICHE LORRAINE

1   envelope onion soup mix
3   tablespoons all-purpose flour
2   (10 ounce) packages frozen creamed spinach, thawed
½   pound cubed boiled ham or diced bacon
2   cups (8 ounces) grated Swiss cheese
2   eggs, lightly beaten
⅔   cup half and half
1   unbaked 9-inch pastry shell

Combine soup mix and flour. Add spinach, ham or bacon, and cheese, mixing well. Stir in eggs and half and half. Spoon mixture into pastry shell. Bake at 350 degrees for 1 hour or until surface is lightly browned.

Yield: 6 servings

SPINACH-MUSHROOM QUICHE

1   unbaked 9-inch pastry shell
1   (10 ounce) package frozen chopped spinach, thawed
¼   pound mushrooms sliced
2   tablespoons butter
2   cups (8 ounces) grated cheese
4   eggs, beaten
1   cup half and half
½   cup milk
¾   teaspoon salt
⅛   teaspoon black pepper
⅛   teaspoon nutmeg

Bake pastry shell at 425 degrees for 15 minutes or until very lightly browned. Place spinach in colander and press to remove excess moisture. Sauté mushrooms in butter. Sprinkle half of cheese in bottom of pastry shell, layer spinach on cheese, add mushrooms and top with remaining cheese. Beat eggs, half and half, milk and seasonings together; carefully pour over cheese layer. Bake at 375 degrees for 40 minutes.

Yield: 6 to 8 servings

BREAKFAST PIE

½   pound bulk pork sausage, cooked, drained and crumbled
1   (12 ounce) carton creamed cottage cheese
1   cup (4 ounces) shredded Cheddar cheese
1   (3 ounce) package cream cheese, softened
4   eggs, divided
1   cup biscuit baking mix
¼   cup chopped green onion
¼   cup milk

Combine sausage, cheese and 2 eggs; mix well and set aside. Combine biscuit mix and green onion; add 2 eggs and milk. Spoon ½ of batter into greased 9x9x2-inch baking pan. Spread sausage filling evenly on batter in pan. Top with remaining batter. Bake at 375 degrees for 20 minutes or until medium golden brown. For larger quantity, double ingredients and bake in 13x9x2-inch baking pan.

Yield: 6 to 9 servings

SPINACH PIE

6   eggs, beaten
4   cups (16 ounces) grated mozzarella
     cheese
4   cups (16 ounces) ricotta cheese
¼   cup grated Romano cheese
2   (10 ounce) packages frozen chopped
     spinach, thawed and drained
1   teaspoon salt
¼   teaspoon garlic powder
1   pound bulk pork sausage, cooked, well
     drained and crumbled
4   unbaked 9-inch pastry shells

Combine eggs, cheese, spinach and seasonings in large bowl. Add sausage and mix thoroughly. Pour mixture into 2 pastry shells. Cover each with remaining pastry, crimping edges to seal. Bake at 350 degrees for 1 hour.

Yield: 8 to 12 servings

CHEESE GRITS SOUFFLÉ

1   cup regular grits, uncooked
4   cups water
1   teaspoon salt
¼   cup butter
3   tablespoons all-purpose flour
1   tablespoon dry mustard
½   cup whipping cream
3   eggs, separated
2   cups (8 ounces) grated sharp Cheddar
     cheese, divided

Prepare grits according to package directions, using 4 cups water seasoned with 1 teaspoon salt. Melt butter in top of double boiler over hot water. Blend in flour and mustard. Add cream, egg yolks, butter mixture and 1¾ cups cheese to cooked grits. Beat egg whites until stiff and fold into grits. Spoon mixture into 2-quart casserole. Bake at 350 degrees for 30 to 40 minutes, sprinkling with remaining cheese 5 minutes before completion of baking time.

Yield: 8 servings

Among the Lilies

GARLIC CHEESE GRITS

1	cup regular grits, uncooked
4	cups water
1½	teaspoons salt
½	cup butter
1	cup (4 ounces) grated sharp cheese
1	teaspoon dried minced garlic or garlic powder
2	tablespoons Worcestershire sauce
	Paprika

Prepare grits according to package directions, using 4 cups water and 1½ teaspoons salt. Add butter, cheese, garlic and Worcestershire sauce to cooked grits; stir until butter and cheese are melted. Spoon grits mixture into greased 1½-quart casserole. Sprinkle with paprika. Bake at 350 degrees for 15 to 20 minutes.

Yield: 6 to 8 servings

BAKED OATMEAL

2	cups regular oatmeal, uncooked
½	cup sugar or firmly-packed brown sugar
1	teaspoon baking powder
¼	teaspoon salt
1	teaspoon cinnamon
¼	cup butter, softened
1	egg, beaten
¾	cup milk
	Chopped nuts, raisins, prunes or dates to taste
	Warm milk
	Homemade fried cinnamon apple slices

Combine oatmeal, sugar, baking powder, salt, cinnamon, butter, egg and milk. Pour into 1-quart casserole. Bake at 350 degrees for 30 minutes. Pour warm milk over individual servings and add apple slices. Dish may be assembled a day in advance and chilled until ready to bake.

Yield: 4 servings

OATMEAL WITH FRUIT

½ cup regular oatmeal, uncooked
¾ cup milk
¼ cup raisins
1 tablespoon frozen lemonade concentrate
2 tablespoons frozen orange juice concentrate
2 tablespoons honey
3 tablespoons whipping cream
1 banana, sliced
1 apple, peeled and diced
Chopped nuts (optional)

Combine oatmeal, milk and raisins in saucepan; bring to a boil. Stir and add juices, honey, cream and fruit. Cook for about 1 minute. Sprinkle individual servings with nuts.

Yield: 2 servings

Ursula Knaeusel

OATMEAL WAFFLES WITH ORANGE-MAPLE SAUCE

1½ cups all-purpose flour
½ cup quick cooking oats, uncooked
1 tablespoon sugar
1 tablespoon baking powder
½ teaspoon salt
2 eggs, beaten
1½ cups milk
¼ cup melted butter or vegetable oil
¼ cup currants or raisins
½ teaspoon cinnamon
1½ cups maple syrup
1 tablespoon grated orange peel
½ cup butter

Combine flour, oats, sugar, baking powder and salt. Beat eggs and milk together; add to dry ingredients and blend thoroughly. Add melted butter or oil. Stir in currants or raisins and cinnamon. Preheat waffle iron. Use about 1/6 of batter for each waffle. Combine syrup, orange peel and butter in saucepan. Bring to a boil, then simmer for 5 minutes. Serve hot over waffles or pancakes.

Yield: 6 servings
2½ cups sauce

SOURDOUGH WAFFLES AND PANCAKES

SOURDOUGH STARTER
Milk
All-purpose flour

Place 1 cup milk in glass container. Let stand, uncovered, at room temperature for 24 hours. Stir in 1 cup flour. Let stand, uncovered, in warm (80 degrees) place for 2 to 5 days; mixture will have sour aroma and be bubbly. When using, add flour and milk specified in waffle or pancake recipes, then reserve ½ cup of mixture. Replenish with equal amounts of milk and flour. Let stand, uncovered, at room temperature for several hours or until bubbly. Cover jar tightly and store in refrigerator.

SOURDOUGH WAFFLES
2   **cups all-purpose flour**
2   **cups milk**
2   **eggs**
2   **tablespoons vegetable oil**
1   **teaspoon baking soda**
1   **teaspoon salt**

The night before preparing waffles, add flour and milk to starter. Cover with damp cloth and let stand overnight. Before adding remaining ingredients, remove ½ cup of mixture to use as starter.
Add eggs, oil, soda and salt; blend well. Bake in preheated waffle iron.
For sourdough pancakes, omit vegetable oil.

Yield: 6 servings

BLENDER POTATO PANCAKES

¼   **cup milk**
1   **egg**
2   **cups diced peeled potatoes**
1   **small onion, quartered**
2   **tablespoons all-purpose flour**
¾   **teaspoon salt**
¼   **teaspoon baking powder**
⅓   **cup vegetable oil**

Place ingredients in blender container in sequence: milk, egg, potatoes, onion, flour, baking powder and salt. Blend at high speed for about 10 seconds; do not overblend. Heat oil in 12-inch skillet over medium heat. Drop scant ¼ cup measures of potato mixture into skillet, forming 4 mounds about 3 inches apart; flatten with spatula to 4-inch diameter. Sauté until pancakes are golden brown; turn to brown both sides. Drain on paper towel and keep warm in 200 degree oven. Serve hot.

Yield: 4 servings

OLD FASHIONED PANCAKES

2	eggs, beaten
2	tablespoons sugar
2	cups buttermilk
2½	cups all-purpose flour
1	teaspoon baking powder
1	teaspoon baking soda
½	teaspoon salt
2	tablespoons vegetable oil

Combine eggs and sugar. Sift flour, baking powder, soda, and salt together; add with milk to eggs. Add shortening. Beat batter well. Pour ¼ cup measures of batter onto hot ungreased griddle. Cook until lightly browned and holes form on upper surface; turn to brown both sides. Serve hot.

Yield: 4 to 6 servings

ORANGE FRENCH TOAST

8	eggs
¾	cup orange juice
3	tablespoons powdered sugar, divided
1	teaspoon vanilla
1	large loaf French or Italian bread, cut in ½-inch slices
	Butter
3	tablespoons brown sugar

Combine eggs, orange juice, sugar and vanilla. Pour over bread slices and let stand for 2 hours. Sauté slices in butter, turning once, until golden on both sides. Sprinkle toast with mixture of brown sugar and 1 tablespoon powdered sugar.

Yield: 8 servings

CHEESE BLINTZ CASSEROLE

FILLING

2	(15 ounce) cartons ricotta cheese
1	(8 ounce) package cream cheese, softened
2	eggs
¼	cup sugar
⅛	teaspoon salt
¼	cup lemon juice

BLINTZES

1	cup margarine, melted
½	cup sugar
2	eggs
¼	cup milk
1	teaspoon vanilla
1	cup sifted all-purpose flour
1	tablespoon baking powder
⅛	teaspoon salt
	Sour cream
¼	cup strawberry jam
12	strawberry fans

Using electric mixer, prepare filling by blending cheeses, eggs, sugar, salt and lemon juice, beating until smooth; set aside. Just before baking, prepare blintz batter by combining margarine and sugar; add eggs, milk and vanilla and mix thoroughly. Add dry ingredients and stir by hand until blended. Pour half of mixture into well-greased 13x9x2-inch baking pan. Carefully spread filling over batter, preserving blintz base. Spoon remaining batter evenly over filling. Bake at 300 degrees for 1½ hours. Cool slightly before serving. Cut into squares and serve each with dollop of sour cream, 1 teaspoon strawberry jam and a strawberry fan.

Yield: 12 servings

44

FUNNEL CAKE

	Vegetable oil
2	cups self-rising flour
1	tablespoon sugar
1	teaspoon baking powder
½	teaspoon salt
2	eggs, beaten
1¼	cups milk
	Powdered sugar
	Cinnamon sugar

Using a large electric skillet, add oil to ¾ inch depth. Heat to 400 degrees; do not let smoke. Oil is ready when drop of batter floats to surface and browns in 5 seconds. Sift flour, sugar, baking powder and salt together. Blend eggs with milk; add to dry ingredients and beat until smooth. Pour batter into funnel (hold fingertip over funnel tip), then quickly release into hot oil, moving crosswise; do not fill entire surface as batter expands as it cooks. Cook until edges are browned, then turn to evenly brown on both sides. Lift from oil. Repeat with remaining batter. Sprinkle with powdered sugar or cinnamon sugar.

Yield: 4 to 6 servings

MAANDAZI (*Kenyan Doughnuts*)

1¼	cups all-purpose flour
2	tablespoons sugar
1	teaspoon baking powder
1	teaspoon ground cardamom
1	egg
¼	cup milk
	Vegetable oil
	Cinnamon sugar

Combine flour, sugar, baking powder and cardamom. Stir in egg and milk. Drop dough by teaspoonfuls into oil heated to 365 degrees; dough may also be rolled to ¾-inch thickness on well-floured surface and cut into triangles before frying. Deep-fry until lightly browned. Roll doughtnuts in cinnamon sugar.

Yield: 12 to 16

MOMBASA TOAST

3	tablespoons margarine, softened
	Cinnamon
1	teaspoon curry powder
8	slices white bread
8	slices Canadian bacon
1	(8¼ ounce) can sliced pineapple, drained
4	slices Swiss cheese

Combine margarine, 1 teaspoon cinnamon and curry powder; blend well. Spread mixture on one side of each bread slice. Broil, spread side up on baking sheet until lightly toasted. Top each bread slice with 1 slice bacon, ½ pineapple slice and ½ slice cheese; sprinkle with cinnamon. Broil until cheese is melted and lightly browned. Serve immediately.

Yield: 4 servings

HOEVER DRINKS OF

THE WATER THAT I

SHALL GIVE HIM SHALL NEVER

THIRST; BUT THE WATER THAT I

SHALL GIVE HIM SHALL BECOME

IN HIM A WELL OF WATER

SPRINGING UP TO ETERNAL LIFE.

John 4:14

BISCUITS

FOR A CROWD

1½	pounds vegetable shortening
5	pounds self-rising flour (soft wheat)
½	gallon buttermilk
	Melted butter

FOR FIVE

½	cup vegetable shortening
4	cups self-rising flour
2	cups buttermilk
	Melted butter

Using pastry blender, cut shortening into flour until mixture is size of peas. Stir in buttermilk and let stand for about 5 minutes. Roll out dough on lightly-floured surface, cut with biscuit cutter and place on baking sheet. Bake at 400 degrees for at least 20 minutes. Brush generously with melted butter, then brush again.

To assure light biscuits, handle dough as little as possible.

Yield: 100/24

CHEESE DILL DROP BISCUITS

2¼	cups biscuit mix
⅔	cup milk
½	cup grated sharp Cheddar cheese
¼ to ½	teaspoon dill weed
	Melted butter

Combine biscuit mix, milk, cheese and dill, blending just until mix is moistened. Drop teaspoonfuls of dough on ungreased baking sheet. Bake at 400 degrees for 8 to 10 minutes or until golden brown. Brush biscuit tops with melted butter.

Yield: 10

LIZA'S BISCUITS

2	cups self-rising flour
2	tablespoons vegetable shortening
⅔	cup milk

Preheat oven to 400 degrees. Using fork, cut flour into shortening. Add milk and mix quickly with fork; do not overwork dough. Shape dough into ball; if too sticky, add small amount of flour. Place dough on lightly-floured surface and roll to ½-inch thickness. Using 1½-inch cutter, cut biscuits and place on ungreased baking sheet. Bake for 10 to 12 minutes or until lightly browned.

Yield: 20 to 24

SWEET POTATO BISCUITS

2	cups self-rising flour
1	teaspoon baking powder
½	teaspoon baking soda
½	teaspoon salt
¼	cup vegetable shortening
2	medium sweet potatoes, cooked and peeled
¾	cup sugar
¾	cup buttermilk, divided

Sift dry ingredients together into mixing bowl. Using pastry blender or fork, cut in shortening. Mash potatoes in separate bowl; add sugar and ½ cup buttermilk and mix well. Add sweet potatoes to flour mixture. Mix, adding ¼ cup buttermilk if necessary, to form soft dough. Roll out dough on lightly floured surface, cut with biscuit cutter and place on baking sheet. Bake at 425 degrees for 15 to 20 minutes or until lightly browned.

Yield: 20 to 24

PUFF PASTRY

2	tablespoons butter
¼	cup boiling water
¼	cup all-purpose flour
⅛	teaspoon salt
1	egg
¼	cup shredded Swiss cheese

Melt butter in boiling water in medium saucepan. Add flour and salt. Cook, stirring vigorously, until mixture forms a ball. Remove from heat and cool slightly. Add egg and beat until smooth. Stir in cheese. Drop level teaspoonfuls of dough on greased baking sheet. Bake at 400 degrees for 20 minutes.

Yield: 10 to 12

CORNBREAD

1	cup all-purpose flour
¾	cup self-rising cornmeal
1	tablespoon sugar
1½	teaspoons baking powder
½	teaspoon baking soda
½	teaspoon salt
1½	cups buttermilk
3	tablespoons butter, melted
2	eggs, beaten

Combine dry ingredients in mixing bowl. Mix milk and butter with eggs; add to dry ingredients, stirring just until moistened. Pour batter into greased 10-inch ovenproof skillet. Bake at 400 degrees for 20 minutes.

Yield: 6 servings

RAISIN SCONES

½	cup golden raisins
	Boiling water
2	cups all-purpose flour
3⅓	tablespoons sugar, divided
2	teaspoons baking powder
½	teaspoon baking soda
¾	teaspoon salt
¼	cup plus 1 tablespoon butter
1	(8 ounce) carton sour cream
1	egg, separated
⅛	teaspoon cinnamon

Soak raisins in boiling water to cover for 5 minutes; drain well and set aside. Combine flour, 3 tablespoons sugar, baking powder, soda and salt. Using pastry blender, cut butter into dry ingredients until mixture resembles coarse crumbs. Add raisins. Combine sour cream and egg yolk; add to dry mixture and knead 10 to 12 strokes to form dough. Roll dough on lightly-floured surface to form 9-inch circle. Cut into 4-inch circles with biscuit cutter and place on ungreased baking sheet. Score each circle into quarters; do not cut completely through dough. Lightly beat egg white; brush on dough. Sprinkle with 1 teaspoon sugar mixed with cinnamon. Bake at 450 degrees for 15 to 18 minutes.

Fresh cranberries may be substituted for raisins.

Yield: 1 dozen

MEXICAN CORNBREAD

1 cup all-purpose flour
1 cup yellow corn meal
2 tablespoons sugar (optional)
1⅓ tablespoons baking powder
½ teaspoon salt
1½ cups (6 ounces) shredded sharp
 Cheddar cheese
1 (8 ounce) can cream-style corn
1 (4 ounce) can chopped green chilies,
 drained
⅓ cup milk
¼ cup vegetable oil
2 large eggs, beaten

Combine dry ingredients in mixing bowl. Add cheese, corn, chilies, milk and oil. Stir in eggs, mixing just until blended. Pour batter into greased 9-inch baking pan. Bake at 400 degrees for 30 to 35 minutes or until golden brown. Serve hot.

Yield: 9 servings

PARAGUAYAN CORNBREAD

2 medium-sized onions, minced
½ cup butter or margarine, divided
1 cup (8 ounces) farmer or cottage cheese
2 cups (8 ounces) shredded Muenster
 cheese
1 (16 ounce) can cream-style corn
2 cups yellow cornmeal
1 teaspoon salt
1 cup milk
6 eggs, separated

Sauté onion in ¼ cup butter until tender; set aside. Cream ¼ cup butter until smooth. Add onion, cheeses, corn, cornmeal, salt and milk; mix thoroughly. Beat egg whites until soft peaks form. Lightly beat egg yolks in separate bowl. Combine yolks and egg whites and stir into cornmeal mixture. Spread batter in greased and floured 13x9x2-inch baking pan. Bake at 400 degrees for 45 minutes or until wooden pick inserted near center comes out clean. Serve hot.

Yield: 12 to 16 servings

Breads

SOUTHERN SPOON BREAD

½ cup cornmeal
1 teaspoon salt
1½ cups milk
1 tablespoon sugar
1 tablespoon butter
2 eggs, well beaten
1 teaspoon baking powder
Butter

Combine cornmeal and salt in saucepan. Add milk and sugar; cook, stirring often, for about 5 minutes or until mixture is smooth and thickened. Stir in 1 tablespoon butter. Cool. Beat eggs and baking powder into cooled cornmeal mixture. Pour batter into buttered 1-quart casserole. Bake at 375 degrees for about 25 to 30 minutes or until firm and browned. Spoon from casserole, topping each serving with pat of butter.

Yield: 4 to 6 servings

HUSH PUPPIES

2 cups self-rising cornmeal
¼ cup pancake mix
1 medium-sized onion, chopped
2 green onions with tops, chopped
1 egg, beaten
1½ cups buttermilk
Vegetable oil

Combine cornmeal and pancake mix in mixing bowl. Stir in onions, egg and buttermilk. Let stand for 15 minutes. Shape mixture into walnut-sized balls. Deep fry in oil at 375 degrees, turning to brown on all sides. Drain well.

Yield: 30 to 36

SPINACH CORNBREAD

1 (10 ounce) package frozen chopped spinach, thawed and drained
4 eggs, beaten
1 (8 ounce) package cornbread mix
1 tablespoon sugar
½ teaspoon salt
1 onion, chopped
⅔ cup cottage cheese
¼ cup melted margarine

Press spinach to remove excess moisture. Add spinach to eggs. Stir in dry ingredients, onion, cottage cheese and margarine; mix well. Pour batter into greased 10-inch square baking pan. Bake at 400 degrees for 30 minutes.

Yield: 9 to 12 servings

APPLE NUT MUFFINS

3	cups all-purpose flour
2½	cups sugar
½	teaspoon baking powder
1½	teaspoons baking soda
1½	teaspoons salt
1	teaspoon ground cloves
2	teaspoons ground cinnamon
1¼	cups vegetable oil
4	eggs, beaten
1	teaspoon vanilla
3	cups chopped unpeeled apples
⅔	cup raisins
½	cup nuts

Combine dry ingredients in mixing bowl. Add oil, eggs, vanilla and fruit; beat for 1 minute. Pour batter into well-greased muffin pans. Bake at 325 degrees for 10 to 15 minutes or until wooden pick inserted near center of muffin comes out clean. Cool before removing from pans.

Yield: 36

BLUEBERRY MUFFINS

½	cup butter, softened
1	cup sugar
2	eggs
2	cups unsifted all-purpose flour, divided
2	teaspoons baking powder
½	teaspoon salt
½	cup milk
1	teaspoon vanilla
2½	cups blueberries
2	teaspoons sugar

Using electric mixer, cream butter and sugar until fluffy. Add eggs, 1 at a time, beating until blended. Reserving 2 tablespoons flour, sift dry ingredients together. Alternately add dry ingredients and milk with vanilla to creamed mixture. Mash ½ cup blueberries; add to batter, stirring by hand. Toss remaining whole blueberries with 2 tablespoons flour, then stir into batter. Spoon batter into well-greased muffin pans (grease cups and top surface of pan), mounding in cups. Sprinkle with sugar. Bake at 375 degrees for 30 minutes. Cool in pan for 30 minutes before removing.

Yield: 12

Breads

ONE GREAT MUFFIN

1	cup high-fiber bran cereal
½	cup oats, uncooked
½	cup hot water
1	egg
¼	cup vegetable oil
¼	cup molasses
¼	cup honey
1	cup buttermilk
1	teaspoon vanilla
¾	cup oat bran cereal, uncooked
1¼	cups all-purpose flour
1	teaspoon baking powder
1	teaspoon baking soda
½	cup raisins

Combine high fiber bran cereal, oats and hot water in large mixing bowl; stir to moisten and set aside. Blend egg, oil, molasses, honey, buttermilk and vanilla. Stir into cereal mixture, mixing thoroughly to moisten cereal. Stir in oat bran cereal. Add flour, baking powder and soda, mixing just until dry ingredients are moistened. Stir in raisins. Spoon batter into muffin pans prepared with non-stick vegetable spray, filling cups ⅔ full. Bake at 400 degrees for 20 minutes. Remove from pans and cool.

Muffins are better if batter is stored in refrigerator overnight before using.

Yield: 24 to 30

ZUCCHINI MUFFINS

3	eggs
1	cup vegetable oil
2	cups sugar
1	teaspoon vanilla
2	cups grated unpeeled zucchini
3	cups all-purpose flour
1	teaspoon baking soda
¼	teaspoon baking powder
½	teaspoon salt
1	tablespoon cinnamon
1	cup chopped pecans

Combine eggs, oil, sugar, vanilla and zucchini, mixing well. Stir dry ingredients together in mixing bowl. Make a well in dry ingredients, pour in liquid mixture and stir just until dry ingredients are moistened. Spoon batter into greased and floured muffin pans, filling cups ½ to ¾ full. Bake at 325 degrees for 25 to 30 minutes or until golden brown.

Yield: 24

PARTY BREAD

1	large loaf unsliced bread
½	cup butter, softened
¼	teaspoon salt
1	teaspoon celery seed
¼	teaspoon paprika
	Dash of red pepper

Trim crust from bread. Cut loaf into 1½-inch thick slices, carefully leaving slices joined at bottom side. Combine butter and seasonings; spread mixture on cut sides and top of loaf. Cut loaf lengthwise but leave slices attached at bottom. Wrap loaf in aluminum foil. Bake at 400 degrees for 15 to 18 minutes.

Yield: 16 to 20 servings

FLOUR TORTILLAS

2	cups all-purpose flour
½	teaspoon salt
¼	cup lard or vegetable shortening
½	cup hot water

Mix flour and salt together. Cut lard or shortening into flour until texture is crumbly. Gradually add water, mixing with fork until dough forms a ball. Knead on lightly-floured surface for about 5 minutes or until dough is elastic and smooth. Let stand, covered, for 10 minutes. Divide dough into 12 balls. On lightly-floured surface, roll each ball to 7-inch diameter. Cook on hot ungreased griddle for 20 to 30 seconds on each side or until spotted and tender. Serve immediately with butter or keep warm in folded towel for up to 1 hour before serving.

Yield: 12

GARLIC ROLLS

1	(16 ounce) package frozen yeast rolls, thawed
½	cup butter
⅓	cup grated Parmesan cheese
2	teaspoons garlic salt
	Sesame seed
	Parsley flakes

Tear rolls in halves; place half of rolls in buttered 10-inch fluted tube pan. Combine butter, cheese and garlic salt in saucepan; heat until melted and blended. Pour half of mixture over dough in pan. Sprinkle with sesame seed and parsley. Place remaining dough in pan, drizzle with remaining butter mixture and add seasonings. Let rise, covered, for 1 hour. Punch down each roll with fingertip just before baking. Bake at 375 degrees for 30 to 35 minutes.

Yield: 12 servings

BROWN BREAD

2	cups bran cereal (not flakes)
2	cups buttermilk
2	teaspoons baking soda
2	eggs
1¾	cup firmly-packed dark brown sugar
2	cups all-purpose flour
1	(15 ounce) package seedless raisins, dusted with flour
½	teaspoon salt

Combine bran, buttermilk and soda in mixing bowl; let stand for 30 minutes. Stir in eggs, sugar, flour, raisins and salt; mix well. Pour batter into 4 greased 20-ounce coffee cans or loaf pans. Bake at 350 degrees for 1 hour or 55 minutes for loaves.

Yield: 4 loaves

STRAWBERRY BREAD

2	(10 ounce) packages frozen strawberries, thawed and mashed
1¼	cups vegetable oil
4	eggs, beaten
2	cups sugar
3	cups all-purpose flour
1	teaspoon baking soda
1	teaspoon salt
1	tablespoon cinnamon
1	cup chopped nuts

Combine strawberries, oil, eggs and sugar, mixing thoroughly. Sift dry ingredients together and add to strawberry mixture. Add nuts and stir until blended. Pour batter into 2 greased 9x5x3-inch loaf pans. Bake at 350 degrees for 1 hour.

Yield: 2 loaves

HERB BREAD

1	envelope dry yeast
¼	cup warm (105 to 115 degrees) water
¼	cup sugar
¼	cup vegetable shortening
1½	teaspoons salt
¾	cup milk, scalded
3 to 3½	cups all-purpose flour
¼	teaspoon ground cloves
½	teaspoon nutmeg
1	teaspoon ground sage
2	teaspoons celery seeds
1	egg, lightly beaten

Dissolve yeast in warm water and set aside. Combine sugar, shortening and salt in large mixing bowl. Stir in milk and let cool to lukewarm. Add about half the flour and mix well. Add seasonings, yeast and egg; beat until smooth. Add remaining flour to make soft dough. Knead for about 8 minutes. Place dough in lightly-greased bowl, turning once to grease all surfaces. Let rise, covered, for about 1½ hours. Punch down, cover and let rest 10 to 15 minutes. Shape dough into round loaf and place in greased 9-inch pie plate. Let rise, covered, in warm place for 45 to 60 minutes or until doubled in bulk. Bake at 400 degrees for 35 minutes.

Dill or caraway seed may be substituted for celery seed and poultry seasoning used instead of sage.

Yield: 1 loaf

HONEY OATMEAL BREAD

½   cup margarine
½   cup honey
2   cups warm milk
1   tablespoon salt
¾   cup oatmeal, uncooked
½   cup bran flakes
2   eggs
5   cups bread flour, divided
2   packages dry yeast

Melt margarine and place in large mixing bowl. Stir in honey, milk, salt, oatmeal, bran flakes, eggs and 2 cups flour. Using electric mixer, mix until well blended. Add yeast and mix thoroughly. Add 3 cups flour and knead for about 10 minutes. Let rise, covered with dish towel, in warm place until doubled in bulk. (Let rise overnight for a yeast flavor.) Punch dough down and divide in two portions. Shape each into loaf and place in greased and floured 9x5x3-inch loaf pans. Let rise, uncovered, on stove top until doubled in bulk. Bake at 250 degrees for 20 minutes; increase oven heat to 325 degrees and bake for 40 minutes or until golden brown. Remove from pans. For soft crust, brush with margarine.

Yield: 2 loaves

OATMEAL BREAD

5   cups lukewarm milk or potato water
½   cup firmly-packed brown sugar
2   tablespoons salt
¼   cup vegetable shortening
4   packages dry yeast or yeast cakes
4   cups regular rolled oats, uncooked
8   cups sifted bread or unbleached flour
3   cups whole wheat flour

Combine milk, brown sugar, salt and shortening in large mixing bowl. Add yeast and stir until dissolved. Stir in oats. Using spoon, add half of flour; work in remaining flour by hand, using just enough to make dough easy to handle. Place dough on lightly-floured surface, cover and let stand for 10 minutes. Knead until smooth. Shape into ball and place in large greased bowl. Let rise, covered with damp cloth, in warm place for about 1 hour or until doubled in bulk. Punch dough down. Divide into 4 portions, shape each into a loaf and place in greased 9x5x3-inch loaf pans. Let rise, covered with damp cloth, for 40 minutes or until doubled in bulk. Bake at 400 degrees for 30 to 40 minutes. Bread may be frozen.

Yield: 4 loaves

RAISIN BATTER BREAD

½ cup milk, scalded
¼ cup vegetable shortening
1 tablespoon sugar
1½ teaspoons salt
1 package dry or cake yeast
¼ cup warm (105 to 115 degrees) water
1 egg
1 teaspoon cinnamon
2 teaspoons grated orange peel
3⅓ cups sifted all-purpose flour, divided
1 cup raisins

POWDERED SUGAR FROSTING

1 cup sifted powdered sugar
2 tablespoons milk or cream
1 teaspoon almond flavoring

Combine milk, shortening, sugar and salt in large bowl of electric mixer. Cool to lukewarm. Dissolve yeast in warm water and add to lukewarm milk mixture. Stir in egg, cinnamon, orange peel and 2 cups flour; beat 2 minutes at medium speed (300 strokes by hand). Stir in 1⅓ cups flour and raisins. Spoon batter into greased 1½-quart casserole. Let rise, covered with damp towel, in warm place for about 1 hour or until doubled in bulk. Bake at 350 degrees for 40 to 45 minutes. Remove from casserole and cool on wire rack. Prepare frosting by blending sugar, cream and flavoring; beat until smooth. Spread over loaf.

Yield: 1 loaf

THREE LOAF BREAD

1 package dry yeast
½ cup plus 1 tablespoon sugar, divided
2½ cups warm (105 to 115 degrees) water, divided
1 egg
½ cup corn oil
1½ teaspoons salt
½ cup sugar
8 to 9 cups unbleached flour
Butter

Dissolve yeast and 1 tablespoon sugar in ½ cup warm water in large mixing bowl; let stand in warm place for 45 minutes. Add egg, oil, 2 cups warm water, salt and ½ cup sugar; beat well. Gradually add flour, beating until thick batter forms. Pour onto well floured surface and knead for about 10 minutes, adding enough flour to make dough easy to handle. Place dough in well-greased bowl and let rise for 1 hour or until doubled in bulk. Knead dough again; return to pan and let rise again until doubled in bulk. Knead, then divide in 2 large or 3 small portions. Shape into loaves and place in well-greased 9x5x3-inch loaf pans. Let rise until doubled in bulk. Bake at 350 degrees for 30 to 35 minutes or until done. Brush with butter.

Yield: 2 or 3 loaves

SOUR DOUGH BREAD

STARTER

1	package dry yeast
2	cups warm (105 to 115 degrees) water, divided
½	cup instant potatoes
½	cup sugar
2	teaspoons salt

FEED

¾	cup sugar
3	tablespoons instant potatoes
1	cup warm water

Dissolve yeast in ½ cup warm water in mixing bowl. Stir in 1½ cups water, ½ cup potatoes, ½ cup sugar and salt; mix well. Let stand at room temperature for 24 hours. Combine ¾ cup sugar, 3 tablespoons potatoes and 1 cup water; mix well and add to starter. Let stand at room temperature for 8 to 12 hours. Remove 1 cup to make bread; store remainder in refrigerator for 3 to 5 days. Feed again; if not making bread after feeding starter, discard 1 cup to avoid deflating the starter.

SOURDOUGH BREAD

¼	cup sugar
½	cup vegetable oil
1	tablespoon salt
1	cup sour dough starter
1½	cups warm water
6	cups bread flour
	Vegetable oil

Combine sugar, oil, salt, starter, water and flour in large mixing bowl; mix well to form stiff batter. Place dough in well-greased bowl, turning to coat on all sides. Cover with aluminum foil and let stand overnight at room temperature. Punch dough down and knead slightly. Divide into 3 portions and knead each on lightly-floured surface 8 to 20 times. Place in greased 9x5x3-inch loaf pans. Brush with oil. Let rise, covered with waxed paper, for 4 to 5 hours or all day. Bake at 350 degrees for 30 to 45 minutes. Remove from pans, brush with butter and cool on wire rack. Wrap and store in refrigerator or freezer.

Yield: 3 loaves

WHOLE WHEAT SPONGE DOUGH

1	package dry yeast
2	cups warm (105 to 115 degrees) water
2	tablespoons sugar
2	teaspoons salt
3	cups bread flour
½	cup hot water
½	cup firmly-packed brown sugar
3	tablespoons vegetable shortening
3	cups whole wheat flour

Dissolve yeast in warm water in large mixing bowl. Add sugar, salt and bread flour; beat until smooth. Let rise in warm place until light and fluffy. Combine hot water, brown sugar and shortening; cool to lukewarm. Add to flour mixture. Stir in whole wheat flour, mix and knead until smooth. Let rise until doubled in bulk. Divide in 3 portions, shape into loaves and place in greased 9x5x3-inch loaf pans. Let rise until doubled in bulk. Bake at 375 degrees for 50 minutes.

Yield: 3 loaves

Breads

WHOLE WHEAT BREAD

9	tablespoons dry yeast
8	cups warm (105 to 115 degrees) water
1	cup vegetable oil
2	cups honey
6 to 7	pounds whole wheat flour
2	tablespoons salt
	Butter, softened

Dissolve yeast in warm water in large mixing bowl. Add oil and honey; mix well. Stir in flour and salt; mix thoroughly. Let rise, covered, until doubled in bulk. Punch dough down and let rise again. Knead dough, divide in 6 portions, shape into loaves and place in greased 9x5x3-inch loaf pans. Let rise. Bake at 400 degrees for 10 minutes; reduce oven heat to 350 degrees and bake for 20 minutes. Brush tops of loaves with butter. Loaves freeze well.

Yield: 6 loaves

HEAVENLY YEAST ROLLS

2	packages dry yeast
⅓	cup warm (105 to 115 degrees) water
½	cup sugar
½	cup vegetable shortening
⅔	cup milk
2	teaspoons salt
5 to 5½	cups sifted all-purpose flour, divided
3	eggs, beaten
¼	cup butter, softened

Dissolve yeast in warm water. Combine sugar, shortening, milk and salt in saucepan; scald until shortening is melted and sugar is dissolved. Cool to lukewarm. Add 1½ cups flour and beat well. Blend in eggs and yeast. Stir in 3½ to 4 cups flour, mixing to form soft dough. Knead on lightly-floured surface until dough is light and elastic. Place in greased bowl, turning once to coat surface. Let rise in warm place for 1½ to 2 hours or until doubled in bulk. Knead slightly on floured surface; let stand for 5 minutes. Divide dough into three portions and roll each into a circle. Spread with butter. Cut each circle in 12 wedges. Beginning with wide edge, roll up wedge toward narrow end. Pinch into crescent shape and place on greased baking sheet. Let rise for 30 to 40 minutes or until doubled in bulk. Bake at 400 degrees for 10 minutes.

Baked rolls may be frozen. Fill with ham and cheese for breakfast.

Yield: 36

WHOLE WHEAT OATMEAL ROLLS

½	cup regular oatmeal, uncooked
½	cup whole wheat flour
2	teaspoons salt
¼	cup vegetable shortening
2	tablespoons molasses
2⅓	tablespoons honey, divided
1	cup boiling water
2	packages dry yeast
½	cup warm (105 to 115 degrees) water
1	egg
2½ to 3½	cups all-purpose flour

Combine oatmeal, whole wheat flour, salt, shortening, molasses and 2 tablespoons honey in mixing bowl. Add boiling water, mix and let stand until cool. Dissolve yeast in warm water with 1 teaspoon honey. Add egg to cooled oatmeal mixture; add flour, mix and knead lightly. Place dough in greased bowl. Let rise, covered with damp cloth, in warm place for about 1 hour or until doubled in bulk. Punch dough down and cut in 12 pieces. Shape each into a ball and place in greased 9-inch square baking pan. Let rise for 45 minutes. Bake at 350 degrees for 40 minutes.

Yield: 12

SKILLET ALMOND COFFEE CAKE

¾	cup butter, melted
1½	cups sugar
2	eggs
1½	cups all-purpose flour
½	teaspoon salt
1	teaspoon almond flavoring
½	cup slivered almonds
	Whipped cream
4	maraschino cherries, halved

Cream butter and sugar until smooth. Add eggs, 1 at a time, beating well after each addition. Add flour, salt and almond flavoring to creamed mixture; mix well. Line ovenproof 10-inch iron skillet with aluminum foil, extending foil above edge. Spray with vegetable oil or non-stick vegetable spray. Pour batter into skillet. Sprinkle with almonds, reserving a few for garnish. Bake at 350 degrees for 30 to 40 minutes. Cool in skillet. Cut into wedges and serve with dollop of unsweetened whipped cream, maraschino cherries and a few almond slivers.
Only an iron skillet should be used.

Yield: 8 servings

Breads

BANANA SOUR CREAM COFFEE CAKE

½	cup butter, softened
1½	cups sugar, divided
2	eggs
3	ripe bananas, mashed
½	teaspoon vanilla
½	cup sour cream
2	cups all-purpose flour
1	teaspoon baking powder
1	teaspoon baking soda
¼	teaspoon salt
½	cup chopped nuts
1	teaspoon cinnamon

Cream butter and 1 cup sugar until smooth. Add eggs, bananas and vanilla; mix thoroughly. Stir in sour cream. Combine flour, baking powder, soda and salt; fold into creamed mixture and set aside. Combine nuts, ½ cup sugar and cinnamon. Spread half of batter in greased 10-inch tube pan, sprinkle with nut mixture and add remaining batter. Bake at 350 degrees for 45 to 50 minutes.

Yield: 12 to 16 servings

BLUEBERRY COFFEE CAKE

2	cups all-purpose flour
1½	cups sugar
⅔	cup margarine
2	teaspoons baking powder
1	teaspoon salt
2	eggs, separated
1	cup milk
1	cup blueberries

Sift flour and sugar together into mixing bowl. Using pastry blender or forks, cut in margarine until pea-sized consistency. Reserve ¾ cup crumbs for topping. To remaining mixture, add baking powder, salt, egg yolks and milk; using electric mixer, beat for 3 minutes. Separately beat egg whites until stiff but not dry; fold into batter, mixing thoroughly but gently. Spread batter in well-greased and lightly floured 12x8x2-inch baking pan or dish. Sprinkle blueberries over batter and top with reserved crumbs. Bake at 350 degrees for 40 to 50 minutes.

Yield: 12 servings

FANCY BREAKFAST BREAD

2	loaves frozen bread dough
½	teaspoon cinnamon
½	cup margarine, melted
¾	cup firmly-packed brown sugar
1	(6 ounce) package regular vanilla pudding mix
¼	cup milk

Allow bread dough to thaw but not rise. Tear 1 loaf into pieces and place in greased 13x9x3-inch baking pan. Sprinkle dough with cinnamon. Combine margarine, brown sugar, pudding mix and milk; beat until smooth. Pour pudding mixture over dough. Tear second loaf into pieces and place in pan, filling any empty spaces. Let rise for about 2 hours or until doubled in bulk. Bake at 375 degrees for 30 minutes. Cool in pan for 3 minutes, then invert on serving plate.

Yield: 12 to 16 servings

CRANBERRY COFFEE CAKE

2¼	cups all-purpose flour
1	cup sugar
1	teaspoon baking powder
1	teaspoon baking soda
¼	teaspoon salt
1	cup chopped nuts
1	cup chopped dates
1	cup fresh cranberries
	Grated peel of 1 orange
2	eggs, beaten
1	cup buttermilk
¾	cup vegetable oil

GLAZE

	Juice of 1 orange
1	cup sugar

Sift dry ingredients together into mixing bowl. Stir in nuts, dates, cranberries and orange peel. Add eggs, buttermilk and oil; mix until well blended. Pour batter into greased and floured 10-inch tube pan. Bake at 350 degrees for 1 hour. Prepare glaze by heating orange juice with sugar in saucepan and cooking until sugar is dissolved. Remove cake from pan and cool on wire rack. Place on serving plate. Pour glaze over cooled cake and chill overnight. Let warm to room temperature before serving.

Yield: 12 to 16 servings

BUTTERSCOTCH ROLLS

1	package dry yeast
1½	cups warm (105 to 115 degrees) water
5	cups all-purpose flour
¾	cup sugar, divided
1	teaspoon salt
½	cup vegetable shortening
2	tablespoons butter, softened
1½	teaspoons cinnamon
¼	cup butter
1	cup firmly-packed brown sugar
½	cup dark corn syrup
⅔	cup pecans

Dissolve yeast in warm water. Sift flour, ¼ cup sugar and salt together in mixing bowl. Cut shortening into dry ingredients. Add dissolved yeast liquid. Mix until well blended and dough forms elastic-like strands when pulled from bowl. Place in greased bowl. Let rise, covered, for 30 minutes. Place half of dough on well-floured surface; do not knead. Using rolling pin, gently spread dough to ¼-inch thick rectangle. Spread with soft butter and sprinkle with ½ cup sugar and cinnamon. Roll, jelly roll fashion, and cut into ½-inch slices. Melt butter in saucepan. Add brown sugar and syrup; heat, stirring often, until blended. Pour syrup mixture into 13x9x3-inch pan prepared with non-stick vegetable spray. Sprinkle pecans on syrup mixture. Place dough slices, cut side down, on pecans. Let rise for 40 to 45 minutes or until light. Bake at 375 degrees for about 25 minutes. Cool in pan for 5 minutes, then invert on serving dish. Remaining dough can be used immediately or stored in refrigerator, well covered, for several days, then prepared in same way.

Yield: 12 to 16 servings

PUMPKIN LOAVES

2	cups unsifted all-purpose flour
½	teaspoon baking powder
1	teaspoon baking soda
½	teaspoon salt
1	teaspoon ground nutmeg
1	teaspoon ground cloves
1	teaspoon cinnamon
¾	cup butter or margarine, softened
2	cups sugar
2	eggs
1	(16 ounce) can pumpkin

Sift flour, baking powder, soda, salt and spices together; set aside. Using electric mixer at medium speed, beat butter and sugar until blended and smooth. Add eggs, 1 at a time, beating well after each; beat mixture until light and fluffy. Add pumpkin and beat well. Gradually add dry ingredients, beating at low speed until combined. Spread batter in 2 lightly-greased 9x5x3-inch loaf pans. Bake at 325 degrees for 1 hour and 15 minutes. Cool in pan for 10 minutes, then remove and cool on rack.

Yield: 2 loaves

CHEESE BRAIDS

1	(8 ounce) carton sour cream, slightly warmed
½	cup sugar
1	teaspoon salt
½	cup melted margarine
2	packages dry yeast
½	cup warm (105 to 115 degrees) water
2	eggs, beaten
4	cups all-purpose flour

FILLING

2	(8 ounce) packages cream cheese, softened
¾	cup sugar
⅛	teaspoon salt
1	egg, beaten
2	teaspoons vanilla

GLAZE

2	cups powdered sugar
¼	cup milk
2	teaspoons vanilla

Combine sour cream, sugar, salt and margarine. Let stand until cool. Dissolve yeast in warm water in large bowl. Add cooled cream mixture, eggs and flour; mix well. Chill, covered tightly, overnight. Divide dough into 4 portions; roll each on well-floured board to form 12x8-inch rectangle. Prepare filling, blending cream cheese, sugar, salt, egg and vanilla until smooth. Spread one-fourth of filling on each dough rectangle, roll up, jelly roll fashion, and place seam side down on baking sheet; slit at 2-inch intervals. Let rise, covered, in warm place for about 1 hour. Bake at 375 degrees for 12 to 15 minutes. Prepare glaze, blending sugar, milk and vanilla until smooth. Drizzle glaze over warm braids.

Yield: 24 servings

PINEAPPLE-DATE LOAF

¼	cup margarine, softened
½	cup sugar
1	egg
1	teaspoon lemon flavoring
1	(8½ ounce) can crushed pineapple
½	cup chopped walnuts or pecans
2½	cups sifted all-purpose flour
2½	teaspoons baking powder
¼	teaspoon baking soda
1	teaspoon salt
¾	cup finely chopped dates
¼	cup water
½	cup chopped red and green maraschino cherries, well drained

Cream margarine and sugar until smooth. Add egg and lemon flavoring. Drain pineapple, reserving liquid; add pineapple and nuts to creamed mixture. Sift dry ingredients together. Add dates to dry ingredients, mixing to separate date pieces. Alternately add dry ingredients and reserved pineapple juice with water to creamed mixture. Fold in cherries. Pour batter into greased 9x5x3-inch loaf pan. Bake at 350 degrees for 55 minutes. Cool in pan for 10 minutes, remove and cool on wire rack.
Fruitcake flavor of loaf improves after standing overnight.

Yield: 1 loaf

ORANGE OR CINNAMON ROLLS

1	cup water
½	cup butter
½	cup vegetable shortening
¾	cup sugar
1½	teaspoons salt
2	packages dry yeast
1	cup warm (105 to 115 degrees) water
2	eggs, lightly beaten
6	cups all-purpose flour

FILLING
6 to 8	tablespoons butter, softened
½	cup sugar
1½	teaspoons grated orange peel or 1 teaspoon cinnamon

GLAZE
2	cups powdered sugar
3 to 5	tablespoons orange juice or milk for cinnamon rolls

Combine 1 cup water, butter and shortening in saucepan; bring to a boil. Stir in sugar and salt. Cool to lukewarm. Sprinkle yeast over 1 cup warm water in large bowl and stir to dissolve. Add cooled shortening mixture with eggs to yeast liquid. Stir in flour, mixing thoroughly to form thick dough. Chill, covered, overnight. Use half of dough, reserving remainder for later use. Divide again and roll each portion on lightly-floured surface to form two 12x8-inch rectangles. Prepare filling, blending butter, sugar, peel or cinnamon, until smooth. Spread half of filling on each dough rectangle. Roll up, jelly roll fashion. Cut into 18 slices and place in buttered pie plates. Let rise for 1½ hours or until light. Bake at 375 degrees for 15 minutes. Prepare glaze by blending sugar and liquid until smooth. Drizzle glaze over warm rolls. Remaining dough may be used immediately or stored, covered, in refrigerator for several days.

Yield: 36

SPICY PINEAPPLE ZUCCHINI BREAD

3	eggs, beaten
1	cup vegetable oil
2	cups sugar
2	teaspoons vanilla
2	cups coarsely shredded zucchini
1	(8½ ounce) can crushed pineapple, drained
3	cups all-purpose flour
½	teaspoon baking powder
2	teaspoons baking soda
1	teaspoon salt
1½	teaspoons cinnamon
¾	teaspoon nutmeg
1	cup chopped nuts
1	cup raisins

Combine eggs, oil, sugar and vanilla; beat until thick and foamy. Stir in zucchini and pineapple. Combine dry ingredients; add with nuts and raisins to zucchini mixture and mix well. Pour batter into 2 greased and floured 9x5x3-inch loaf pans. Bake at 350 degrees for 1 hour or until wooden pick inserted near center comes out clean. Cool loaves in pan.

Yield: 2 loaves

OR I AM PERSUADED,

THAT NEITHER

DEATH, NOR LIFE, NOR ANGELS,

NOR PRINCIPALITIES, NOR

POWERS, NOR THINGS PRESENT,

NOR THINGS TO COME, NOR

HEIGHT, NOR DEPTH, NOR ANY

OTHER CREATURE, SHALL BE ABLE

TO SEPARATE US FROM THE LOVE

OF GOD WHICH IS IN CHRIST JESUS

OUR LORD.

Romans 8:38-39

ASPARAGUS SOUP PHILIPPINE STYLE

1	chicken breast
¼	pound pork
5	cups chicken broth
	Garlic clove, to taste
1	medium-sized onion, thinly sliced
1	teaspoon vegetable oil
	Salt to taste
1	(8 ounce) can asparagus, drained and liquid reserved
3	tablespoons milk

Simmer chicken and pork in broth in large saucepan until tender. Reserve broth; cut meat into small pieces and set aside. Mash garlic. Sauté garlic and onion in oil until golden brown. Add chicken and pork; sauté for about 2 minutes. Season with salt and cook for 2 minutes. Stir in chicken broth and asparagus liquid. Cut asparagus into 1-inch lengths and add to broth mixture. Cook for about 20 minutes. Stir in milk.

Yield: 4 servings

BLACK BEAN SOUP

1	(16 ounce) package black beans
	Cold water
2	large onions, minced
1	stalk celery, finely chopped
3	large cloves garlic, crushed
1	red bell pepper, minced
¼	cup olive oil
½	teaspoon crushed oregano
8	cups chicken broth
1¾	pounds ham hocks or ham bones
	Salt and black pepper to taste
2	bay leaves
2	whole cloves
8	whole black peppercorns
2	tablespoons red wine vinegar
	Sour cream to garnish
	Chopped green onion to garnish

Soak beans overnight in water. Drain. Sauté minced onion, celery, garlic and pepper in oil in large heavy saucepan for 10 minutes. Stir in oregano, broth, beans, ham hocks or bones and seasonings. Bring to a boil, then simmer for 2 hours or until beans are tender. Remove bay leaves and bones from soup. Remove 1 cup beans, mash into a paste and return to soup. Check seasoning. Before serving, add vinegar. Ladle into bowls, garnish with dollop of sour cream and sprinkle with green onion.

Yield: 8 servings

LENTIL SOUP

1	(16 ounce) package lentils
	Cold water
2	large onions, chopped
4	cloves garlic, chopped
3	tablespoons olive oil
3	carrots, diced
4	stalks celery with leaves
1	red bell pepper, chopped
8	oil-packed sun-dried tomatoes, drained and chopped
1	(28 ounce) can crushed tomatoes
2	tablespoons tomato paste
2	teaspoons dried basil
6	cups water
1	ham bone
	Salt to taste
	Black pepper to taste

Soak lentils in water overnight. Drain. In heavy 4-quart saucepan, sauté onion and garlic in oil for 10 minutes. Stir in carrots, celery and pepper; cook for about 6 minutes or until pepper is tender. Add tomatoes, tomato paste, basil and 6 cups water. Bring to a boil. Stir in lentils and add ham bone. Simmer for about 1½ hours or until lentils are tender, adding water as needed. Season with salt and pepper to taste.

Yield: 6 to 8 servings

BROCCOLI CHEESE SOUP

2	(10 ounce) packages frozen chopped broccoli
3½	cups chicken broth, divided
10	large mushrooms, sliced
⅔	cup finely chopped celery
⅓	cup chopped green onion
1	tablespoon parsley
2	tablespoons butter
2	teaspoons garlic powder
1½	cups (6 ounces) grated mild Cheddar cheese
½	cup sour cream
½	teaspoon hot pepper sauce

Prepare broccoli according to package directions; drain. Place broccoli in blender with 1½ cups broth; blend until puree forms. Mix pureed broccoli with 2 cups broth in medium saucepan; simmer over medium heat. In large skillet, sauté mushrooms, celery, onion and parsley in butter until onion is transluscent. Season with garlic powder and add broccoli. Simmer for 30 minutes. Stir in cheese and sour cream and season with hot pepper sauce. Serve when cheese is melted.

Yield: 4 to 6 servings

CORN CHOWDER

1	cup diced ham
½	cup chopped onion
½	cup chopped celery
½	cup chopped green bell pepper
3	tablespoons butter or margarine
1	(14 ounce) can or 2 cups fresh chicken broth
3	medium potatoes, cubed
1	(16 ounce) can whole kernel corn, drained
1	(16 ounce) can cream style corn
1	(2 ounce) jar pimientos
1	cup (4 ounces) shredded Cheddar cheese
1	cup whipping cream, unwhipped
	Salt to taste
	Black pepper to taste

Sauté ham, onion, celery and pepper in butter in large saucepan until onion is transluscent. Stir in broth, potatoes, corn and pimientos. Simmer for 30 minutes. Add cheese and stir until melted. Blend in cream. Season with salt and pepper. To reheat, warm thoroughly but do not boil.

Yield: 6 servings

POTATO SOUP DELUXE

2	stalks celery, sliced
1	medium-sized onion, chopped
2	tablespoons butter
6	medium potatoes, cubed
2	carrots, sliced
3	cups water
5	chicken bouillon cubes
¼	teaspoon seasoned salt
½	teaspoon dried thyme
½	teaspoon crushed rosemary
	Dash of garlic powder
	Dash of black pepper
2	cups milk
1	cup (4 ounces) shredded longhorn Cheddar cheese

Sauté celery and onion in butter in large Dutch oven until celery is tender. Add vegtables, water, bouillon and seasonings. Simmer, covered, for 20 minutes or until vegetables are tender. Remove from heat and mash vegetables with potato masher. Stir in milk and cheese. Cook, stirring constantly, until cheese is melted.

Yield: 6 to 8 servings

Soups

POTATO TOMATO SOUP

2	cups sliced onion
¼	cup butter
2	cups sliced potatoes
6	cups boiling water
5	cups seeded, sliced tomatoes or 3 cups canned tomatoes
2	teaspoons sugar
1	teaspoon salt
⅛	teaspoon paprika
	Pinch of chervil
1	cup whipping cream, unwhipped

Sauté onion in butter until transluscent. Add onion and potatoes to boiling water in large stock pot. Simmer for about 30 minutes. Add tomatoes, sugar and seasonings. Simmer, covered, for about 20 minutes. Puree vegetable mixture through fine strainer, blender or food processor. Reheat and check seasoning. Heat cream. Stir vegetable mixture into cream and serve immediately.

Yield: 10 servings

VICHYSSOISE

4	leeks, white part only, sliced
1	medium-sized onion, sliced
¼	cup butter
5	medium potatoes, thinly sliced
4	cups chicken broth
1	tablespoon salt or to taste
3	cups milk
2	cups half and half, divided
	Chopped chives for garnish

Lightly sauté leeks and onion in butter in large saucepan. Add potatoes, broth and salt. Bring to a boil, reduce heat and cook for 35 minutes or until potatoes are very tender. Using electric blender, puree vegetables with broth until smooth. Return puree to saucepan and add milk and 1 cup half and half. Bring to a boil and add remaining half and half. Remove from heat. Chill thoroughly. Serve cold, garnished with chives.

Yield: 8 servings

VEGETABLE CHOWDER

1	pound zucchini squash
½	cup chopped onion
2	tablespoons chopped parsley
½	teaspoon basil leaves
1	tablespoon margarine
3	tablespoons all-purpose flour
2½	cups water
2	teaspoons chicken bouillon granules
1	teaspoon lemon juice
½	teaspoon black pepper
1	cup frozen whole kernel corn
1	(16 ounce) can tomatoes, drained and diced
1	(12 ounce) can evaporated skim milk
1	cup (4 ounces) cubed American cheese

Cut zucchini in half lengthwise, then cut into ⅛-inch thick slices. Sauté zucchini, onion, parsley and basil in margarine in large saucepan; cook for about 6 minutes, stirring occasionally. Stir in flour. Add water, bouillon, lemon juice and pepper. Bring to a boil, stirring frequently. Add corn and bring to a boil, stirring to prevent sticking. Stir in tomatoes. Add milk and heat to just boiling. Add cheese and stir until melted; do not boil.

Yield: 4 to 6 servings

WILLIE'S WONDERFUL SOUP

1	ham bone
4½	quarts water
2	chicken bouillon cubes
1	teaspoon peppercorns
3	bay leaves
2	(10 ounce) cans tomato soup, undiluted
2	(16 ounce) cans stewed tomatoes
2	(16 ounce) cans French-style green beans
1 or 2	medium-sized onions, chopped
4 or 5	carrots, sliced
	Salt to taste
	Black pepper to taste
	Herbs to taste

Cook ham bone in water in large stock pot with bouillon, peppercorns and bay leaves for 30 to 40 minutes. Add vegetables; use no other vegetables. Simmer for 15 to 20 minutes or until carrots are tender. Season with salt, pepper and preferred soup spices such as thyme, marjoram and lemon pepper.

Yield: 12 to 20 servings

Soups

ZUCCHINI SOUP

2¼   **pounds zucchini, peeled**
2   **chicken bouillon cubes**
     Water
     Salt to taste
1   **(3 ounce) package cream cheese**

Cook zucchini with bouillon in water until tender. Season with salt. Reserving cooking liquid, remove zucchini and place in blender container. Blend to puree consistency. Pour puree in pan and add enough cooking liquid to form desired consistency. Simmer until hot. Cut cream cheese into chunks, add to hot soup and stir until melted.

Yield: 4 servings

BUTTERNUT SQUASH SOUP

1   **cup chopped onion**
1   **tablespoon chopped sage or 1 teaspoon dried sage**
     Pinch of allspice or cloves
2   **tablespoons unsalted butter**
1   **small apple, diced**
4   **cups chicken broth**
2   **cups butternut squash pulp**
     Fresh lemon juice to taste
     Salt and black pepper to taste
¼   **cup yogurt or sour cream (optional) for garnish**
¼   **cup toasted slivered almonds**

Sauté onion and herbs in butter in medium saucepan over medium heat for about 10 minutes; do not brown onion. Add apple and broth; simmer for 15 minutes. Stir in squash and simmer for 5 minutes. Pour into blender container and puree until very smooth. Add lemon juice, salt and pepper. Garnish with dollops of yogurt or sour cream and sprinkle of almonds.

Yield: 6 servings

73

ROMAN EGG AND SPINACH SOUP

1	pound ground beef round
3	eggs, divided
¾	cup freshly grated Parmesan cheese, divided
¼	cup breadcrumbs
1	clove garlic, minced
½	teaspoon oregano
	Boiling water
4	(11 ounce) cans chicken broth
1	pound mild Italian sausage, browned and cut in 1-inch pieces
1	medium head escarole, torn in bite-sized pieces
1	pound spinach, torn in bite-sized pieces
	Freshly ground black pepper

Combine ground beef, 1 egg, ¼ cup cheese, breadcrumbs, garlic and oregano, mix and shape into 1-inch balls. Place in boiling water, simmer for 15 minutes, remove and drain. Mix 2 eggs with ½ cup cheese. Bring broth to a boil in large saucepan. Add meatballs, sausage, escarole and spinach. Pour egg and cheese mixture into broth; simmer for 3 to 4 minutes. Serve with additional Parmesan cheese if desired and pepper.

Yield: 8 servings

MANHATTAN SUPPER SOUP

1	pound ground beef
2	cups chopped cabbage
1	large onion, thinly sliced
3	carrots, cut in 1-inch pieces
1	potato, cubed
1	(16 ounce) can tomatoes
1	(10 ounce) can beef broth
2	broth cans water
½	(6 ounce) can tomato paste
1	tablespoon parsley flakes
1½	teaspoons salt
¼	teaspoon black pepper
1½	teaspoons sugar
1	(10 ounce) package frozen English peas

Cook beef until lightly browned; drain excess grease. In large stock pot, combine beef, cabbage, onion, carrots, potato, tomatoes, broth, water, tomato paste and seasonings. Bring to a boil, then simmer, uncovered, for 50 minutes. Add peas and cook, covered, for 10 minutes or until peas are tender. Soup may be frozen.

Yield: 6 to 8 servings

SIX HOUR STEW

2	pounds boneless beef stew meat, cubed
1	(26 ounce) can tomatoes
4 or 5	new potatoes, cut in large pieces
4	stalks celery, cut in 1-inch pieces
4 or 5	carrots, cut in 1-inch pieces
1	large onion, cut in large pieces
3	tablespoons tapioca
1½	teaspoons salt
½	teaspoon basil
½	teaspoon oregano
¼	teaspoon marjoram
1	small bay leaf
2	tablespoons plus 2 teaspoons Worcestershire sauce

Combine vegetables, meat, tapioca, seasonings and Worcestershire sauce in large roasting pan. Bake, covered, at 250 degrees for 6 hours.

Yield: 4 to 6 servings

SOUTH GEORGIA BRUNSWICK STEW

2	pounds beef shoulder
3	pounds pork butt roast
	Water
1	(4 pound) chicken, cut up
4	(16 ounce) cans tomatoes
2	(15 ounce) cans cream-style or 4 cups fresh corn
1	pound onions, chopped
4	cups fresh lima beans
2	cups ketchup
1	(4 ounce) bottle Worcestershire sauce
	Hot pepper sauce

Simmer pork and beef in water to cover until tender; separately cook chicken in water until tender. Remove meat from cooking liquid, reserving broth. Cool, remove bones, chop and mix together. Combine broth, tomatoes, corn, onions and beans in large stock pot. Mix ketchup, Worcestershire sauce and hot pepper sauce until smooth. Add sauce and meat to vegetable mixture. Simmer for at least 1 hour. Stew may be frozen.

Yield: 20 to 25 servings

CHICKEN VEGETABLE SOUP

1	(3 pound) chicken, cooked and boned
5	cups chicken broth
1	medium-sized onion, chopped
2	cups chopped carrots
2	cups chopped celery
2	cups diced potatoes
1	teaspoon salt
¼	teaspoon black pepper
1	bay leaf
4	chicken bouillon cubes
1	(16 ounce) package processed cheese spread

Combine chicken, broth, vegetables and seasonings in large stock pot. Simmer until vegetables are tender. Cut cheese into chunks and add to soup, stirring until melted.

Yield: 8 servings

RITZ-CARLTON CLAM CHOWDER

2	cups diced potatoes
	Water
3	tablespoons diced salt pork
1	cup unsalted butter
1	cup diced onion
¾	cup all-purpose flour
6	cups clam juice
2	pounds fresh clam meat, coarsely chopped
2	cups half and half
1	cup whipping cream, unwhipped

Place potatoes in water to cover in saucepan; bring to a boil, then simmer for 3 minutes. Plunge into cold water, drain and set aside. In heavy stock pot, sauté salt pork in butter over low heat for 5 to 7 minutes or until lightly browned. Add onions and sauté until transluscent. Stir in flour and cook for 5 minutes, stirring constantly to avoid scorching. Warm clam juice in a saucepan. Gradually ladle warm clam juice into stock pot over medium heat, stirring constantly until roux and juice are completely blended and mixture is thick and smooth. Add clams and cook over medium heat for 5 minutes. Stir in half and half, whipping cream and potatoes. Season with salt and pepper. Reduce heat and simmer for 15 minutes, stirring occasionally to prevent sticking.

Yield: 8 to 10 servings

SEAFOOD GUMBO

1	cup vegetable oil or shortening
1½	cups all-purpose flour
8	cups water
1	(16 ounce) can tomatoes
1	(8 ounce) can tomato sauce
3	stalks celery, chopped
1	green bell pepper, chopped
2	(10 ounce) packages frozen okra
2	large onions, chopped
3	cloves garlic, minced
¼	cup chopped parsley
½	cup chopped green onion
3	pounds peeled shrimp
3	cups oysters
1	(6½ ounce) can crab meat
	Salt to taste
	Black pepper to taste
	Hot pepper sauce to taste
	Rice, cooked
	Filé powder

Heat oil in heavy iron skillet over medium heat. Stir in flour and cook, stirring constantly, until deeply browned; do not scorch. Place in large stock pot. Add water, tomatoes and tomato sauce; cook for 5 minutes. Stir in celery, peppers, okra, onion and garlic; cook for 10 minutes. Add parsley, green onion and seafood. Season with salt, pepper and hot pepper sauce. Cook for 30 minutes, adding water if too thick. To serve, place serving of rice in large soup bowl; pour gumbo over rice and sprinkle with filé powder.

Yield: 10 to 12 servings

OR GOD SO LOVED

THE WORLD, THAT HE

GAVE HIS ONLY BEGOTTEN SON,

THAT WHOEVER BELIEVES IN HIM

SHOULD NOT PERISH, BUT HAVE

ETERNAL LIFE.

John 3:16

ARTICHOKE AND HEARTS OF PALM SALAD

SALAD

2   (15 ounce) cans artichoke hearts, drained and quartered
2   (14 ounce) cans hearts of palm, drained and sliced
1   (2 ounce) jar chopped pimiento, drained
½   pound mushrooms, sliced
¼   cup ripe olives, chopped (optional)

DRESSING

2   teaspoons prepared mustard
1   tablespoon Worcestershire sauce
1   teaspoon salt
½   teaspoon black pepper
½   cup tarragon vinegar
½   cup olive oil
    Juice of ½ lemon
    Pinch of oregano
    Pinch of basil

Combine vegetables in a bowl. Prepare dressing in separate bowl, blending mustard, Worcestershire sauce, salt and pepper. Add vinegar, oil, lemon juice and herbs, mixing thoroughly. Just before serving, pour dressing over vegetables and lightly toss. Serve over leaf lettuce.

Salad, with dressing added, may be stored in refrigerator for additional meals.

Yield: 8 to 10 servings

MARINATED ASPARAGUS

1   (15 ounce) can asparagus spears, drained
½   cup sugar
¼   cup water
¼   cup tarragon vinegar
3   whole cloves
1   stick cinnamon
½   teaspoon salt
½   teaspoon celery seed

Arrange asparagus in serving dish. Combine water, vinegar and seasonings in saucepan. Bring to a boil, then pour marinade over asparagus. Chill, covered, for at least 12 hours.

Yield: 4 servings

AVOCADO AND GRAPEFRUIT SALAD

SALAD

2   medium avocados, peeled and sliced
2   medium-sized pink grapefruit, peeled and cut in sections
1   head Boston or Bibb lettuce

YOGURT DRESSING

1   cup plain yogurt
3 to 4   tablespoons honey
½   teaspoon vanilla

Arrange avocado slices and grapefruit sections on lettuce leaves on individual plates. Prepare dressing by blending yogurt, honey and vanilla until smooth. Drizzle over fruit.

Yield: 4 to 6 servings

BLACK EYED PEA SALAD

SALAD
2	(15 ounce) cans black eyed peas, drained
½	cup thinly sliced purple onion
½	cup green pepper strips

DRESSING
¼	cup vinegar
¼	cup salad oil
¼	cup sugar
1	clove garlic, minced
½	teaspoon salt
¼	teaspoon black pepper
⅛	teaspoon hot pepper sauce

Combine vegetables in bowl. Prepare dressing by blending vinegar, oil, sugar, garlic and seasonings, mixing until sugar is dissolved. Pour dressing over vegetables. Chill, covered, for 12 to 24 hours.

Yield: 6 to 8 servings

BROCCOLI-BACON SALAD

SALAD
1	bunch broccoli, chopped
½	pound bacon, cooked and crumbled
¾	cup chopped celery
½	cup raisins
½	cup chopped red onion
½	cup chopped walnuts

DRESSING
1	cup mayonnaise
¼	cup vinegar
¼	cup sugar

Combine broccoli, bacon, celery, raisins, onion and walnuts in bowl. Prepare dressing by blending mayonnaise, vinegar and sugar until smooth. Pour dressing over broccoli mixture.

Yield: 5 or 6 servings

FRESH BROCCOLI SALAD

SALAD
1	bunch broccoli, chopped
4	hard-cooked eggs, diced
1	small onion, grated
⅔	cup pimiento-stuffed olives, chopped

DRESSING
1½	teaspoons lemon juice
½	teaspoon sugar
1	cup mayonnaise

Combine broccoli, eggs, onion and olives in bowl. Prepare dressing by mixing lemon juice, sugar and mayonnaise together; fold into vegetable mixture. Chill before serving.

Yield: 6 to 8 servings

CAULIFLOWER SALAD

1	large head lettuce, shredded
1	large Bermuda onion, thinly sliced in rings
1	pound bacon, cooked and crumbled
1	large head cauliflower, separated in flowerets
2	cups mayonnaise
¼	cup sugar
⅓	cup grated Parmesan cheese

Layer lettuce, onion, bacon and cauliflower in bowl. Spread mayonnaise over cauliflower, sprinkle with sugar and top with cheese. Chill, covered, overnight. Toss lightly before serving.

Yield: 12 servings

SWEET AND SOUR SLAW

SLAW
1	medium head cabbage, shredded
2	large onions, thinly sliced
¾	cup plus 2 tablespoons sugar

DRESSING
1	tablespoon salt
1	teaspoon dry mustard
1	teaspoon celery seed
2	teaspoons sugar
¾	cup vegetable oil
1	cup vinegar

Alternate layers of cabbage and onion in bowl. Sprinkle with sugar. Prepare dressing by combining salt, mustard, celery seed and sugar in saucepan. Stir in oil and vinegar. Bring to a boil; pour hot dressing over vegetables. Chill for at least 4 hours.
Salad may be stored in refrigerator indefinitely and flavor improves with storage.

Yield: 10 servings

Salads

SOUR CREAM CUCUMBERS

SALAD
- ½ teaspoon salt
- ½ teaspoon sugar
- ½ teaspoon red pepper
- ¼ cup garlic wine vinegar

DRESSING
- 1 cup sour cream
- 2 teaspoons chopped chives
- 1 teaspoon celery seed
- 2 or 3 cucumbers

Combine salt, sugar, red pepper and vinegar; stir until sugar and salt are dissolved. Prepare dressing by whipping cream until smooth and stiff. Add chives, celery seed and vinegar mixture and blend until smooth. Score cucumbers with fork tines, then slice and place in bowl. Add dressing and mix thoroughly. Chill for at least 2 hours before serving.

Yield: 4 to 6 servings

MANDARIN SALAD

SALAD
- ½ cup sliced almonds
- 3 tablespoons sugar
- ½ head iceberg lettuce, cut in bite-sized pieces
- ½ head Romaine lettuce, cut in bite-sized pieces
- 1 cup chopped celery
- 2 green onions, chopped
- 1 (11 ounce) can mandarin oranges, drained

DRESSING
- 2 tablespoons vinegar
- 2 tablespoons sugar
- ¼ cup vegetable oil
- ½ teaspoon salt
- Dash of pepper
- Dash of hot pepper sauce
- 1 tablespoon chopped parsley or 1 teaspoon parsley flakes

Combine almonds and sugar in saucepan. Over medium heat, cook almonds, stirring constantly, just until almonds are coated. Remove from heat immediately. Spread glazed almonds on waxed paper. Cool, then store in air-tight container. Prepare dressing by combining vinegar, sugar, oil, salt, pepper, hot pepper sauce and parsley; blend thoroughly. Toss vegetables and oranges in bowl. Just before serving, add almonds. Drizzle dressing over vegetable mixture.

Yield: 4 to 6 servings

Among the Lilies

ORANGE WALNUT SALAD

SALAD

2	small heads Bibb lettuce, shredded
1	pound spinach, shredded
2	oranges, peeled, seeded and sectioned
½	medium-sized onion, sliced in rings
½	cup coarsely chopped walnuts
2	teaspoons butter

DRESSING

1	cup vegetable oil
½	cup vinegar
½	cup sugar
1	teaspoon salt
1	teaspoon paprika
1	teaspoon grated onion
1	teaspoon dry mustard
1	teaspoon celery seed

Place lettuce, spinach, oranges and onion in bowl. Sauté walnuts in butter until lightly browned; add to vegetable mixture. Prepare dressing by combining oil, vinegar, sugar and seasonings; blend until sugar and salt is dissolved. Pour dressing over vegetable mixture and toss to coat thoroughly.

Yield: 6 to 8 servings

BLEU CHEESE APPLE SALAD

DRESSING

1	cup vegetable oil
½	cup sugar
½	cup cider vinegar
½	teaspoon salt
½	teaspoon dry mustard
¾	teaspoon paprika

SALAD

1	red Delicious apple, sliced
2	Granny Smith apples, sliced
1	bunch red leaf lettuce
¼	cup (2 ounces) bleu cheese, crumbled

Combine oil, sugar, vinegar and seasonings in jar with tight-fitting lid; shake until thoroughly blended. Chill overnight. Arrange apple slices on lettuce leaves and sprinkle with cheese. Pour dressing over apples.

Yield: 3 or 4 servings

RASPBERRY ROMAINE

RASPBERRY DRESSING

½	cup mayonnaise
⅓	cup sugar
¼	cup milk
2	tablespoons raspberry vinegar
1	teaspoon poppy seed

SALAD

1	head Romaine lettuce, torn in bite-sized pieces
2	cups strawberries, sliced
1	medium-sized purple onion, sliced
½	cup toasted slivered almonds

Combine mayonnaise, sugar, milk, vinegar and poppy seed in jar with tightly-fitting lid and shake until blended. Chill for 4 hours. Combine lettuce, strawberries, onion and almonds in bowl. Pour dressing over lettuce mixture.

Yield: 4 to 6 servings

POTATO SALAD

DRESSING

1	cup half and half
1	cup mayonnaise
1	teaspoon salt
1	teaspoon mustard seed
1	teaspoon celery seed

SALAD

6	potatoes, cooked, peeled and cubed
½	onion, diced
1	cup chopped celery
2	hard-cooked eggs, chopped

Combine half and half, mayonnaise and seasonings; blend thoroughly. Place vegetables and eggs in bowl. Add dressing and mix lightly but thoroughly.

Yield: 8 servings

Potato Salad Mold

1   (8 ounce) package cream cheese, softened
⅔   cup olive oil and vinegar salad dressing
⅓   cup cider vinegar
⅓   cup mayonnaise
1   tablespoon prepared mustard
2   teaspoons lemon pepper
2   teaspoons horseradish
½   green bell pepper
½   red bell pepper
½   Granny Smith or tart apple
1   medium-sized onion
3   stalks celery
3   hard-cooked eggs, chopped
2   large potatoes, cooked, peeled and diced
2   teaspoons unflavored gelatin
1   tablespoon water

Combine cream cheese, dressing, vinegar, mayonnaise and seasonings; mix thoroughly. Place peppers, apple, onion and celery in food processor; process until chopped. Add vegetables to cream cheese mixture. Fold in eggs and add potatoes. Soften gelatin in water; heat until dissolved. Add small portion of vegetable mixture to gelatin; then add gelatin mixture to remaining vegetable mixture. Spread in salad mold. Chill, uncovered, for 5 hours or up to 5 days if covered. Serve with Stuffed Ham Rolls, page 141.

Yield: 8 servings

Ursula Knaeusel

Sausage-Potato Salad

Salad
½   pound smoked beef sausage, cut in ¼-inch slices
8   large red potatoes, cooked and cubed
½   cup grated carrots
1   small onion, chopped
1   cup (8 ounces) cubed mozzarella cheese
2 to 3   tablespoons capers

Dressing
½   cup mustard
2   tablespoons mayonnaise
2   teaspoons dill weed
¼   teaspoon salt
¼   teaspoon black pepper

Combine sausage, vegetables, cheese and capers in bowl. Prepare dressing by blending mustard, mayonnaise and seasonings until smooth. Fold dressing into sausage mixture, mixing lightly but thoroughly.

Yield: 10 to 12 servings

Salads

SAUERKRAUT SALAD

DRESSING
1	cup sugar
½	cup vinegar

SALAD
1	(10 ounce) can sauerkraut, drained
1	cup grated carrots
½	cup sliced olives
½	cup chopped celery
¼	cup chopped green bell pepper
¼	cup chopped red bell pepper
¼	cup chopped onion
1	tablespoon chopped pimiento
¼	teaspoon celery seed
⅛	teaspoon black pepper

Combine sugar and vinegar in saucepan. Bring to a boil; cook for 5 minutes. Let cool slightly. Place sauerkraut in bowl. Pour vinegar mixture over kraut. Stir in vegetables and seasonings and mix well. Chill for several hours or overnight.

Yield: 6 servings

JELLIED GAZPACHO

2	cups finely chopped tomatoes
½	cup finely chopped celery
½	cup finely chopped green bell pepper
½	cup minced onion
1	(4 ounce) can sliced mushrooms
2	tablespoons tarragon vinegar
1	tablespoon chopped parsley
1½	teaspoons salt
1½	teaspoons garlic salt
1	teaspoon chopped chives
¼	teaspoon black pepper
¼	teaspoon Worcestershire sauce
2	(3 ounce) packages lemon gelatin
2	cups boiling water
1	tablespoon unflavored gelatin
1½	cups ice water
2	tablespoons lemon juice
1	envelope ranch style salad dressing mix
1	teaspoon Worcestershire sauce
1½	cups (12 ounces) cottage cheese
	Lettuce leaves
	Cherry tomatoes for garnish
	Shredded Cheddar cheese for garnish

Combine vegetables and seasonings in bowl. Dissolve lemon gelatin in boiling water; set aside. Soften unflavored gelatin in ice water and add lemon juice; add to lemon gelatin. Pour gelatin mixture into vegetables. Spoon into individual molds and chill until firm. Combine salad dressing mix, Worcestershire sauce and cottage cheese in blender container; blend until smooth. To serve, unmold salad on lettuce leaf. Drizzle with dressing and garnish with tomatoes and cheese.

Yield: 6 to 8 servings

Among the Lilies

Korean Salad

Salad

1	pound spinach, chopped
1	(8 ounce) can bean sprouts, drained
1	(8 ounce) can sliced water chestnuts, drained
5	slices bacon, cooked and crumbled
2	hard-cooked eggs, sliced

Dressing

1	cup vegetable oil
¾	cup sugar
⅓	cup ketchup
¼	cup vinegar
1	small onion, chopped

Combine spinach, bean sprouts, water chestnuts, bacon and eggs in bowl. Prepare dressing by combining oil, sugar, ketchup, vinegar and onion in blender; blend at medium speed for 10 seconds. Just before serving, pour dressing over vegetable mixture.

Yield: 8 servings

Savory Summer Salad

¼	pound button mushrooms
1	pint cherry tomatoes
1	(8 ounce) can whole water chestnuts, cut in halves
1	(2¼-ounce) can ripe olives, drained
1	(14 ounce) can quartered artichoke hearts
1	onion, sliced
1	sprig dill
1	(8 ounce) bottle Italian salad dressing
	Romaine lettuce leaves
½	cup (4 ounces) crumbled feta cheese
4	slices bacon, cooked and crumbled
¼	teaspoon oregano

Combine vegetables, dill and salad dressing in bowl. Chill overnight. To serve, spoon salad on lettuce leaf, garnish with cheese and bacon and sprinkle with oregano.

Yield: 6 servings

Honey Mustard Dressing

½	cup mayonnaise
2	teaspoons prepared mustard
2	tablespoons honey

Combine mayonnaise, mustard and honey; beat until smooth. Serve as a salad dressing, dip or sandwich spread.

Yield: ⅔ cup

DAVE'S BLEU CHEESE SPECIAL DRESSING

1	(8 ounce) carton sour cream
1	cup mayonnaise
½	cup (4 ounces) bleu cheese, crumbled
	Juice of 1 lemon
	Dash of garlic salt
	Dash of Worcestershire sauce
	Paprika

Combine sour cream, mayonnaise, cheese, lemon juice, garlic salt and Worcestershire sauce. Chill overnight to blend flavors. To serve, pour dressing over lettuce wedges and sprinkle with paprika.

Yield: 2½ cups

CELERY SEED DRESSING

⅓	cup sugar
1	teaspoon salt
1	teaspoon celery seed
1	teaspoon dry mustard
1	teaspoon paprika
1	teaspoon grated onion
¼	cup cider vinegar
1	cup corn oil

Place sugar and seasonings in food processor. Process at low speed, adding onion and vinegar. Gradually add oil and continue to process for 30 seconds. *Dressing is excellent with fruit and with avocado and spinach salads.*

Yield: 1½ cups

CRANBERRY WALDORF

2	cups cranberries, chopped
3	cups miniature marshmallows
¾	cup sugar
2	cups diced, unpeeled apples
½	cup seedless grapes
½	cup chopped pecans or walnuts
1	cup whipping cream, whipped
1	(9 ounce) carton frozen whipped topping, thawed

Combine cranberries, marshmallows and sugar in bowl. Chill, covered, overnight. Add apples, grapes and nuts to cranberry mixture. Fold in whipped cream and topping. Chill before serving.

Yield: 8 to 10 servings

FROZEN CRANBERRY SALAD

1	(14 ounce) can sweetened condensed milk
¼	cup lemon juice
1	(16 ounce) can whole cranberry sauce
1	(20 ounce) can pineapple tidbits, drained
½	cup chopped nuts
1	(9 ounce) carton frozen whipped topping, thawed

Combine milk and lemon juice in bowl. Add sauce, pineapple and nuts, mixing thoroughly. Fold in whipped topping. Pour salad into 12x9x2-inch baking dish or into individual molds. Freeze before serving.

Yield: 10 to 12 servings

CRANBERRY SALAD RING

¾	cup sugar
1	cup boiling water
2	(3 ounce) packages raspberry gelatin
¼	cup cold water
1	cup ground cranberries
1	orange, unpeeled, seeded and ground
1	apple, unpeeled, cored and ground
1	(7½ ounce) can crushed pineapple, undrained
½	cup chopped pecans
	Orange slices for garnish

Combine sugar and boiling water; add gelatin and stir until dissolved. Add cold water. Chill until partially thickened. Combine fruit and pecans; fold into gelatin. Pour into lightly-oiled 5-cup mold. Chill until firm. Invert on lettuce leaves, unmold and garnish with orange slices.

Yield: 8 to 10 servings

FROZEN FRUIT SALAD A L'ORANGE

1	(16 ounce) carton sour cream
2	tablespoons lemon juice
¾	cup sugar
1	(9 ounce) can crushed pineapple
¼	cup chopped cherries
¼	cup chopped nuts
2	bananas, sliced
	Dash of salt
1	cup orange juice
½	cup sugar
2	tablespoons cornstarch
	Grated peel of 1 orange

Combine sour cream, lemon juice, sugar, pineapple, cherries, nuts, bananas and dash of salt; mix well. Spoon mixture into paper-lined muffin cups. Freeze; when firm, remove and store in plastic bag in freezer until ready to use. Combine orange juice, sugar, cornstarch, orange peel and dash of salt in saucepan. Cook until thickened. Let stand until cool. To serve, place frozen fruit cup on lettuce leaf and pour orange sauce over fruit.

Yield: 6 servings

FROZEN FRUIT SALAD

1	(8 ounce) package cream cheese, softened
¾	cup sugar
1	(9 ounce) can crushed pineapple, drained
1	(10 ounce) package frozen strawberries, thawed
2	bananas, sliced
1	cup chopped walnuts
1	(9 ounce) carton frozen whipped topping, thawed

Combine cream cheese and sugar, beating until smooth. Fold fruit and walnuts into sweetened cream cheese, then fold in whipped topping. Spread mixture in 13x9x2-inch baking pan. Freeze overnight. Cut into squares to serve.

Yield: 12 servings

FRESH FRUIT SALAD WITH LIMEADE DRESSING

LIMEADE DRESSING

⅓	cup frozen limeade concentrate, thawed
⅓	cup honey
⅓	cup vegetable oil

SALAD

2	medium unpeeled apples, cut in ¼-inch slices
2	bananas, sliced
1	pound seedless green grapes
2	oranges, peeled and sliced
8	lettuce cups or leaves
½	cup fresh or frozen blueberries

Using electric mixer, combine limeade, honey and oil, beating until smooth. Chill before using. Arrange apples, bananas, grapes and oranges in lettuce cups or on leaves; sprinkle with blueberries. Pour dressing over fruit. Serve with toasted snack rye bread.

Yield: 8 servings

HEAVENLY HONEYDEW SALAD WITH MARSHMALLOW DRESSING

DRESSING

4	egg yolks
1	tablespoon butter
1	tablespoon sugar
¼	cup vinegar
½	teaspoon salt
	Dash of red pepper
12	marshmallows
1	cup whipped cream

SALAD

½	honeydew melon, sliced
½	large pineapple, peeled and cut in chunks
2	kiwi, peeled and sliced
1	cup fresh red raspberries
2	peaches, sliced (optional)
4	Bibb lettuce leaves
1	cup walnut pieces

Combine egg yolks, butter, sugar, vinegar, salt and pepper in saucepan. Cook, stirring constantly, until thickened. Add marshmallows and beat until smooth. Set aside to cool. Fold whipped cream into dressing before using. Arrange fruit on lettuce leaves on individual salad plates. Pour dressing over fruit and sprinkle with walnuts.

Yield: 4 servings

KIWI AND STRAWBERRY SALAD

6	kiwi, peeled and sliced
2	(13 ounce) cans mandarin oranges, drained
2	(20 ounce) cans pineapple chunks, drained
3	cups sliced strawberries
2	cups sliced green grapes

Combine fruit, tossing lightly to mix. If fruit requires sweetening, drizzle lightly with honey.

Yield: 12 servings

FRUIT SALAD UNIQUE

1	(20 ounce) can pineapple chunks, drained
	Juice of 1 lemon
3	tablespoons all-purpose flour
1	cup sugar
1	egg, beaten
2	teaspoons prepared mustard
1	(20 ounce) can fruit salad mix, drained
3	Delicious apples, peeled and diced
12	large or 1½ cups miniature marshmallows
1	cup (4 ounces) grated American cheese
1	(3½ ounce) can flaked coconut

Combine pineapple, lemon juice, flour, sugar and egg in saucepan. Cook until thickened. Cool slightly, add mustard and let stand to cool completely. Stir in fruit and marshmallows. Cover until ready to use. Store overnight in refrigerator. Just before serving, sprinkle fruit mixture with cheese and coconut.

Yield: 10 to 12 servings

Salads

CHICKEN SALAD ORIENTAL

SALAD
2 to 3	cups diced cooked chicken
1	apple, diced
1	cup pineapple chunks, drained and juice reserved
⅓	cup chopped dates
¼	cup golden raisins
1½	cups shredded coconut, divided
	Lettuce leaves

ORIENTAL DRESSING
1	tablespoon curry powder
2	tablespoons instant chicken bouillon granules or 1 cube
1	cup mayonnaise
½	teaspoon salt
2	tablespoons chutney

Combine chicken, apple, pineapple, dates, raisins and ½ cup coconut in bowl. In saucepan, prepare dressing by blending curry powder and bouillon with enough pineapple juice to form smooth paste. Simmer for 2 minutes. Add mayonnaise, salt and chutney. Fold dressing into chicken mixture. Spoon salad onto lettuce leaves placed on individual salad plates and sprinkle with remaining coconut.

Yield: 4 to 6 servings

CHICKEN SALAD ALMONDINE

SALAD
10	chicken breast halves, cooked, boned and cut in bite-sized chunks
2	cups chopped celery
1½	cups toasted slivered almonds

DRESSING
1½	cups mayonnaise
1	(8 ounce) carton sour cream
1	teaspoon lemon juice
¾	teaspoon salt
½	teaspoon pepper

Combine chicken, celery and almonds in bowl. Prepare dressing by blending mayonnaise, sour cream, lemon juice and seasonings together. Fold dressing into chicken mixture.

Yield: 10 to 12 servings

Among the Lilies

TOMATO LUNCHEON SALAD

1	(10½ ounce) can tomato soup, undiluted
1	envelope unflavored gelatin
½	cup mayonnaise
1	(3 ounce) package cream cheese, softened
½	cup whipping cream or evaporated milk
1	tablespoon lemon juice
2½ to 3	cups cooked shrimp, tuna, salmon or chicken
2½	cups diced celery
½	cup chopped green pepper
2	tablespoons chopped green onion tops
2	tablespoons chopped pimiento
	Avocado, cucumber, tomato wedges and olives for garnish

Pour tomato soup in saucepan. Sprinkle with gelatin. Heat until gelatin is dissolved. Let stand until cool. Combine mayonnaise and cream cheese, beating until smooth. Add cream and lemon juice. Fold fish or chicken, vegetables and soup into cream cheese mixture, mixing lightly but thoroughly. Pour into 5½-cup fish shaped mold. Chill for several hours or until gelatin is firm. Unmold and garnish with avocado, cucumbers, tomato and olives.
For a firmer salad, use 8 ounces cream cheese instead of 3 ounces and omit cream or milk.

Yield: 4 to 6 servings

PUFFED SALAD CUP

¾	cup water
¼	cup butter
1	cup biscuit baking mix
4	eggs
2	cups cubed baked ham
1	cup cubed Cheddar cheese
1	(10 ounce) package frozen green peas, thawed
1	cup diced celery
½	cup sweet pickle relish, drained
1	teaspoon grated onion
½	cup mayonnaise-type salad dressing
½	teaspoon dry mustard

Combine water and butter in saucepan; bring to a boil. Add biscuit mix and beat quickly to blend. Remove from heat. Beat in eggs, 1 at a time. Drop batter onto greased baking sheet in 6 mounds. Bake at 400 degrees for 15 to 20 minutes or until golden. Cool before using. Combine ham, cheese, peas, celery, relish, onion, salad dressing and mustard. Chill, covered, until ready to serve. Mound salad in puffed cups.

Yield: 6 servings

FRANKFURTER SALAD

SALAD

1	(12 ounce) package frankfurters, thinly sliced
1	tablespoon butter
2	(16 ounce) cans red kidney beans, drained
4	green onions, chopped
½	cup chopped green bell pepper
½	cup chopped celery
2	ripe tomatoes, peeled and cut in wedges

DRESSING

½	cup cider vinegar
¼	cup olive oil
	Salt to taste
	Pepper to taste

Sauté frankfurters in butter until lightly browned. Mix frankfurters with vegetables. Prepare dressing by combining vinegar, oil and seasonings; pour over vegetable mixture and toss lightly to mix. Chill before serving.

Hickory smoked beef frankfurters are especially good in this salad.

Yield: 6 servings

AM THE LIGHT OF

THE WORLD; HE WHO

FOLLOWS ME SHALL NOT WALK

IN THE DARKNESS, BUT SHALL

HAVE THE LIGHT OF LIFE.

John 8:12

BUTTER HERB BAKED FISH

½	cup butter
⅔	cup crushed saltine crackers
¼	cup grated Parmesan cheese
½	teaspoon salt
½	teaspoon basil
½	teaspoon oregano
¼	teaspoon garlic powder
1	pound sole or flounder fillets

Place butter in 13x9x2-inch baking pan; bake at 350 degrees for 5 to 7 minutes or until melted. Combine crumbs, cheese and seasonings in 9-inch pie plate. Dip fish in butter, then dredge in crumb mixture. Arrange fillets in baking pan. Bake for 25 to 30 minutes or until tender.

Yield: 3 or 4 servings

FRIED CATFISH

4 to 6	small catfish fillets
1	cup buttermilk
¾	cup cracker meal
¾	cup self-rising cornmeal
	Salt to taste
	Pepper to taste
	Vegetable oil
	Lemon pepper to taste

Soak fish in buttermilk for 5 to 10 minutes. Combine cracker meal, cornmeal, salt and pepper in paper bag and shake to mix. Add fish and shake to thoroughly coat each piece. Deep fry in hot oil, cooking until golden brown. Sprinkle with lemon pepper.

Yield: 2 or 3 servings

HERB-CRUSTED ORANGE ROUGHY

¼	cup fresh orange juice
4	orange roughy fillets
	Safflower or olive oil
1	tablespoon dried tarragon
1	tablespoon coarsely ground black pepper
	Grated peel of 2 oranges

Pour orange juice into 12x8x2-inch baking dish. Brush fish lightly with oil and place in dish. Combine tarragon, pepper and orange peel; sprinkle on fish, patting lightly to form a thin crust. Bake at 325 degrees for 20 to 25 minutes or until fish flakes easily when probed with fork. Carefully transfer fish to serving dish, discarding cooking liquid. Serve immediately.

Yield: 4 servings

WHITE FISH SUPREME

1½	pounds white fish fillet
1	(3 ounce) package cream cheese, cubed
1	(12 ounce) package sliced mozzarella cheese
1	medium zucchini, sliced diagonally
1	medium carrot, sliced diagonally

Place fish in greased 9x5x3-inch baking dish. Sprinkle cheese cubes on fish and cover with mozzarella slices. Arrange vegetables around edges of dish. Bake, covered, at 350 degrees for 20 to 30 minutes.

Yield: 4 or 5 servings

GRILLED SWORDFISH

4   (1-inch thick) swordfish steaks
½   cup mayonnaise
¼   cup melted butter
    Juice of 1 lemon
    Chopped parsley for garnish

Preheat grill for 20 to 30 minutes; fire must be very hot. Spread 1 side of each steak with mayonnaise; place mayonnaise side down on grill and cook 6 minutes. Spread top side with mayonnaise, turn that side down on grill and cook additional time to equal 10 minutes per inch thickness of steaks. Blend butter and lemon juice; serve with steaks. Garnish with parsley.

Yield: 4 servings

GRILLED SALMON TERIYAKI

⅓   cup teriyaki sauce
⅓   cup firmly-packed brown sugar
4   salmon steaks
4   slices lemon

Blend teriyaki sauce with brown sugar until smooth. Marinate steaks in sauce for 15 minutes. Grill, basting occasionally with marinade, until fish begins to flake. Serve with lemon slices.
Tuna may be substituted for salmon.

Yield: 4 servings

TUNA TOASTIES

2   (6½ ounce) cans tuna, flaked
4   hard-cooked eggs, chopped
⅔   cup mayonnaise or salad dressing
½   cup ripe olives, chopped
24   slices sandwich bread
½   cup margarine
2½ cups (10 ounces) grated sharp cheese
2   eggs

Combine tuna, eggs, mayonnaise and olives. Use tuna can to cut circles from bread slices. Spread tuna mixture on bread rounds, using 3 rounds per sandwich. Melt margarine in saucepan over low heat. Add cheese and stir until melted. Stir in eggs and mix well. Quickly spread cheese mixture on sandwiches and place on baking sheet. Chill overnight. Bake at 400 degrees for 20 minutes or until lightly browned.

Yield: 8 servings

PASTA WITH SHELLFISH

½	cup butter
½	cup olive oil
1	cup de-alcoholized white wine
2 to 4	cloves garlic, cut in halves
1	teaspoon crushed rosemary
1 to 2	pinches dried oregano
1	large onion, chopped
1	(28 ounce) can Italian plum tomatoes, drained and chopped
3	cups cooked shellfish
½	cup minced parsley
½	teaspoon sugar
	Salt and black pepper to taste
1	(12 ounce) package pasta, cooked

Melt butter and oil together in large saucepan over medium-high heat. Stir in wine, garlic, seasonings and onion. Cook, stirring frequently, until wine evaporates and butter is golden but not browned. Add tomatoes, shellfish, parsley, sugar, salt and pepper. Cook over medium heat, just until shellfish is thoroughly heated. Serve over pasta.

Yield: 5 or 6 servings

LOBSTER THERMIDOR

3 or 4	celery tops
1	small onion, sliced
	Juice and peel of 1 lemon
1	teaspoon salt
	Dash of cayenne pepper
1	bay leaf
6 to 8	whole cloves
	Water
1	tablespoon butter
2	(9 ounce) packages frozen African lobster tails
1	tablespoon all-purpose flour
1¼	cups half and half
¼	teaspoon salt
	Cayenne pepper to taste
2	tablespoons lemon juice
1	(4 ounce) can sliced mushrooms, drained
½	cup (2 ounces) grated Cheddar cheese
2	tablespoons breadcrumbs

Combine celery, onion, lemon juice and peel and seasonings in 6 quarts water in stockpot; bring to a boil. Cook lobster in seasoned water, according to package directions. Remove from water and cool. Remove lobster meat from shells and dice; reserve shells. Melt butter in saucepan. Stir in flour and blend well; add cream, salt and pepper and cook to form white sauce. Add lemon juice. Stir in lobster and mushrooms. Spoon lobster with sauce into shells. Sprinkle with cheese and breadcrumbs. Broil until golden brown.

Yield: 2 servings

Low Country Boil

1   cup ketchup
2   teaspoons lime juice
     Worcestershire sauce to taste
     Horseradish to taste
     Water
1   envelope shrimp-crab boil
1   lemon or lime
2   pounds Polish sausage, cut in 1-inch
     pieces
8   onions
8   new potatoes
4   ears corn on the cob, cut in halves
2½   pounds large or jumbo shrimp in the
     shell

Combine ketchup, lime juice, Worcestershire sauce and horseradish; blend well. Chill. Fill large stockpot with water. Add shrimp-crab boil and bring water to a boil. Squeeze juice from lemon or lime, then add fruit to water. Add sausage and vegetables to boiling water; cook until just tender. Drop in shrimp and cook for 2 to 3 minutes or until bright pink and tender. Lift vegetables, sausage and shrimp from cooking liquid; serve on platters with cocktail sauce.

Yield: 8 servings

Shrimp Creole

1   large onion, chopped
1   large clove garlic, minced
½   cup chopped green bell pepper
½   cup chopped celery
2   tablespoons all-purpose flour
¼   cup butter or margarine
4   small green onions, minced
1   tablespoon minced parsley
3½   cups canned tomatoes
½   cup water
1   teaspoon salt
½   teaspoon black pepper
¼   teaspoon red pepper
1   pound shelled, deveined shrimp

Sauté onion, garlic, green pepper and celery in butter in large skillet until onion is lightly browned. Blend in flour. Add green onion, parsley, tomatoes, water and seasonings, mixing thoroughly. Simmer, covered, for 20 minutes. Stir in shrimp and cook, covered, for 10 minutes. Serve over rice.

Yield: 6 servings

ELEGANT SHRIMP

1	(10 ounce) can cream of shrimp soup, undiluted
1	(5 ounce) can evaporated milk
½	cup mayonnaise
½	cup (2 ounces) grated sharp cheese
1	pound cooked shelled and deveined shrimp

Combine soup, milk, mayonnaise and cheese in saucepan; cook until bubbly. Stir in shrimp and heat thoroughly. Serve over rice or in pastry shells.

Yield: 3 or 4 servings

TENDER FRIED SHRIMP

6	cups ice water
3½	cups sifted all-purpose flour, divided
2	teaspoons baking powder
	Salt to taste
	Pepper to taste
1½ to 2	pounds large shelled shrimp
	Vegetable oil

Combine water, 2 cups flour, baking powder, salt and pepper. Stir in shrimp and let stand for 30 minutes. Drain shrimp. Mix 1½ cups flour with salt and pepper. Dredge shrimp in seasoned flour. Deep fry in hot oil for 5 to 7 minutes or until golden brown.

Yield: 4 servings

SIMPLE SHRIMP CURRY

½	cup chopped onion
1	tablespoon butter or margarine
1	(10 ounce) can cream of shrimp soup, undiluted
½	teaspoon curry powder
2	cups cooked shrimp
1	(8 ounce) carton sour cream

Sauté onion in butter for 5 to 7 minutes or until onion is tender. Add soup, curry powder and shrimp. Simmer for 5 to 10 minutes, stirring occasionally, until bubbly. Stir in sour cream and heat; do not boil. Serve immediately over rice.

Shrimp sauce may be prepared through simmer stage, then chilled until ready to serve; reheat until bubbly and add sour cream.

Yield: 3 or 4 servings

MARINATED SHRIMP

2 to 3	pounds medium shrimp, cooked and shelled
1	cup mayonnaise
¼	cup olive oil
¼	cup chili sauce
1	clove garlic, crushed
1	small onion, grated
1	tablespoon fresh dill
1	teaspoon celery seed
½	pineapple

Combine shrimp, mayonnaise, oil, sauce, garlic, onion and seasonings. Chill, covered, for several hours or overnight. Cut pineapple to form bowl, removing pulp. Fill with shrimp mixture.
Shrimp may also be served as appetizer.

Yield: 4 to 6 servings

PICKLED SHRIMP

6	cups water
1	(3 ounce) package crab boil
3½	teaspoons salt
1	bay leaf
2½	pounds shrimp, shelled
1	cup vegetable oil
¾	cup white vinegar
1	teaspoon salt
2½	teaspoons celery seed
	Dash of hot pepper sauce
2	large onions, sliced
1	(6 ounce) jar green olives, drained
1	(6 ounce) can black olives, drained

Bring water to a boil in saucepan; add crab boil, salt and bay leaf. Add shrimp and cook until bright pink and tender; do not overcook. Drain shrimp. Combine oil, vinegar, salt, celery seed and hot pepper sauce. Alternate layers of shrimp, onion and olives in container with tight-fitting lid. Pour marinade over shrimp and vegetables. Chill for 24 hours, turning container occasionally. Shrimp may be stored in refrigerator for several weeks.

Yield: 10 to 12 servings

Poultry

CAST YOUR BURDEN

UPON THE LORD AND

HE WILL SUSTAIN YOU. HE WILL

NEVER ALLOW THE RIGHTEOUS

TO BE SHAKEN.

Psalm 55:22

CHICKEN AND DUMPLINGS

 6   whole cloves
 1   medium-sized onion
 1   (4 pound) fryer
 2   stalks celery
 1   carrot
 4   teaspoons salt, divided
 1   teaspoon black peppercorns
     Water
 2   cups all-purpose flour
 1   teaspoon baking powder
 1   egg
 2   tablespoons chicken fat
     Milk
     Parsley sprigs for garnish

Press cloves into onion. Place onion, chicken, vegetables, 3 teaspoons salt and peppercorns in water to cover in large sauce pot. Bring to a boil, then simmer, covered, for 1½ hours. Cool chicken in broth. Remove skin and bone; cut in bite-sized pieces. Chill. Remove all fat from top, reserving 2 tablespoons for dumplings. Strain and reserve broth. Combine flour, baking powder and 1 teaspoon salt. Add egg and chicken fat with enough milk (about ½ cup) to form dough. Roll dough to thickness of pie pastry. Cut into 1 to 2 inch wide strips. Holding strip above boiling broth, tear pieces to drop into broth. Simmer, covered, for about 15 minutes or until dumplings are cooked. Mix with chicken. Garnish with parsley.

Yield: 4 servings

CHICKEN FLORENTINE

 10   chicken breast halves, boned
 ½   cup butter, melted
 1½   cups grated Parmesan cheese, divided
 2   large onions, sliced
 ¾   pound mushrooms, chopped
 6   tablespoons butter
 2   (10 ounce) packages frozen chopped spinach
 3   tablespoons Italian seasoned breadcrumbs
 1   teaspoon salt (optional)
 ½   teaspoon cracked pepper
 1   teaspoon soy sauce
 2   tablespoons mayonnaise
 1   (8 ounce) package cream cheese, softened

Using a meat mallet or rolling pin, pound chicken breasts to ¼-inch thickness. Dip in melted butter, then in 1½ cups cheese, reserving 3 tablespoons cheese for topping, and place in single layer on baking sheet prepared with non-stick vegetable spray. Broil near heat source for 2 minutes on one side only. Sauté onion in 6 tablespoons butter. Add mushrooms and cook for 5 minutes. Stir in spinach, breadcrumbs, seasonings, soy sauce and reserved cheese. Remove from heat. Add mayonnaise and cream cheese and mix well. Spoon spinach sauce on chicken. Bake at 375 degrees for 20 minutes; do not overcook. Chicken and sauce may be prepared in advance and stored in refrigerator; bake for 30 minutes.

Yield: 10 servings

Ursula Knaeusel

106

CHICKEN PAPRIKASH

2   (3 pound) fryers, cut up and skin removed
½   cup margarine, melted
¾   cup sifted all-purpose flour, divided
1   tablespoon salt
¼   teaspoon black pepper
2   tablespoons paprika
1   cup water
1   (8 ounce) carton sour cream

Dip chicken in margarine. Combine ½ cup plus 2 tablespoons flour, salt, pepper and paprika. Roll chicken in seasoned flour and place in single layer in baking pan. Drizzle remaining margarine over chicken. Bake at 400 degrees for 1 hour. Remove chicken to hot platter. Stir 2 tablespoons flour and water into pan drippings. Stir, cooking over medium heat, until thickened. Add sour cream and heat thoroughly; do not boil. Serve gravy over chicken.

Yield: 8 servings

CHICKEN PARMIGIANA

6   chicken breast halves, boned and skin removed
2   eggs, lightly beaten
1   teaspoon salt
⅛   teaspoon black pepper
¾   cup fine dry breadcrumbs
½   cup vegetable oil
1   (15 ounce) can Italian style tomatoes
¼   teaspoon dried or 1 tablespoon fresh basil
⅛   teaspoon garlic powder
1   teaspoon sugar
1   tablespoon butter or margarine
½   cup grated Parmesan cheese
1   (8 ounce) package mozzarella cheese, thinly sliced and cut in triangles

Using a meat mallet or rolling pin, pound chicken breasts to ¼-inch thickness. Combine eggs, salt and pepper. Dip chicken into egg mixture and roll in breadcrumbs. Sauté in oil in skillet and drain on paper towels. Place chicken in lightly greased 12x9x2-inch baking dish. Remove oil from skillet. Combine tomatoes, basil, garlic powder and sugar in skillet; bring to a boil and simmer for 10 minutes or until thickened. Stir in butter. Pour tomato mixture over chicken and sprinkle with Parmesan cheese. Bake, covered, at 350 degrees for 30 minutes. Arrange mozzarella cheese slices on chicken and bake, uncovered, for 10 minutes.

Yield: 6 servings

COUNTRY CAPTAIN CHICKEN

6	chicken breast halves, boned
¼	cup butter or margarine
1	cup chopped onion
¾	cup chopped green bell pepper
2	cloves garlic, minced
1	tablespoon vegetable oil
½	teaspoon salt
2	teaspoons curry powder
½	teaspoon thyme
1	(16 ounce) can tomatoes
1	tablespoon chopped parsley
2	tablespoons currants
¼	cup toasted slivered almonds

Sauté chicken in butter until lightly browned on both sides. Place in 13x9x2-inch baking dish. Sauté onion, pepper and garlic in oil until onion is transluscent. Stir in seasonings and mix well. Add tomatoes and parsley. Heat tomato mixture thoroughly and pour over chicken. Sprinkle with currants. Bake, covered, at 350 degrees for 30 minutes. Sprinkle with toasted almonds. Serve over rice or noodles.

Yield: 6 servings

CASHEW CHICKEN STIR-FRY

2	chicken breast halves, cut in bite-sized pieces
1	egg white, lightly beaten
4	teaspoons cornstarch, divided
4	teaspoons soy sauce, divided
1	tablespoon cold water
1	cup cashews
2	tablespoons vegetable oil
1	small onion, chopped
1	small green bell pepper, cut in ¾-inch pieces
1	(8 ounce) can sliced water chestnuts
¼	cup chicken broth

Combine chicken, egg white, 1 teaspoon cornstarch and 1 teaspoon soy sauce. Chill, covered, for 20 minutes. Combine remaining cornstarch, soy sauce and water; set aside. Stir-fry cashews in oil until lightly browned; remove and drain. Stir-fry chicken until chicken turns white; remove and drain. Stir-fry onion. Add chicken, pepper, water chestnuts and chicken broth to onion. Bring to a boil. Stir in cornstarch mixture and cook just until thickened. Add cashews. Serve over rice.

Yield: 4 servings

CHINESE CHICKEN

4	chicken breast halves, cut in bite-sized pieces
3 or 4	green onions with tips, sliced
½	red bell pepper, sliced
½	green bell pepper, sliced
1	(12 ounce) can pineapple chunks, drained
1	clove garlic, sliced
½	cup walnut halves
2	tablespoons butter
2	tablespoons vegetable oil
1	(6 ounce) jar apricot preserves
½	(8 ounce) bottle Russian dressing
	Dash of hot pepper sauce

Sauté chicken, vegetables, pineapple, garlic and walnuts in butter mixed with oil until chicken is tender and cooked. Stir in preserves, dressing and hot pepper sauce; heat thoroughly. Serve over rice.

Yield: 4 servings

CURRY GLAZED CHICKEN

2	tablespoons butter
¼	cup honey
3	tablespoons Dijon prepared mustard
½	teaspoon salt
2	teaspoons curry powder
4	chicken breast halves, boned

Place butter in 13x9x2-inch baking pan; place in oven at 375 degrees and heat until butter is melted. Remove and stir in honey, mustard and seasonings, blending well. Add chicken and turn to coat with butter sauce on all sides. Bake, covered, for 50 minutes; remove cover and bake for 15 to 20 minutes until browned. Serve with rice.

Yield: 4 servings

PRALINE CHICKEN

6	chicken breast halves, boned
2	teaspoons Cajun seasoning
¼	cup butter
1	tablespoon vegetable oil
⅓	cup maple syrup
2	tablespoons brown sugar
1	cup sliced pecans

Sprinkle chicken with seasoning. Sauté in butter mixed with oil, cooking until chicken is tender. Remove from pan and keep warm. Add syrup and brown sugar to pan drippings; bring to a boil. Stir in pecans. Place chicken in serving dish and pour sauce over chicken.

Yield: 6 servings

ALMOND CHICKEN

6	chicken breast halves, boned and skin removed
¼	cup butter
1	tablespoon vegetable oil
½	cup slivered almonds
1	clove garlic, chopped
2	tablespoons chopped onion
2	tablespoons all-purpose flour
1½	cups chicken broth
	Salt to taste
	Black pepper to taste
2	tablespoons grated Parmesan cheese

Variation:

ALMOND CHICKEN STROGANOFF

1½	teaspoons tarragon
¾	cup sour cream

Sauté chicken in butter mixed with oil until browned; remove and set aside. Sauté almonds until golden; add garlic and onion and cook over low heat for 3 minutes. Add flour and stir until smooth. Stir in broth and cook until thickened, stirring constantly. Season with salt and pepper. Add chicken to sauce and cook until chicken is tender; do not overcook. Serve with rice, sprinkling cheese over chicken pieces. For Almond Chicken Stroganoff, prepare chicken according to Almond Chicken directions. Just before serving, stir in tarragon and sour cream; do not boil. Pour stroganoff over noodles and sprinkle with Parmesan cheese.

Yield: 6 servings

LEMON SAUCY CHICKEN

6	chicken breast halves, boned and skin removed
¾	cup butter, divided
1	tablespoon vegetable oil
½	cup butter
½	cup lemon juice
1	teaspoon sugar
1	clove garlic, minced
1	teaspon salt
1	teaspoon paprika
½	teaspoon dried thyme
½	teaspoon curry powder
1	lemon, sliced, for garnish
3	sprigs parsley for garnish

Sauté chicken in ¼ cup butter mixed with oil until tender; remove and set aside. Combine ½ cup butter, lemon juice, sugar, garlic and seasonings in sauté pan; simmer until well blended. Add chicken to sauce. Serve over angel hair pasta and garnish with twisted lemon slices and parsley.

Yield: 6 servings

Orange Saucy Chicken

6	chicken breast halves, boned and skin removed
¼	cup butter
1	tablespoon vegetable oil
½	cup sugar
½	cup firmly-packed brown sugar
¾	cup orange juice
1½	tablespoons grated orange peel
¼	cup julienne-cut orange peel
½	teaspoon salt
⅛	teaspoon cayenne pepper
½	cup walnut halves
3 or 4	maraschino cherries for garnish

Sauté chicken in butter mixed with oil until tender; remove and set aside. Combine sugar, juice, peel, seasonings and walnuts in sauté pan; simmer until well blended. Add chicken to sauce. Serve over yellow or wild rice and garnish with cherries.

Yield: 6 servings

Imperial Chicken Bake

½	cup dry breadcrumbs
6	tablespoons grated Parmesan cheese
1½	tablespoons minced parsley
½	teaspoon salt
⅛	teaspoon black pepper
6	chicken breast halves, boned and skin removed
¼	cup milk
¼	cup butter or margarine, melted
1	small clove garlic, crushed
	Juice of 1 lemon
	Paprika to taste

Combine breadcrumbs, cheese, parsley, salt and pepper. Dip each chicken piece in milk, then dredge in seasoned crumbs. Place in lightly-greased 12x8x2-inch baking dish. Combine butter, garlic and lemon juice; drizzle over chicken. Sprinkle with paprika. Bake at 350 degrees for 40 minutes or until tender.

Yield: 6 servings

REUBEN CHICKEN

8	chicken breast halves, boned
¼	teaspoon salt
⅛	teaspoon black pepper
1	(16 ounce) can sauerkraut, well drained
4	slices Swiss cheese
1¼	cups prepared Thousand Island dressing
1	tablespoon chopped parsley

Place chicken in greased 13x9x2-inch baking dish. Season with salt and pepper. Place sauerkraut on chicken and top with cheese slices. Pour dressing over cheese layer. Bake, covered with aluminum foil, at 375 degrees for 45 minutes or until chicken is tender. Sprinkle with parsley.

Yield: 8 servings

SPITZAD CHICKEN

6	chicken breast halves
2	cloves garlic, crushed
½	teaspoon rosemary
¼	cup olive oil
¼	cup lemon juice

Place chicken in lightly-greased 12x8x2-inch baking dish. Combine garlic, rosemary and oil; brush mixture on all sides of chicken. Bake at 400 degrees for 40 to 45 minutes or until tender, basting occasionally. Pour lemon juice over chicken and bake for 5 minutes. Serve with rice, drizzling pan liquids over chicken.

Yield: 6 servings

TANGY CHICKEN GRILL

¾	cup vegetable oil
¼	cup plus 2 tablespoons soy sauce
2	tablespoons Worcestershire sauce
¼	cup wine vinegar
⅓	cup fresh lemon juice
1	clove garlic, crushed
1	teaspoon salt
½	teaspoon coarsely ground black pepper
1	tablespoon dry mustard
1	teaspoon parsley flakes
4	chicken breast halves, skin removed

Combine all marinade ingredients in a glass jar with tight-fitting lid. Shake well. Pour marinade over chicken arranged in single layer in glass baking dish. Marinate, covered with plastic wrap, for at least 6 hours in refrigerator. Drain chicken before grilling. *Slice grilled chicken for use in chicken salad.*

Yield: 4 servings

SPICY CHICKEN GRILL

	Juice and pulp of 1 lemon
1	cup cider vinegar
⅔	cup prepared mustard
½	cup butter
2	tablespoons horseradish
2	teaspoons Worcestershire sauce
2	teaspoons chili powder
	Salt and black pepper to taste
6	chicken breast halves, skin removed

Combine lemon juice, vinegar, mustard and butter in saucepan. Add seasonings. Cook over medium heat until butter is melted. Brush sauce on chicken before grilling.

Yield: 6 servings

ORIENTAL CHICKEN GRILL

⅓	cup pineapple juice
¼	cup soy sauce
¼	cup Worcestershire sauce
2	tablespoons vinegar
1	clove garlic, pressed
1	tablespoon sugar
1	tablespoon black pepper
1	tablespoon ginger, grated
4	chicken breast halves, skin removed

Combine all ingredients in glass jar with tight-fitting lid. Shake well. Pour marinade over chicken arranged in single layer in glass baking dish. Marinate, covered with plastic wrap, for at least 6 hours in refrigerator. Drain chicken before grilling.

Yield: 4 servings

LEMON CURRY CHICKEN GRILL

½	cup margarine or butter
½	cup lemon juice
1	clove garlic, crushed
1	teaspoon sugar
1	teaspoon salt
1	teaspoon paprika
½	teaspoon dried thyme
½	teaspoon curry powder
4	chicken breast halves, skin removed

Melt margarine in saucepan over low heat. Add lemon juice, garlic and seasonings; mix well. Bring to a boil. Remove from heat and let stand until warm. Pour marinade over chicken arranged in single layer in glass baking dish. Marinate, covered with plastic wrap, for at least 6 hours in refrigerator. Drain chicken before grilling.

Yield: 4 servings

CHICKEN ALMOND PIE

½   pound mushrooms, sliced
¼   cup grated onion
5   tablespoons butter or margarine,
      divided
4   chicken breast halves, cooked, boned
      and chopped
1   (10¾ ounce) can cream of chicken soup,
      undiluted
2   teaspoons chopped pimiento
      Salt to taste
      Black pepper to taste
1   baked 9-inch pastry shell
¾   cup breadcrumbs
¾   cup slivered almonds

Sauté mushrooms and onion in 3 tablespoons butter until onion is transluscent. Combine sautéed vegetables, chicken, soup, pimiento and seasonings, mixing thoroughly. Spoon mixture into pastry shell. Melt 2 tablespoons butter in sauté pan; stir in breadcrumbs. Sprinkle buttered crumbs over chicken mixture and top with almonds. Bake at 350 degrees for 15 to 20 minutes or until hot. Let stand 10 minutes before cutting.

Yield: 6 servings

CHICKEN ARTICHOKE CASSEROLE

1   cup butter or margarine
½   cup all-purpose flour
3½   cups milk
¾   cup (3 ounces) grated Swiss cheese
2   cups (8 ounces) grated Cheddar cheese
1   teaspoon seasoning salt
½   teaspoon red pepper
2   cloves garlic, pressed
1   (3 pound) fryer or breasts, cooked,
      boned, skin removed and cut into large
      pieces
2   (8 ounce) cans button mushrooms,
      drained
1   (12 ounce) can artichoke hearts, drained

Melt butter in saucepan; add flour and stir until blended. Gradually add milk, stirring until sauce is smooth. Add cheese and seasonings; stir until cheese is melted and sauce is bubbly. Add chicken and vegetables. Pour mixture into 3-quart casserole. Bake at 350 degrees for 30 minutes.

Yield: 8 to 10 servings

CHICKEN DIVAN CRÊPES

2 (10 ounce) packages frozen broccoli
  spears
¼ cup butter
¼ cup all-purpose flour
2 cups chicken broth
2 teaspoons Worcestershire sauce
3 cups (12 ounces) grated Cheddar cheese,
  divided
2 cups (16 ounces) sour cream
2 cups chopped cooked chicken
12 crêpes

Prepare broccoli according to package directions, cooking until tender crisp; drain and set aside. Melt butter in small saucepan over medium heat. Stir in flour and cook until bubbly. Add broth and Worcestershire sauce; cook, stirring, until thickened. Stir in 2 cups cheese. Place sour cream in bowl and gradually add hot cheese sauce, stirring constantly. On each crêpe, place broccoli and chicken; spoon 1 tablespoon sauce over chicken and fold crêpe to enclose; place in shallow baking dish. Pour remaining sauce over folded crêpes and sprinkle with 1 cup cheese. Bake, covered, at 350 degrees, for 20 to 30 minutes.

Yield: 6 servings

CHICKEN ENCHILADAS

1 cup chopped onion
¼ cup butter or margarine
¼ cup all-purpose flour
2½ cups water
3 chicken bouillon cubes
1 (8 ounce) carton sour cream, at room
  temperature
½ cup (2 ounces) shredded Cheddar
  cheese
1½ cups (6 ounces) shredded Monterey Jack
  cheese, divided
1 (4 ounce) can chopped green chilies,
  drained
½ teaspoon chili powder
3 cups chopped cooked chicken
10 (8 inch) flour tortillas
  Paprika to taste

Sauté onion in butter in saucepan until tender. Stir in flour. Add water and bouillon; cook, stirring frequently, until thickened and bouillon is dissolved. Remove from heat and stir in sour cream. Combine 1 cup sauce, Cheddar cheese, ½ cup Monterey Jack cheese, chilies, chili powder and chicken; mix thoroughly. Spoon chicken mixture on tortillas; roll up and place in lightly-greased 13x9x3-inch baking dish. Pour remaining sauce over enchiladas, sprinkle with 1 cup Monterey Jack cheese and season with paprika. Bake, uncovered, at 350 degrees for 25 minutes.

Yield: 5 servings

CHICKEN FAJITAS

½ cup fresh lime juice
6 tablespoons olive oil, divided
2 tablespoons soy sauce
3 or 4 cloves garlic, minced
    Cajun seasoning
1½ pounds skinless, boned chicken
2 onions, sliced
2 green bell peppers, cut in strips
6 flour tortillas

Combine lime juice, 4 tablespoons oil, soy sauce, garlic and seasoning. Pour over chicken in glass baking dish. Chill for 4 to 6 hours. Remove chicken from marinade and grill over hot charcoal for 8 to 10 minutes on each side. Cut chicken in ¼-inch strips. Sauté onion and pepper in 2 tablespoons oil until tender. Serve chicken and vegetables in warm tortillas.

Yield: 6 servings

CHILI-CHICKEN CASSEROLE

½ (8 ounce) package tortilla chips, lightly crushed
1 pound boneless chicken breast, cut in 1-inch cubes
1 small onion, diced
1 clove garlic, minced
2 tablespoons vegetable oil
1 (15 ounce) can tomato sauce
1 (17 ounce) can whole-kernel corn, drained and rinsed
1 (15 ounce) can red kidney beans, drained and rinsed
½ cup sliced green olives
½ cup sliced ripe olives
1 teaspoon black pepper or to taste
3 tablespoons chili powder or to taste
¼ teaspoon red pepper flakes or to taste
1 tablespoon basil
1 tablespoon chopped parsley
1 cup (4 ounces) shredded Monterey Jack cheese
1 cup (4 ounces) shredded Cheddar cheese

Arrange chips evenly in bottom of 13x9x3-inch baking dish. In large skillet, sauté chicken, onion and garlic in oil until chicken is opaque. Stir in vegetables and seasonings, blending well. Pour chicken mixture over chips and sprinkle with cheese. Bake at 350 degrees for 30 minutes or until thoroughly heated and cheese is melted.

Yield: 6 servings

GEORGIA-TEX CHICKEN CASSEROLE

1   dozen tortillas
1   (3 pound) chicken, cooked, boned and cut into bite-sized pieces
1   onion, chopped
1   (10 ounce) can tomatoes with green chilies
1   (10¾ ounce) can cream of chicken soup, undiluted
1   (10¾ ounce) can mushroom soup, undiluted
½   soup can chicken broth
2   cups (8 ounces) grated cheese

Tear tortillas into strips and place in bottom of greased 13x9x2-inch baking dish. Place chicken on tortillas. Sprinkle onion on chicken. Blend tomatoes, soups and broth; pour over onion layer. Bake, covered, at 350 degrees for 45 minutes. Remove from oven, sprinkle with cheese, and bake for 5 minutes or until cheese is melted.

Yield: 5 or 6 servings

HERBED CHICKEN SUPREME

1   (8 ounce) package herb-seasoned stuffing mix
3   cups cubed cooked chicken
½   cup butter or margarine
½   cup all-purpose flour
¼   teaspoon salt
   Dash of black pepper
4   cups chicken broth
6   eggs, lightly beaten
1   (10¾ ounce) can mushroom soup, undiluted
¼   cup milk
1   (8 ounce) carton sour cream
¼   cup chopped pimiento

Prepare stuffing mix according to package directions for dry stuffing. Spread stuffing in greased 13x9x3-inch baking dish. Place chicken on stuffing layer. Melt butter in large saucepan. Blend in flour and seasonings to form smooth paste. Gradually add broth, stirring constantly, and cook until mixture is thickened. Beginning with a small amount, add hot sauce to eggs, gradually adding up to half the sauce; then add remainder and pour egg-sauce mixture over chicken. Bake at 325 degrees for 40 to 45 minutes or until knife tip inserted near center comes out clean. Let stand for 5 minutes before cutting into squares. Combine soup, milk, sour cream and pimiento in saucepan; heat thoroughly, stirring constantly, but do not boil. Pour sauce over each chicken square.

Yield: 6 to 8 servings

CHICKEN PIE

FILLING

1	(4 pound) stewing chicken, cut up
1	stalk celery, cut in large chunks
1	onion
2	cloves
1	bay leaf
4	sprigs parsley
	Water
2 or 3	carrots, thinly sliced
1	cup peas
12	small white onions
	Salt
2	tablespoons butter
1	tablespoon all-purpose flour
½	cup half and half
	Salt and black pepper to taste

PASTRY

½	cup butter, softened
2	cups (8 ounces) grated Cheddar cheese
2	cups sifted all-purpose flour
¼	teaspoon baking powder
¼	teaspoon dry mustard

Place chicken, celery, onion pierced with cloves, bay leaf and parsley in stock pot; add water just to cover chicken. Bring to a boil and simmer until chicken is tender. Let stand until cool to touch. Remove chicken, strain stock and reserve it. Discard skin and bones from chicken and cut meat into small pieces. Cook carrots, peas and onions in small amount of salted water until tender; drain thoroughly. Melt butter in saucepan. Add flour and stir until smooth, cooking over low heat until bubbly. Add 2 cups reserved broth and cream. Season with salt and pepper. Cook, stirring constantly, until sauce is smooth and slightly thickened. Combine chicken, vegetables and sauce in deep 9-inch pie dish. Prepare pastry by blending butter and cheese until mixture is creamy. Sift flour with baking powder and mustard; add to cheese mixture and blend with hands until dough sticks together. On lightly floured surface, roll pastry to ¼-inch thickness; pierce with fork tines. Place over chicken mixture, pressing along edges to seal. Bake at 425 degrees for 10 minutes, reduce heat to 350 degrees and bake for 25 to 30 minutes.

Yield: 6 servings

CRAZY CAJUN RICE

5	cups uncooked brown rice
¾	cup butter or margarine
7	cups chicken broth
1	(6½ ounce) package cashews
7	cups chopped cooked chicken, skin removed
1	cup chopped green onion
	Salt to taste
1	tablespoon curry powder
1	teaspoon red or cayenne pepper
½	cup plus 2 tablespoons chopped parsley

Sauté rice in butter in large heavy pan until rice is deeply browned. Gradually add broth, being careful to avoid steam. Chop ⅔ of cashews, leaving remainder whole; add with chicken, onion and seasonings to rice mixture. Stir to blend flavors. Simmer, covered, until broth is absorbed and rice is chewy-tender.

Yield: 10 to 12 servings

HOLIDAY CHICKEN DIVAN

1 (16 ounce) package frozen chopped broccoli
1 cup sliced celery
2 cups seasoned croutons
1 cup diced green onion
1 cup sliced mushrooms
2 cups sliced water chestnuts
4 to 5 cups cubed cooked chicken breast
3 (10¾ ounce) cans cream of chicken soup, undiluted
¼ cup milk
1 tablespoon Worcestershire sauce
Salt to taste
Black pepper to taste
½ cup grated Parmesan cheese
1 (4 ounce) package slivered almonds
Dash of nutmeg

Steam broccoli and celery for a few minutes or just until crisp; drain. Place vegetables in 13x9x3-inch baking pan. Layer, in order, croutons, onion, mushrooms, chestnuts and chicken on vegetables. Combine soup, milk, Worcestershire sauce, salt and pepper in saucepan; cook until hot, stirring to blend. Pour sauce over chicken. Sprinkle with cheese, almonds and nutmeg. Bake at 350 degrees for 30 to 40 minutes or until cheese is golden and casserole is bubbly.

Yield: 8 servings

HOT CHICKEN SALAD

4 to 6 cups diced cooked chicken
6 hard-cooked eggs, grated
2 cups chopped celery
½ cup chopped pimiento
2 tablespoons chopped onion
1 (4 ounce) can sliced mushrooms
½ cup slivered almonds
1 cup breadcrumbs
2 (10¾ ounce) cans cream of chicken soup, undiluted
1 (10¾ ounce) can mushroom soup, undiluted
1 cup mayonnaise
2 tablespoons lemon juice
Worcestershire sauce to taste
Salt to taste
Black pepper to taste
2 cups crushed potato chips
2 cups (8 ounces) grated Cheddar cheese

Combine chicken, eggs, vegetables, almonds and breadcrumbs. Mix soups, mayonnaise and lemon juice; fold into chicken mixture. Add Worcestershire sauce and season with salt and pepper. Spread mixture in 13x9x2-inch baking dish. Sprinkle potato chips over mixture, then top with cheese. Bake at 325 degrees for 40 minutes.

Yield: 12 servings

SAVORY CRESCENT CHICKEN SQUARES

1   (3 ounce) package cream cheese, softened
3   tablespoons margarine or butter, melted, divided
2   cups cubed cooked chicken or 2 (5 ounce) cans boned chicken
¼   teaspoon salt
⅛   teaspoon black pepper
2   tablespoons milk
1   tablespoon chopped pimiento (optional)
1   tablespoon chopped chives or onion
1   (8 ounce) can refrigerated crescent roll dough
¾   cup crushed seasoned croutons

Blend cream cheese and 2 tablespoons margarine until smooth. Add chicken, seasonings, milk, pimiento and onions; mix thoroughly. Separate dough into 4 rectangles, pressing perforations to seal. Spoon ½ cup chicken mixture into center of each rectangle, pull corners of dough to middle and press firmly to seal. Brush with 1 tablespoon margarine and dip in croutons. Place on ungreased baking sheet. Bake at 350 degrees for 20 to 25 minutes or until browned.

Yield: 4 servings

DEEP FRIED WHOLE TURKEY

1   (10 to 11 pound) turkey
   Soy sauce
   Shrimp boil seasoning
   Black pepper
   Garlic powder
   Chives
2   medium-sized onions, quartered
4 to 6   stalks celery, cut in 3-inch pieces
1   cup water
2   gallons peanut oil (no substitute)
   Cajun poultry seasoning

Pierce turkey surface with fork tines. Place in roasting pan. Season with soy sauce, shrimp boil, black pepper, garlic powder and chives, sprinkling on all surfaces and in turkey cavities. Place some of vegetables inside turkey and place remainder alongside turkey. Add water to pan. Chill, covered with pan lid or aluminum foil, in coldest area of refrigerator for 1 to 3 days. Occasionally turn turkey, basting with pan liquids. Heat oil in large heavy pot until very hot. Remove turkey from marinade, remove vegetables and drain excess liquid. Sprinkle generously with poultry seasoning. Using two forks or holding turkey by legs, lower carefully into hot oil. Cook, breast side down, for about 20 minutes; turn and cook for about 15 minutes or until browned and turkey floats. Carefully remove with two forks and place on wire rack to drain. Serve hot or cold.

Cooking time is about 2 minutes per pound; do not overcook or turkey will fall apart when removed from oil. If undercooked, complete cooking in microwave oven. Peanut oil may be strained and reused.

Yield: 12 to 16 servings

BREAST OF TURKEY SUPREME WITH RICE DRESSING

1	turkey breast

DRESSING

1	medium-sized onion, chopped
½	cup shredded carrot
1	cup diced celery
¼	cup butter
4	cups instant rice, cooked without salt
½	cup milk
1	(13½ ounce) can chicken broth
1	egg, lightly beaten
1	teaspoon salt
1	teaspoon poultry seasoning

SAUCE

½	cup butter
½	cup all-purpose flour
2	cups hot chicken broth
1	teaspoon salt
⅛	teaspoon white pepper
1	cup milk
1	cup half and half
3	tablespoons chopped toasted almonds

Roast turkey, using own preferred method. While turkey is roasting, prepare dressing. Sauté onion, carrot and celery in butter until tender. Mix vegetables with rice, milk, broth, egg, salt and poultry seasoning. Pour into greased 9x9x2-inch baking dish. Bake at 350 degrees for 20 to 25 minutes or until liquid is absorbed. Just before serving, prepare sauce. Melt butter in saucepan, add flour and stir until smooth. Add hot broth and stir until smooth. Stir in salt and pepper. In separate saucepan, heat milk and half and half. Add to broth mixture and simmer for 10 minutes, stirring frequently. Serve hot sauce over sliced turkey and rice dressing. Sprinkle individual servings with almonds.

Yield: 10 servings

MARINATED GRILLED TURKEY

1	turkey breast, boned and skin removed
¼	cup firmly-packed brown sugar
¼	cup vinegar
¼	cup pineapple juice
¼	cup soy sauce
¼	teaspoon garlic salt
¼	teaspoon ground ginger
¼	teaspoon paprika
⅛	teaspoon black pepper

Place turkey halves, smooth side up, on cutting surface; cut diagonally into ½-inch slices and place in baking dish. Combine brown sugar, vinegar, juice, soy sauce and seasonings; pour over turkey. Store, covered, in refrigerator, for 2 days. Grill turkey slices for 2 to 3 minutes on each side; do not overcook. Grilled turkey may be frozen.

Yield: 10 servings

SK, AND IT SHALL BE
GIVEN TO YOU; SEEK,
AND YOU SHALL FIND; KNOCK,
AND IT SHALL BE OPENED TO
YOU. FOR EVERYONE WHO ASKS
RECEIVES, AND HE WHO SEEKS
FINDS, AND TO HIM WHO KNOCKS
IT SHALL BE OPENED.

Matt. 7:7-8

Beef Tenderloin with Sauce

Beef with Stuffing

1	clove garlic, crushed
2	medium-sized onions, chopped
¼	cup butter
1	cup chopped fresh spinach
1	pound mushrooms, sliced
1	cup herb-seasoned stuffing mix
1	egg
½	teaspoon salt
1	tablespoon paprika, divided
1	teaspoon marjoram
2	tablespoons olive oil
1	tablespoon soy sauce
1	(4 pound) beef tenderloin
6 to 8	slices center cut bacon

Sauce

¼	cup butter
½	(6 ounce) can tomato paste
1	teaspoon garlic pepper
2	teaspoons oregano
1	teaspoon Dijon mustard
1	tablespoon Worcestershire sauce
1	tablespoon soy sauce
½	cup beef bouillon
¾ to 1	cup half and half

Sauté garlic and onion in butter until onion is soft. Add mushrooms and cook until soft. Remove from heat and add spinach, stuffing mix, egg, salt, 1 teaspoon paprika and marjoram. Line baking pan with aluminum foil. Sprinkle oil and 1 tablespoon soy sauce on foil. Place meat on oiled surface, turning to coat on all sides. Spoon mushroom stuffing into slit in meat. Braid bacon across meat and stuffing. Bake at 450 degrees for 55 to 65 minutes. Prepare sauce by melting butter in saucepan. Stir in tomato paste, seasonings, Worcestershire sauce, soy sauce and bouillon; blend and heat for 2 to 3 minutes. Just before serving, add half and half. Let meat stand 8 to 10 minutes after roasting. Serve sauce in side dish.

Yield: 12 servings

Ursula Knaeusel

Yost's Beef Tenderloin

Marinade

2	cups vegetable oil
1½	cups prepared mustard
2	cloves garlic, minced
4	drops hot pepper sauce
1	tablespoon salt
	Dash of pepper
½	teaspoon smoke flavored salt
2½	teaspoons cumin
1	tablespoon seasoned salt

Meat

1	whole beef tenderloin

Combine oil, mustard, garlic and seasonings, blending well. Rub marinade on meat, coating all sides. Let stand for 6 hours. Cook over hot coals for 1½ hours, turning every 15 minutes; use meat thermometer to determine doneness to medium rare.

Yield: 3½ cups

STANDING RIB OR SIRLOIN TIP ROAST WITH YORKSHIRE PUDDING

1	clove garlic
1	(4 or 5 pound) standing rib or sirloin tip roast
	Lemon pepper

YORKSHIRE PUDDING

1	cup all-purpose flour
	Pinch of salt
1	egg
1	cup milk, divided
1 to 2	tablespoons pan drippings

Thoroughly rub garlic on bottom and sides of cast iron skillet and on rack to fit in skillet. Trim all fat from roast. Place on rack in skillet. Roast, uncovered, at 450 degrees for 15 minutes to brown surface and seal in juices. Reduce oven temperature to 325 degrees. Using meat thermometer, roast meat to desired doneness. While meat roasts, prepare Yorkshire pudding batter. Sift flour and salt into bowl. Make a well in center of dry ingredients, add egg and beat well. Gradually add ½ cup milk, beating constantly. When thick batter develops, beat for about 5 minutes. Stir in ½ cup milk. Chill, covered, for 30 minutes. Place roasted meat on platter and rub with several tablespoons of pan liquid. Sprinkle with lemon pepper. Cover with aluminum foil until ready to carve and serve. Pour drippings from beef roast into shallow baking dish and heat in oven. Pour batter into very hot dish. Bake at 425 degrees for 20 to 25 minutes or until well browned.

Cooled and fat-skimmed pan juices may also be used to make au jus or gravy.

Yield: 12 to 16 servings roast
4 servings pudding

EYE OF ROUND ROAST

	Freshly ground black pepper
	Garlic pepper
1	(3 to 5 pound) eye of round beef roast

Preheat oven at 500 degrees. Rub pepper into surface of roast. Place roast in pan and bake for 5 minutes per pound. Turn oven heat off; keep roast in oven for two hours without opening oven door. Remove roast and serve with au jus made from small amount of water heated with pan drippings.

Yield: 8 to 12 servings

ROAST A LA DANNY

1	(3 to 4 pound) beef roast
¼	cup Worcestershire sauce
2	tablespoons soy sauce
1	small onion, minced
¼	teaspoon rosemary
¼	teaspoon thyme
¼	teaspoon oregano
¼	teaspoon basil
2	bay leaves

Brown roast in Worcestershire sauce and soy sauce in Dutch oven, turning to sear both sides. Add onion and seasonings to meat. Simmer, covered, for 2 hours or roast at 350 degrees for 2 hours. Pan liquid may be strained and thickened for gravy.

Yield: 10 to 12 servings

BEEF AND CAULIFLOWER STIR-FRY

1	pound top round steak, cut in bite-sized pieces
2	tablespoons butter or margarine
4	cups cauliflowerets
1	green bell pepper, cut in ¾-inch pieces
¼	cup teriyaki sauce
1	clove garlic, minced (optional)
2	tablespoons cornstarch
½	teaspoon sugar
1½	cups beef broth or water
1	cup sliced green onion with tops

Sauté meat in butter for about 5 minutes. Add cauliflower, pepper, teriyaki sauce and garlic; stir to coat meat and vegetables with sauce. Simmer, covered, for about 10 minutes or until vegetables are just tender. Blend cornstarch, sugar and broth; add with green onion to beef mixture. Cook, stirring constantly, until thoroughly heated and thickened. Serve over rice or noodles.

Yield: 6 servings

GREEN PEPPER STEAK

MARINADE

½	cup soy sauce
½	teaspoon ground ginger
1	clove garlic, crushed

MEAT

1	pound boneless round or London broil steak, thinly sliced
2	tablespoons olive oil
2	green bell peppers, cut in thin strips
2	(16 ounce) cans tomatoes
1 or 2	onions, sliced
1	(16 ounce) can bean sprouts
1	(8 ounce) can bamboo shoots
1	(8 ounce) can water chestnuts
½ to ¾	pound mushrooms, thinly sliced
1	tablespoon cornstarch
	Garlic powder to taste
	Salt to taste
	Seasoned pepper to taste

Blend soy sauce, ginger and garlic. Pour marinade over meat in bowl and let stand, covered, for 30 minutes. Remove meat and drain, reserving marinade. Sauté meat in oil. Add vegetables and simmer, covered, for 5 minutes, stirring often. Blend cornstarch with reserved marinade, stir into meat mixture and cook, stirring constantly, until sauce is thickened. Serve over white or yellow rice.
If rare meat is desired, add after sauce is thickened. Precooked meat may be used; do not sauté.

Yield: 4 to 6 servings

PEPPER STEAK FOR SLOW-COOKER

2	pounds round steak, cut in ¼-inch strips
	Vegetable oil
1	tablespoon cornstarch
¼	cup soy sauce
1	(16 ounce) can tomatoes plus ½ cup water OR 2 fresh tomatoes plus 1 cup water
2	medium-sized green bell peppers, cut in strips
1	medium-sized onion, sliced
½	teaspoon salt
½	teaspoon black pepper

Sauté meat in oil until browned. Blend cornstarch and soy sauce, mixing until smooth. Place meat, vegetables, seasonings and cornstarch mixture in slow-cooker. Cook at medium-high setting for 4 to 5 hours. Serve over rice or with mashed potatoes.

Yield: 4 to 6 servings

GRILLED FLANK STEAK WITH CREAMED MUSHROOMS

MARINADE

¼	cup vegetable oil
¼	cup plus 2 teaspoons soy sauce, divided
2	teaspoons Worcestershire sauce
1	clove garlic, minced
1	teaspoon prepared mustard
½	teaspoon dry mustard
½	teaspoon salt
¼	teaspoon black pepper

MEAT

1½ to 2	pounds flank steak

CREAMED MUSHROOMS

1	pound mushrooms, sliced
2	tablespoons all-purpose flour
¼	cup plus 2 tablespoons butter
	Salt to taste
	Black pepper to taste
1½	cups half and half

Combine oil, ¼ cup soy sauce, Worcestershire sauce, garlic, mustard, salt and pepper in blender container; blend for 3 minutes. Pour into shallow baking dish or zip-seal plastic bag. Place meat in dish or bag. Marinate overnight in refrigerator. Remove meat from marinade and grill to desired doneness. Dredge mushrooms in flour. Sauté in butter over low heat for 10 minutes. Stir in 2 teaspoons soy sauce, season with salt and pepper and add cream. Simmer until hot. Serve with grilled meat.

Yield: 6 to 8 servings

PIQUANT FLANK STEAK

MARINADE
1	cup tomato juice
¼	cup minced onion or green onion
¼	cup minced green bell pepper
¼	cup minced celery
¼	cup olive oil
1	tablespoon vinegar
1 or 2	cloves garlic, minced
1	tablespoon chili powder
¼	teaspoon salt

MEAT
1	(2 pound) flank steak, fat trimmed

Combine tomato juice, vegetables, oil, vinegar, garlic and seasonings in small saucepan. Bring to a boil, then simmer, covered, for 15 minutes. Cool. Place meat in shallow baking dish. Pour cooled marinade over meat. Marinate in refrigerator for 4 hours. Remove meat from marinade, reserving marinade. Grill meat about 4 inches from coals for 3 to 4 minutes on each side for rare doneness; baste with marinade. Carve meat on diagonal into thin slices.

Yield: 4 to 6 servings

STEAK FAJITAS

MARINADE
½	cup fresh lime juice
6	tablespoons olive oil, divided
2	tablespoons soy sauce
3 or 4	cloves garlic, minced
	Cajun seasoning

MEAT
1½	pounds flank steak
2	onions, sliced
2	green bell peppers, cut in strips
6	flour tortillas

Combine lime juice, 4 tablespoons oil, soy sauce, garlic and seasoning. Pour over steak in baking dish. Chill for 4 to 6 hours. Remove steak from marinade and grill over hot charcoal for 4 to 5 minutes on each side or until preferred doneness. Cut, across grain, in ¼-inch slices. Sauté onion and pepper in 2 tablespoons oil until tender. Serve steak and vegetables in warm tortillas.

Yield: 6 servings

Meats & Main Dishes

TERIYAKI STEAK

MARINADE
1	cup soy sauce
½	cup firmly-packed brown sugar
4	cloves garlic, minced
2	teaspoons ground ginger
1	teaspoon seasoned salt (optional)
½	teaspoon black pepper

MEAT
1	(3 pound) (2½-inch thick) round steak

Combine soy sauce, brown sugar, garlic and seasonings. Marinate meat in mixture for 24 hours, turning once. Grill meat to desired doneness. Cut in thin slices.

Steak slices are especially good in sandwiches.

Yield: 6 to 8 servings

BARBECUE BRISKET

	Celery salt
	Onion salt
	Garlic salt
1	whole beef brisket
3 to 4	tablespoons liquid smoke
1	(16 ounce) bottle barbecue sauce

Sprinkle seasonings generously over meat, covering all sides. Place meat in 13x9x3-inch baking dish and sprinkle with liquid smoke. Cover with plastic wrap and chill overnight; remove wrap before baking. Bake at 275 degrees for 5 hours. Drain excess fat from dish. Let meat cool before slicing. Pour barbecue sauce over slices and reheat at 300 degrees for 20 minutes.

Yield: 20 servings

KOREAN BARBECUE BEEF

MARINADE
3	tablespoons soy sauce
1	tablespoon vegetable oil
2	tablespoons sugar
½	green bell pepper, cut in strips
2	tablespoons sliced green onion
3	cloves garlic, minced
2	tablespoons sesame seed

MEAT
1	pound top round of beef, thinly sliced

Combine soy sauce, oil, sugar, pepper, onion, garlic and sesame seeds; blend well. Add meat and toss to coat thoroughly. Marinate for 1 hour in refrigerator. Drain meat, reserving marinade. Stir-fry meat in wok at 350 degrees just until done; do not overcook. Pour marinade over meat. Serve with rice and vegetable side dishes.

Yield: 3 or 4 servings

SAUERBRATEN

1	(3 to 4 pound) beef brisket
1	clove garlic
	Salt to taste
	Pepper to taste
2	tablespoons vegetable oil
1	medium-sized onion, chopped
1	(8 ounce) can tomato sauce
½	cup beef broth
6 to 8	gingersnaps, crushed

Rub meat with garlic and season with salt and pepper. Sauté meat in oil in large skillet, turning to brown all sides. Add onions and cook until transparent. Add tomato sauce and broth. Simmer, covered, for about 3 hours or until meat is tender. Remove meat from skillet. Add gingersnaps to pan liquid to thicken for gravy. Serve with rice.

Yield: 8 to 10 servings

FRUITED BEEF

3 to 4	pounds cubed stew beef
2	tablespoons butter
1	clove garlic, minced
¼	teaspoon cinnamon
2½	teaspoons salt
¼	teaspoon black pepper
1	(11 ounce) package mixed dried fruit
2	onions, sliced in rings
1	(8 to 10 ounce) package dried apple rings
1	beef bouillon cube
1¾	cup water
¼	cup firmly-packed dark brown sugar
2	bay leaves
1	teaspoon parsley flakes

Sauté meat in butter until lightly browned, seasoning with garlic, cinnamon, salt and pepper. Reserving half of the dried fruit, alternate layers of meat, fruit and onions in slow-cooker. Place apples on top of layers. Dissolve bouillon in water. Add brown sugar and stir until dissolved. Pour over apples. Sprinkle bay leaves and parsley flakes over apples. Cook at low setting for 6 to 8 hours, adding reserved dried fruit for the last 30 minutes of cooking time. Serve with wild and white rice mixture.

Yield: 6 to 8 servings

THAI STYLE STEW

1	pound stew beef
1	teaspoon minced garlic
1	teaspoon salt
½	teaspoon black pepper
1	tablespoon vegetable oil
1	tablespoon sugar
2	tablespoons soy sauce
1	cup water
1	(1 inch) piece ginger root, peeled and grated
2	medium potatoes, peeled and quartered
½	cup green beans

Rub meat with garlic, salt and pepper; let stand for 1 hour. Sauté meat in oil in heavy saucepan, turning several times to brown all sides. Add sugar, soy sauce and water. Check seasonings and add ginger. Bring to a boil, then simmer, covered, for 1 hour or until meat is tender. Add potatoes and green beans; simmer, covered, for 20 minutes. Serve with rice.

Yield: 3 or 4 servings

LASAGNA FANTASTICO

1	pound ground chuck
½	pound Italian sausage, casing removed
2	cloves garlic, chopped
1	onion, chopped
½	cup pine nuts
2	tablespoons olive oil
2	pounds tomatoes, chopped
2	(6 ounce) cans tomato paste
1½	teaspoons salt
½	teaspoon black pepper
1	teaspoon basil
1	teaspoon oregano
½	(16 ounce) package lasagna noodles
2	cups (16 ounces) ricotta or cottage cheese
½	cup grated Romano cheese
2	tablespoons parsley flakes
1	egg
1	(16 ounce) package shredded mozzarella cheese

Sauté meats, garlic, onion and pine nuts in oil, stirring to crumble meat. Add tomatoes, tomato paste and seasonings. Simmer meat mixture for 30 minutes. Prepare noodles according to package directions, drain and rinse. Combine ricotta cheese, Romano cheese, parsley and egg. Alternately layer noodles, ricotta filling, mozzarella cheese and meat sauce in 13x9x3-inch baking dish. Bake at 375 degrees for 30 minutes. Let stand 10 minutes before serving.

Yield: 6 to 8 servings

Cabbage Casserole

1   medium head cabbage, chopped
     Water
1   pound ground meat
1   cup chopped onion
1   cup chopped green bell pepper
1   cup chopped celery
1   (10 ounce) can tomatoes with green
     chilies
1   cup breadcrumbs, divided

Cook cabbage in water until tender; drain. Sauté meat until browned. Add onion, pepper, celery and tomatoes. Simmer for 45 minutes. Add ½ cup breadcrumbs to meat mixture; stir in cabbage. Spoon into 2-quart casserole and sprinkle with ½ cup breadcrumbs. Bake at 350 degrees until browned.

Yield: 4 servings

Green Enchiladas

1   (10¾ ounce) can cream of chicken soup,
     undiluted
1   (5 ounce) can evaporated milk
1   (8 ounce) package processed cheese
     spread
1   (4 ounce) can green chilies, chopped
1   (2 ounce) can pimiento
1   pound ground beef
2   cups (8 ounces) longhorn cheese, grated
1   cup chopped onion
12   tortillas

Combine soup, milk and cheese spread in double boiler; heat over boiling water until cheese is melted. Stir in chilies and pimiento. Cook meat until browned; drain excess grease. Add cheese and onion and mix thoroughly. Spoon meat mixture into each tortilla and roll tightly; place in 13x9x3-inch baking dish. Pour cheese sauce over rolled tortillas. Bake, covered, at 350 degrees for 30 minutes.

Yield: 6 servings

BOBOTIE

2	onions, thinly sliced
1	apple, diced
2	tablespoons butter or margarine
2	pounds ground beef
2	slices bread, soaked in water and pressed
2	eggs, divided
2	tablespoons vinegar
¼	cup raisins
1	teaspoon turmeric
2	tablespoons curry powder
2	tablespoons sugar
2	teaspoons salt
½	teaspoon black pepper
12	almonds, blanched, skin removed and quartered
6	lemon or bay leaves
1	cup milk

Sauté onion and apple in butter until onion is transluscent. Separately sauté meat until browned. Combine onion, apple, meat, bread, 1 egg, vinegar, raisins and seasonings; mix thoroughly. Stir in almonds. Spoon mixture into greased 2-quart casserole. Roll lemon leaves and insert them vertically in meat mixture; if using bay leaves, do not roll but insert in mixture. Bake at 350 degrees for 30 to 45 minutes. Combine 1 egg and milk; beat well and pour over meat mixture about 10 minutes before cooking time is completed. Remove bay leaves. Serve with rice and toppings of coconut, tomatoes, bananas, almonds and raisins.

Yield: 6 to 8 servings

GROUND BEEF STEAK WITH MUSHROOM SAUCE

MEAT

2	pounds ground sirloin
½	teaspoon salt

MUSHROOM SAUCE

3 to 5	tablespoons margarine or butter
2	teaspoons onion powder
¼	teaspoon garlic powder
1	(8 ounce) can mushrooms, drained
3 or 4	(¼-inch thick) slices processed cheese spread
¼	teaspoon Worcestershire sauce
1	teaspoon summer savory

Shape meat into 4 (1½-inch thick) patties. Pan broil patties in hot iron skillet seasoned with salt, searing on both sides and cooking to desired doneness. Remove from skillet and keep warm. Prepare sauce by melting margarine in skillet. Add onion and garlic powders, mixing well. Add mushrooms and sauté until browned. Stir in cheese, mixing until melted. Add Worcestershire sauce and mix well. Remove from heat and let stand to thicken. Serve sauce over patties and sprinkle with savory.

Yield: 4 servings

ITALIAN MEAT SAUCE WITH MEATBALLS

SAUCE
1½	pounds ground beef
2	tablespoons olive oil, divided
1	cup chopped onion
4	cloves garlic, minced
½	pound mushrooms, sliced
½	pound Italian sausage, cut in 1-inch pieces
2	(29 ounce) cans Italian tomatoes
2	(8 ounce) cans tomato sauce
2	chicken bouillon cubes
2	beef bouillon cubes
2	tablespoons minced parsley
1½	teaspoons sugar
1	teaspoon black pepper
2	tablespoons dried basil
1	tablespoon oregano
2	(6 ounce) cans tomato paste
1	paste can water

MEATBALLS
1	pound ground beef
¼	pound ground pork
1	cup Italian-seasoned breadcrumbs
½	cup grated Parmesan or Romano cheese
1	tablespoon minced parsley
1	clove garlic, crushed
¼	cup milk
1	small onion, chopped
1	egg, beaten
	Salt to taste
	Black pepper to taste
1	tablespoon olive oil

Sauté meat in 1 tablespoon oil until browned. Drain excess fat and transfer meat to slow-cooker set on low heat. Sauté onion, minced garlic and mushrooms in 1 tablespoon oil until onions are transluscent. Place vegetable mixture on meat in slow-cooker. Sauté sausage until browned, drain excess fat and place on vegetables in slow-cooker. Set cooker on high heat. Place tomatoes in large saucepan and mash with potato masher. Add tomato sauce, bouillon cubes, 2 tablespoons parsley and other seasonings, mixing well. Heat until bubbly, then pour into slow-cooker. In saucepan, heat tomato paste and water until thickened and bubbly; add to slow-cooker and stir. Cook for up to 12 hours at high setting. About 1 hour before sauce is done, prepare meatballs. Combine ground beef, pork, breadcrumbs, cheese, parsley, garlic, milk, onion, egg, salt and pepper. Mix thoroughly and shape into lemon-sized balls. Sauté meatballs in oil, turning to brown on all sides. Transfer to slow-cooker. Stir sauce and meatballs occasionally and check seasonings. Serve over spaghetti or with stuffed shells and a tossed salad.

Yield: 12 to 16 servings

MEAT LOAF WITH PIQUANT SAUCE

MEAT LOAF

¾	cup dry breadcrumbs or corn flake crumbs
1	cup milk
1½	pounds ground chuck
2	eggs, lightly beaten
¼	cup grated or minced onion
1	teaspoon salt
⅛	teaspoon black pepper
½	teaspoon sage

PIQUANT SAUCE

¼	cup ketchup
3	tablespoons brown sugar
1	teaspoon dry mustard
¼	teaspoon nutmeg

Soak crumbs in milk. Add meat, eggs, onion and seasonings; mix well. Shape mixture into 1 or 2 loaves and place in greased pan. Combine ketchup, brown sugar and seasonings; blend thoroughly and pour over meat loaves. Bake 2 loaves at 350 degrees for 45 minutes or 1 loaf for 1 hour.

Yield: 4 servings

SLOPPY JOES

1	pound ground beef
1	small onion, chopped
½	cup chopped celery or green bell pepper
1	(8 ounce) can tomato sauce
½	cup ketchup
1	tablespoon vinegar
1	tablespoon Worcestershire sauce
1	teaspoon dry mustard
¼	teaspoon black pepper

Sauté meat until browned. Add onion and celery or pepper; cook until vegetables are tender. Drain excess grease. Stir in tomato sauce, ketchup, vinegar, Worcestershire sauce and seasonings. Simmer for 15 to 20 minutes. Serve on buns or in pita bread pockets.

Yield: 4 servings

Veal Parmesan

6	thinly-sliced veal cutlets (about 1½ pounds)
1	clove garlic
½	cup all-purpose flour
2	teaspoons salt, divided
1	teaspoon pepper, divided
1½ to 2	cups fine dry Italian breadcrumbs
½	cup grated Parmesan cheese
3	eggs
½	cup olive oil
2	(8 ounce) cans tomato sauce
1	(6 ounce) can tomato paste
6	thin slices mozzarella cheese

Rub cutlets with garlic. Place flour, 1 teaspoon salt and ½ teaspoon pepper in paper bag. Add cutlets, 2 pieces at a time, to seasoned flour and shake briefly to coat. Mix breadcrumbs and cheese on platter. Beat eggs with 1 teaspoon salt and ½ teaspoon pepper and pour into shallow bowl. Slowly heat skillet over medium heat, add olive oil and allow to smoke briefly. Dip cutlets in egg mixture, then in crumbs. Sauté in oil, slowly browning both sides. Arrange cutlets in baking dish. Mix tomato sauce and paste; pour over cutlets and top each with cheese slice. Bake at 350 degrees for 15 to 20 minutes or until cheese is melted and lightly browned.

Yield: 6 servings

Veal Scaloppine

¼	cup butter, divided
½	pound mushrooms, sliced
2	large onions, sliced
2	cloves garlic, minced
1½	tablespoons lemon juice
1½	pounds boneless veal
½	cup all-purpose flour
	Salt
	Pepper
1	beef bouillon cube
¼	cup water
½	cup de-alcoholized white wine
	Minced parsley for garnish

Melt 2 tablespoons butter in large skillet. Add mushrooms, onion and garlic; sprinkle with lemon juice. Cook over medium heat until mushrooms are soft; remove from skillet and set aside. Pound veal and cut in 1-inch strips. Dust with flour and season with salt and pepper; shake to remove excess. Sauté meat in 2 tablespoons butter in skillet over high heat, turning to brown both sides. Remove from skillet and set aside. Dissolve bouillon in water; add with de-alcoholized wine to browned particles in skillet to form sauce. Return meat and mushrooms to skillet and heat thoroughly. Garnish servings with parsley.

Yield: 6 servings

LAMB STUFFED SQUASH

1	medium-sized onion, chopped
2	tablespoons butter, divided
1	tablespoon salt, divided
1	teaspoon black pepper
¼	teaspoon cinnamon
¼	teaspoon nutmeg
¼	teaspoon allspice
1	cup uncooked regular rice
1	pound ground lamb
4¼	cups water, divided
10	medium to large yellow squash
1	onion, sliced
1	(16 ounce) can tomatoes
2	tablespoons tomato paste
½	teaspoon minced garlic
1	teaspoon dried mint

Sauté chopped onion in 1 tablespoon butter until soft. Mix onion, 2 teaspoons salt and other seasonings with rice. Add lamb and ¼ cup water; mix thoroughly. Cut top from each squash. Scoop out pulp, being careful to avoid breaking the skin. Spoon lamb mixture into squash shells, filling ¾ full. In saucepan in which squash will be cooked, sauté sliced onion in 1 tablespoon butter until lightly browned. Add garlic and tomatoes to onion. Place squash in pan. Combine tomato paste and 4 cups water; pour over squash. Sprinkle with mint. Place a heatproof plate over squash to keep in place during cooking. Bring to a boil, then simmer, covered, for 1 to 1½ hours. Cool in pan juices and reheat before serving.

Yield: 4 to 6 servings

PORK ADOBO

2	pounds pork, cut in 1-inch cubes
1	tablespoon vegetable oil or shortening
2	large cloves garlic, quartered
¼	cup cane, coconut or pineapple vinegar
1	large bay leaf
1	whole peppercorn, crushed
½	teaspoon salt
1	tablespoon soy sauce
1	teaspoon brown sugar
1½	cups water

Sauté meat and garlic in oil until browned. Add vinegar, seasonings, soy sauce, brown sugar and water. Simmer until meat is tender, adding more water if necessary. Check seasoning, adding more sugar or vinegar if desired.

Pan liquid may be thickened with flour to make gravy.

Yield: 6 servings

PORK ROAST WITH VEGETABLES

1   (5 to 7 pound) pork roast
1   (8 ounce) package dried seedless prunes
1½   teaspoons salt
1½   teaspoons lemon pepper
½   teaspoon cracked pepper
3   medium-sized onions, quartered
3   carrots, quartered
10   whole allspice
6   juniper berries
5   whole cloves
3   bay leaves
1   clove garlic
1   cup boiling water
2   apples, quartered

Cut several slits in meat and insert prunes. Place meat in baking dish lined with heavy duty aluminum foil. Sprinkle meat with salt, lemon pepper and pepper. Arrange vegetables and other seasonings around meat; add water. Close foil over meat, folding to seal tightly. Bake at 400 degrees for 1 hour. Cut a slit in foil and pull to side. Add apples. Bake for 1 hour. Remove meat and vegetables from dish. Place vegetables in saucepan, add cooking liquid and simmer for 5 minutes. Serve with meat.

Yield: 10 to 12 servings

Ursula Knaeusel

SPRING ROLLS

1½   teaspoons chopped garlic
1   tablespoon vegetable oil
1   cup ground pork
½   cup cooked shrimp, chopped (optional)
½   cup cooked crabmeat (optional)
1   cup bean sprouts
4   eggs, lightly beaten, fried and chopped
2   tablespoons chopped green onion
2   tablespoons chopped celery leaves
6   dried black mushrooms, chopped (optional)
½   cup jelly noodles
1   tablespoon soy sauce
1   tablespoon nampla (fish sauce)
1   tablespoon sugar
2   teaspoons salt
1   teaspoon black pepper
     Egg roll wrappers
1   egg yolk
2   cups vegetable oil

Sauté garlic for 2 minutes in 1 tablespoon oil. Add pork, shrimp, crabmeat, sprouts, eggs, onion, celery, mushrooms and noodles; cook for about 5 minutes. Stir in soy sauce, nampla and seasonings. Place about 2 tablespoons of meat mixture on egg roll wrapper, roll up and seal with egg yolk. Deep fry in oil for 5 to 10 minutes. Drain on paper towel and serve hot.
Extra salt can be substituted for nampla. The noodles should be available at an Oriental grocery.

Yield: 24 to 30 servings

Meats & Main Dishes

THAI SWEET AND SOUR PORK

- 1 egg, beaten
- 1 tablespoon sugar
- 1 teaspoon salt
- 1 tablespoons soy sauce
- 1 pound lean pork, cubed
  Cornstarch
- ¼ cup vegetable oil
- 1 clove garlic, minced
- 1 green bell pepper, cut in pieces
- 1 onion, cut in wedges
- 4 slices ginger root, minced (optional)
- 1 tomato, cut in wedges
- ¾ cup pineapple chunks

SAUCE

- 3 tablespoons vinegar
- 2 tablespoons soy sauce
- ¾ cup pineapple juice
- 3 tablespoons brown sugar
- 1 tablespoon cornstarch

Combine egg, sugar, salt and 1 tablespoon soy sauce. Add meat to marinade and let stand for 20 to 30 minutes. Prepare sauce by combining vinegar, 2 tablespoons soy sauce, pineapple juice, brown sugar and 1 tablespoon cornstarch; set aside. Drain meat, then dredge in cornstarch. Sauté in oil, turning to brown all sides. Remove from skillet and keep warm. Remove excess grease, leaving about 2 tablespoons in skillet. Add garlic, pepper, onion and ginger; stir-fry 2 to 3 minutes. Add tomato, pineapple and sauce. Cook just until sauce is thickened and clear. Add meat to sauce mixture and heat until bubbly; onion and peppers should be tender crisp. Serve immediately with rice.

Yield: 4 to 6 servings

GRILLED PORK TENDERLOIN

- 2 pork tenderloins, fat trimmed
- 1 (8 ounce) bottle Italian salad dressing

Marinate tenderloins in dressing overnight. Grill over hot charcoal until tenderloin reaches internal temperature of 185 degrees. Cut in ¼-inch slices. Serve as entree or on small pumpernickel bread rounds for sandwiches.

Yield: 8 to 12 servings

GRILLED PORK CHOPS

- 6 (1 to 1¼-inch thick) loin pork chops
  Lemon pepper
  Salt
  Coarsely ground black pepper
  Worcestershire sauce

Sprinkle chops with dry seasonings to taste; let stand at room temperature for 1 hour before grilling. Prepare charcoal; add several pieces of presoaked hickory chips when coals are red and flaming. Sear chops for 1½ to 2 minutes on each side and baste with Worcestershire sauce. Close top of grill to extinguish flames. Open every 2 minutes to baste with sauce and turn; total cooking time, including searing, should be 11 to 12 minutes.

Yield: 6 servings

Ritzy Pork Chops

4	(¾-inch thick) center cut pork chops
2	tablespoons melted butter, divided
	Garlic salt to taste
	Lemon pepper to taste
½	cup crushed round buttery crackers

Brush each chop lightly with melted butter. Sprinkle with seasonings. Place in baking dish, sprinkle with crumbs and drizzle with remaining butter. Bake, uncovered, at 325 degrees for 1 hour.

Yield: 4 servings

Smothered Pork Chops

6	pork chops
½	cup apple jelly
¼	cup soy sauce
¼	cup ketchup
1	clove garlic, minced
1	tablespoon cornstarch
1	tablespoon water

Place chops in shallow baking dish. Combine jelly, soy sauce, ketchup and garlic, mixing well (jelly will not competely blend). Pour sauce over pork chops. Bake at 350 degrees for 50 to 60 minutes or until tender. Remove chops from dish and keep warm. Combine cornstarch and water. Stir into cooking juices and cook over low heat, stirring constantly, until mixture boils and is thickened. Serve over pork chops with rice.

Yield: 6 servings

Belgian Endives and Ham au Gratin

8	large Belgian endives
1	tablespoon lemon juice
1	teaspoon salt
	Water
2	tablespoons butter
2	tablespoons all-purpose flour
1¼	cups milk
½	cup (2 ounces) grated Swiss cheese
1	egg yolk
	Salt to taste
	Freshly ground black pepper to taste
8	slices boiled ham
2	tablespoons grated Parmesan cheese

Trim endives at stalk and remove brown edged leaves. Place in saucepan with lemon juice, salt and water just to cover. Simmer, covered, for 10 to 15 minutes or until endives are just tender. Drain well and set aside. Melt butter in saucepan; stir in flour and cook for about 2 minutes, stirring constantly. Add milk and cook, stirring constantly, until sauce is thickened and smooth. Add Swiss cheese and cook until cheese is melted. Remove from heat and beat in egg yolk. Season with salt and pepper. Wrap endives in ham slices and place in buttered shallow baking dish. Pour cheese sauce over vegetable bundles and sprinkle with Parmesan cheese. Bake at 375 degrees for about 20 minutes or until browned and bubbly (may be browned under broiler).

Yield: 4 servings

RAISIN STUFFED HAM STEAKS

2	cups soft breadcrumbs
½	cup raisins
½	cup dry roasted peanuts, chopped
2	tablespoons dark corn syrup
½	teaspoon dry mustard
¼	cup butter, melted
2	(½-inch thick) center cut ham slices
½	cup carbonated cola drink
1	tablespoon brown sugar

Combine breadcrumbs, raisins, peanuts, syrup, mustard and butter. Place 1 ham slice in baking pan lined with aluminum foil; spread slice with crumb mixture. Top with second ham slice. Baste with cola and sprinkle with brown sugar. Bake at 350 degrees for about 20 minutes or until thoroughly heated.

Yield: 4 to 6 servings

STUFFED HAM ROLLS

12	slices Danish ham
1	cup chopped cooked chicken
1	(6 ounce) jar marinated artichokes, drained and oil reserved
1	(8 ounce) can water chestnuts, chopped
1	stalk celery, chopped
1	(8 ounce) package frozen peas, thawed
2	tablespoons dried onion
2	teaspoons seasoned salt
2	teaspoons lemon pepper
2	teaspoons prepared mustard
2 to 3	tablespoons mayonnaise
12	shrimp for garnish
12	olives for garnish
12	stalks asparagus for garnish
	Parsley for garnish

Place ham slices on surface covered with plastic wrap. Pour artichoke oil over chicken in bowl; chop artichokes and add with water chestnuts to chicken. Stir in celery, peas, onion and seasonings; add enough mayonnaise for spreading consistency. Divide chicken mixture among ham slices. Roll each, jelly roll fashion; slice into three sections. Place on serving tray. Garnish each with a shrimp, an olive cut in 3 slices, an asparagus stalk and parsley sprig. Extra chicken mixture can be served in tomato or on lettuce. Serve with Potato Salad Mold, page 86.

Yield: 8 servings

Ursula Knaeusel

141

TERRIFIC ITALIAN SAUSAGE

1	pound sweet Italian pork sausage
	Salt
2	tablespoons extra virgin olive oil
1	yellow onion, chopped
3	large green bell peppers, diced
2 or 3	Italian plum tomatoes, quartered and seeded
	Salt to taste
	Black pepper to taste
1	lemon

Separate sausage links. Spread thin layer salt in large iron skillet; heat over high flame. Add sausages, reduce heat and cook slowly until brown and crisp on all sides. In separate skillet, heat oil. Add onion and peppers; cook over low heat, stirring. Press tomatoes through sieve; add to vegetables and cook, stirring often, until thickened. Season with salt and pepper. Drain sausages on paper towel to remove excess salt and grease; place on serving plate. Squeeze lemon juice over sausages. Serve sauce as side dish or spoon over sausages. Serve with narrow noodles.

Yield: 4 servings

CORN DOGS

1	cup sifted all-purpose flour
2	tablespoons sugar
1½	teaspoons baking powder
1	teaspoon salt
⅓	cup cornmeal
2	tablespoons vegetable oil
1	egg
¾	cup milk
1	(16 ounce) package frankfurters
	Vegetable oil for deep frying

Sift flour, sugar, baking powder and salt together. Blend in cornmeal. Add oil, egg and milk; stir just until dry ingredients are moistened. Cook frankfurters in boiling water for 5 minutes; drain well. Dip frankfurters in batter, coating on all sides. Deep fry for 5 minutes or until golden. Drain and serve immediately.

Yield: 5 or 6 servings

SOUTHERN BEANS SUPREME

1	pound ground beef
½	pound link sausage, sliced
3	slices bacon, diced
1	(32 ounce) can baked beans
1	(52 ounce) can baked beans
1	medium-sized onion, diced
½	cup barbecue sauce
1	cup firmly-packed brown sugar
½	cup ketchup
1	tablespoon Worcestershire sauce
1	tablespoon prepared mustard

Sauté meat until browned; drain excess grease. Combine meats, vegetables, barbecue sauce, brown sugar, ketchup, Worcestershire sauce and mustard in slow-cooker. Cook on low setting for 9 hours or until onions are tender.

Yield: 16 to 20 servings

ITALIAN EGGPLANT CASSEROLE

2	medium eggplants, peeled and cut in ¼-inch slices
	Salt
	Water
	Olive oil
1	(16 ounce) can Italian tomatoes
1	clove garlic
1	tablespoon olive oil
2	cups (8 ounces) grated Parmesan cheese
1	(8 ounce) package mozzarella cheese slices
1	pound salami, sliced

Soak eggplant in salted water for 30 minutes. Drain and dry. Sauté eggplant in oil until light golden brown; remove and keep warm. In separate pan, simmer tomatoes and garlic in 1 tablespoon oil until sauce consistency. In oiled baking pan, layer eggplant, tomato sauce, Parmesan cheese, mozzarella and salami, repeating layers until all ingredients are used and ending with a sprinkling of Parmesan cheese. Bake at 350 degrees for 15 minutes or until hot and bubbly.

Yield: 8 to 10 servings

BAKED MANICOTTI WITH CHEESE FILLING

SAUCE

1½	cups minced onion
1	clove garlic, crushed
⅓	cup olive or vegetable oil
1	(35 ounce) can Italian tomatoes, undrained
1	(6 ounce) can tomato paste
2	tablespoons chopped parsley
1	tablespoon sugar
1	tablespoon salt
¼	teaspoon black pepper
1	teaspoon dried oregano
1	teaspoon dried basil

CRÊPES

6	eggs, at room temperature
1½	cups all-purpose flour
¼	teaspoon salt

FILLING

4	cups (32 ounces) ricotta cheese
1	(8 ounce) package mozzarella cheese, diced
⅓	cup plus ¼ cup grated Parmesan cheese, divided
2	eggs
1	teaspoon salt
¼	teaspoon black pepper
1	tablespoon chopped parsley

Sauté onion and garlic in oil until transluscent. Stir in tomatoes, tomato paste, parsley, sugar, salt, pepper, oregano and basil; simmer for 3 hours. Combine eggs, flour and salt in blender container; blend until well mixed. Chill for several hours. Heat a 6 or 7-inch crêpe pan or iron skillet until water drop sizzles. Grease pan, pour scant ¼ cup batter into pan and swirl quickly to cover bottom with batter; immediately pour off batter that does not adhere. Cook until browned. Lift edge with fingers to turn and cook for a few seconds on second side. Repeat with remaining batter, regreasing pan for each crêpe. Combine ricotta cheese, mozzarella cheese, ⅓ cup Parmesan cheese, eggs, salt, pepper and parsley. Spoon filling on each crêpe and roll to enclose. Pour some sauce into bottom of 13x9x2-inch baking dish. Place filled crêpes in single layer and cover with remaining sauce. Sprinkle with ¼ cup Parmesan cheese. Bake, uncovered, at 350 degrees for 20 to 30 minutes or until bubbly.

Yield: 8 servings

THE LORD'S

LOVINGKINDNESSES

INDEED NEVER CEASE, FOR HIS

COMPASSIONS NEVER FAIL. THEY

ARE NEW EVERY MORNING;

GREAT IS THY FAITHFULNESS.

Lamentations 3:22-23

Mustard Mousse

1	envelope unflavored gelatin
¼	cup lemon juice
4	eggs, lightly beaten
¾	cup sugar
½	teaspoon salt
¼	cup prepared mustard
½	cup cider vinegar
½	cup water
1	cup whipping cream, whipped

Soften gelatin in lemon juice in small bowl; let stand 5 minutes. Combine eggs, sugar, salt, mustard, vinegar and water in saucepan; beat until blended. Add gelatin. Cook over medium heat, stirring constantly, until mixture begins to thicken; do not boil or it will separate. Chill until nearly firm. Fold whipped cream into gelatin mixture. Pour into oiled 4-cup mold. Chill, covered with plastic wrap, for about 4 hours or until firm. Invert on platter and serve small wedges with ham or pork. Mousse may be stored in refrigerator for up to 3 days.

Yield: 4 cups

Specialty Mustard

1	cup dry mustard
1	cup champagne wine vinegar
1	cup sugar
1	teaspoon salt
2	eggs

Combine mustard and vinegar. Let stand overnight. Combine mustard mixture, sugar, salt and eggs in saucepan. Cook until thickened. Serve with ham.

Yield: 2 cups

Barbecue Sauce

3	tablespoons ketchup
1½	tablespoons vinegar
¼	cup water
1 to 2	tablespoons butter
2	tablespoons Worcestershire sauce
1	tablespoon lemon juice
1 to 3	drops hot pepper sauce (optional)
2 to 3	tablespoons brown sugar
1	teaspoon grated lemon peel
1	teaspoon salt
⅛	teaspoon black pepper
1	teaspoon dry mustard
1	teaspoon chili powder
¼	teaspoon ginger
2	bay leaves

Combine all ingredients in saucepan. Simmer, covered, for 20 to 30 minutes. If ingredients are doubled, limit vinegar to 2 tablespoons.

Yield: 1 cup

HOLLANDAISE SAUCE

⅓	cup butter or margarine
2	egg yolks
1	tablespoon lemon juice
¼	teaspoon salt
¼	teaspoon dry mustard
	Dash of hot pepper sauce

Place margarine in 1-quart microwave proof measuring cup; microwave on high setting for 45 to 60 seconds or until melted. Stir in egg yolks, lemon juice and seasonings; beat with whisk to blend well. Cook at medium high setting for 1½ minutes or until thickened, stirring 4 or 5 times during cooking time. Serve over vegetables.

Yield: ½ cup

FRESH TOMATO SALSA

5	medium tomatoes, diced
⅓	cup tomato sauce
¼	cup minced purple onion
3	cloves garlic, minced
1 or 2	small jalapeno peppers, seeded and minced
2	tablespoons minced cilantro or parsley
1	tablespoon minced oregano or 1 teaspoon dried oregano
2	tablespoons lime juice
1	teaspoon salt

Combine tomatoes, sauce, onion, garlic and peppers. Add cilantro, oregano, lime juice and salt; stir lightly until mixed. Chill, covered. Serve with tortilla chips, fish or chicken or toasted French bread.

Yield: 3⅓ cups

ZUCCHINI RELISH

10	cups ground zucchini
4	cups ground fresh onion
1	green bell pepper, ground
1	red bell pepper, ground
1	hot pepper, ground
3	tablespoons salt
4	cups sugar
½	teaspoon black pepper
1	tablespoon cornstarch
2¼	cups white or cider vinegar
1	teaspoon tumeric
1	teaspoon celery salt

Combine ground vegetables and salt in large container. Chill overnight. Place small portions of mixture in cloth bag and press to remove liquid. Rinse pulp in cold water, then press through cloth bag again to remove liquid. Combine sugar, pepper and cornstarch. Add tumeric and celery salt. Stir dry mixture into squash mixture in large pan. Bring to a boil, then cook for 5 minutes, stirring continuously and scraping the bottom of the pan to avoid sticking. Spoon into sterilized ½ pint or pint jars and seal. Serve with vegetables or meat.

Relish is slightly sweet with a yellow-green color and unique flavor.

Yield: 7 cups

MIXED PEPPER SALSA

¼ cup white vinegar
2 tablespoons vegetable oil
2 teaspoons sugar
¼ teaspoon salt
¼ teaspoon black pepper
1 medium-sized red bell pepper, diced
1 medium-sized yellow bell pepper, diced
1 medium-sized green bell pepper, diced
2 tablespoons chopped parsley

Combine vinegar, oil, sugar, salt and pepper in small saucepan; bring to a boil, stirring until sugar is dissolved. Remove from heat. Combine peppers and parsley in glass bowl. Pour hot vinegar mixture over peppers and stir gently. Let stand until cool. Chill, covered. Serve with pork or ham.

Yield: 1⅔ cups

PEACH SALSA

½ teaspoon minced gingerroot
5 peaches, peeled and chopped
¼ cup minced green onion
1½ tablespoons sugar
½ teaspoon dry mustard
1½ tablespoons lime juice
⅛ teaspoon salt
⅛ teaspoon white pepper

Combine gingerroot and ¼ of peaches in blender container; process until smooth. Combine remaining puree, remaining peaches, onion, sugar, mustard, lime juice, salt and pepper, stirring gently. Chill, covered, for up to 4 hours. Serve with ham, pork, chicken or seafood.

Yield: 2½ cups

GOLDEN FRUIT SAUCE

1	teaspoon butter or margarine
¼	cup orange juice
¼	cup pineapple juice
1	tablespoon lemon juice
⅓	cup sugar
3	egg yolks, beaten
½	cup whipping cream, whipped
	Mint leaves and orange peel strips for garnish

Melt butter in small saucepan. Add orange, pine-apple and lemon juice and sugar. Simmer until sugar is dissolved. Gradually add about ¼ hot juice mixture to egg yolks, stirring constantly; add egg yolks to remaining hot juice and cook over medium heat for about 5 minutes or until thickened. Chill. Before serving, fold in whipped cream. Serve over fruit or pound cake. Garnish individual servings with mint and orange peel.

Yield: 1¼ cups

STRAWBERRY BUTTER

¾	cup strawberries
¼	cup plus 2 tablespoons powdered sugar
1	cup unsalted butter, cubed and softened.

Place strawberries and sugar in food processor bowl; process using on/off turns. Add butter and process until combined. Press teaspoonfuls of butter into candy molds and chill.

Butter may be prepared a week in advance; store, covered, in refrigerator and return to room temperature before using. Cranberry butter may be prepared by substituting cranberries for strawberries and adding 2 teaspoons grated lemon peel with sugar.

Yield: 1½ cups

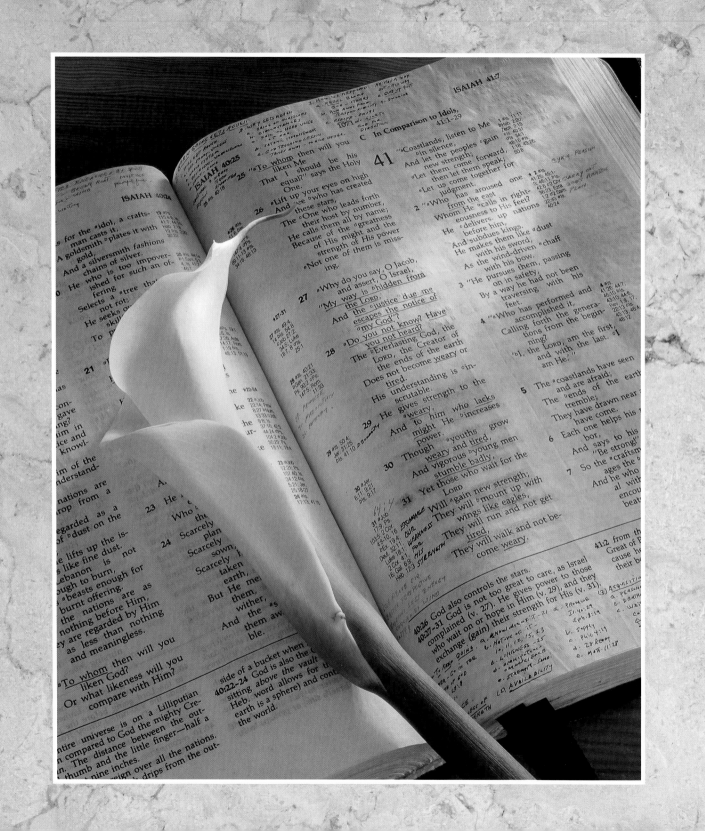

HE UNFOLDING OF

THY WORD GIVES

LIGHT; IT GIVES UNDERSTANDING

TO THE SIMPLE.

Psalm 119:130

ASTOUNDING ASPARAGUS

2	pounds asparagus
1	(14 ounce) can artichoke hearts, drained
1	clove garlic, diced
4	tablespoons butter, divided
3	green onions with tops, sliced
1	pound mushrooms, thickly sliced
	Seasoned salt to taste
1	cup buttered cracker crumbs, divided
2	tablespoons all-purpose flour
1	cup whipping cream
⅛	teaspoon salt
⅛	teaspoon black pepper
⅛	teaspoon cayenne pepper
⅛	teaspoon paprika
1½	cups (6 ounces) grated sharp cheese

Cut stems from asparagus, reserving stems. Cook asparagus according to preferred method; drain and set aside. Sauté artichoke hearts and garlic in 2 tablespoons butter until garlic is soft. Add green onion, mushrooms and asparagus stems; cook until stems are tender. Season with seasoned salt. Pour ¾ cup crumbs in 1½-quart casserole. Spoon artichoke mixture on crumbs and top with asparagus. Melt 2 tablespoons butter in saucepan. Add flour and cook to paste consistency. Stir in cream and seasonings; cook until thickened. Pour sauce over vegetables. Sprinkle ¼ cup crumbs on sauce and sprinkle with cheese. Bake at 350 degrees for 25 to 30 minutes or until sauce is bubbly and cheese is melted.

Yield: 6 to 8 servings

APPLE CURRIED BEANS

1	medium-sized red onion, chopped
½	cup green bell pepper, chopped
½	cup red bell pepper, chopped
1	Granny Smith apple, chopped
¼	cup butter
1	(28 ounce) can tomatoes, drained
2	(15 ounce) cans kidney beans, drained
1	cup firmly-packed brown sugar
1	tablespoon white vinegar
	Salt to taste
	Black pepper to taste
1	teaspoon curry powder
¼	cup grated Parmesan cheese

Sauté onion, peppers and apple in butter in large skillet until onion is translucent. Add tomatoes, beans, brown sugar, vinegar and seasonings; mix thoroughly. Pour into buttered 2½-quart casserole. Bake at 350 degrees for 30 minutes. Sprinkle with cheese.

Yield: 10 servings

Vegetables & Side Dishes

BLACK BEANS

1	(16 ounce) package black beans, rinsed
4	cups water
2	medium-sized yellow onions, chopped
1	medium-sized red bell pepper, chopped
3	cloves garlic, crushed
1	pound smoked ham hocks, cut in 1½-inch pieces
2	teaspoons paprika
1	tablespoon ground cumin
¼	teaspoon chili powder
2	bay leaves
4	cups chicken broth
1	tablespoon red wine vinegar
	Salt and freshly ground black pepper to taste

Place beans and water in heavy 6-quart sauce pan. Cover, bring to a boil and boil for 2 minutes; shut off heat and let stand for 1 hour. Add vegetables, ham, paprika, cumin, chili powder, bay leaves and broth. Simmer, covered, adding water as necessary to keep beans covered, for 2 hours or until beans are tender. Remove ham hocks, discard bones, chop meat and return to bean mixture. Stir in vinegar and season with salt and pepper. Simmer until thoroughly heated.

Yield: 6 servings

GOURMET BAKED BEANS

2	(18 ounce) jars baked beans
1	(4 ounce) can mushroom stems and pieces, drained
1	cup chopped onion
1	cup chopped green bell pepper
½	cup molasses
1½	teaspoons garlic powder
1	teaspoon salt
	Dash of black pepper
2 or 3	slices bacon

Combine vegetables, molasses and seasonings; mix thoroughly and pour into buttered 1½-quart casserole. Arrange bacon slices on top of vegetables. Bake at 350 degrees for 1 hour.

Yield: 4 to 6 servings

REFRIED BEANS

1	cup dried beans
4	cups water
2	tablespoons vegetable shortening
1	teaspoon salt or to taste

Combine beans and water; bring to a boil and cook until tender. Drain most of liquid from beans, retaining a small amount. Mash beans. Fry beans in shortening in skillet, stirring constantly. Season with salt. Refried beans may be topped with grated cheese just before serving.

Yield: 4 to 6 servings

SAVORY PINTO BEANS

1	pound dried pinto beans
	Water
1	tablespoon sugar
½	teaspoon salt
¼	teaspoon black pepper
1	tablespoon chili powder
2	teaspoons cumin
1½ to 2	teaspoons garlic salt
3	cloves garlic, minced
2	teaspoons hot pepper sauce (optional)
½	cup ketchup

Soak beans overnight in water to cover. Drain, place in Dutch oven and add water to cover. Stir in seasonings and ketchup. Bring to a boil, then simmer, covered, for 6 to 8 hours. Add more water if necessary.

Yield: 10 to 12 servings

HARVARD BEETS

¼	cup sugar
1	tablespoon cornstarch
¼	teaspoon salt
½	cup vinegar
¼	cup grape jelly
1	(16 ounce) can sliced beets, drained
2	tablespoons butter or margarine

Combine sugar, cornstarch and salt in saucepan. Blend in vinegar and jelly. Cook, stirring constantly, over medium heat until thickened and smooth. Add beets and butter; heat thoroughly, stirring occasionally.

Yield: 6 servings

BROCCOLI CASSEROLE

1	(16 ounce) package frozen chopped broccoli
1	(10¾ ounce) can mushroom soup, undiluted
1¼	cups (5 ounces) grated Cheddar cheese, divided
½	cup sour cream
½	cup mayonnaise
1	tablespoon fresh lemon juice
½	cup coarsely crumbled buttery round crackers

Prepare broccoli according to package directions, cooking for 12 minutes. Drain and place on paper towel to thoroughly dry. Combine soup, 1 cup cheese, sour cream, mayonnaise and lemon juice. Place broccoli in 2-quart casserole. Pour sauce over broccoli and sprinkle with ¼ cup cheese. Top with broken crackers. Bake at 375 degrees for 35 to 40 minutes.

Yield: 6 servings

BROCCOLI AU GRATIN

1	pound fresh broccoli
3	tablespoons butter
3	tablespoons all-purpose flour
1	teaspoon salt
¼	teaspoon dry mustard
1	cup plus 2 tablespoons milk
¾	cup (3 ounces) grated sharp Cheddar cheese
3	tablespoons grated Parmesan cheese

Steam broccoli until tender. Place in buttered 2-quart casserole. Melt butter in saucepan. Add flour, salt and mustard; cook until blended. Gradually add milk, cooking over medium heat and stirring constantly, until sauce is thickened. Stir in Cheddar cheese. Pour sauce over broccoli. Sprinkle with Parmesan cheese. Bake at 350 degrees for 20 minutes.

Yield: 4 to 6 servings

ROTKRAUT

3	tablespoons margarine
2	pounds red cabbage, shredded
1	onion, minced
1	teaspoon salt
3 to 4	tablespoons vinegar
1	cup water
1	unpeeled apple, sliced
1	tablespoon all-purpose flour
1	teaspoon sugar

Melt margarine in large saucepan with tight-fitting lid. Add cabbage, onion, salt and vinegar; simmer until onion is transluscent. Stir in water, apple, flour and sugar. Simmer for 1½ hours or until vegetables are soft.

Yield: 6 to 8 servings

BROCCOLI WITH ZESTY SAUCE

1	large bunch broccoli
¾	cup sour cream
½	teaspoon prepared horseradish
½	teaspoon prepared mustard
	Dash of salt
	Paprika

Steam broccoli until crisp-tender. Place in serving dish. Combine sour cream, horseradish, mustard and salt; pour over hot broccoli and sprinkle with paprika.

Yield: 6 to 8 servings

CHEESY CABBAGE CASSEROLE

6	cups shredded cabbage
	Boiling water
3⅓	tablespoons butter, divided
3	tablespoons all-purpose flour
2	cups milk
	Salt to taste
	Black pepper to taste
1	(4 ounce) can sliced mushrooms
1	cup (4 ounces) grated sharp cheese

Place cabbage in saucepan, cover with boiling water, bring to a boil and cook for 3 minutes. Drain well and place in buttered 2-quart casserole. Melt 3 tablespoons butter in saucepan; stir in flour and cook to form paste. Gradually add milk, stirring and cooking until thickened and smooth. Sauté mushrooms in 1 teaspoon butter; add to white sauce. Pour sauce over cabbage. Sprinkle with cheese. Bake at 350 degrees for about 30 minutes or until cheese is melted and sauce is bubbly.

Yield: 4 to 6 servings

DIJON CARROTS

1½	pounds baby carrots
	Water
3	tablespoons margarine, melted
1½	tablespoons Dijon mustard
1½	tablespoons honey
⅜	teaspoon ground or minced ginger

Cook carrots in small amount of water in saucepan until crisp-tender. Drain and keep warm. Combine margarine, mustard, honey and ginger; mix well. Pour sauce over carrots and toss gently to coat.

Yield: 6 servings

CARROTS WITH ORANGE SAUCE

3 to 4	cups cooked sliced carrots
½	cup sugar
1	tablespoon cornstarch
1	teaspoon salt
½	cup orange juice
1	tablespoon grated orange peel
2	tablespoons butter, melted

Place carrots in buttered 2-quart casserole. Combine sugar, cornstarch, salt, orange juice and peel; pour over carrots. Add butter, mixing lightly. Bake at 350 degrees for 30 minutes.

Yield: 6 to 8 servings

CORN WITH TAMALES

1	(15 ounce) can hot tamales
1	onion, chopped
½	green bell pepper, diced
1	(4 ounce) jar pimientos
1	(16 ounce) can creamed corn
	Salt to taste
	Black pepper to taste
1	cup (4 ounces) shredded sharp Cheddar cheese

Drain tamales, reserving liquid. Cut tamales into bite-sized pieces and set aside. Cook onion, pepper and pimientos in tamale liquid. Add corn, tamales and seasonings to vegetables. Pour mixture into greased 1½-quart casserole. Bake at 350 degrees for 1 hour or until mixture is thickened. Sprinkle with cheese and bake for a few minutes until cheese is melted.

Yield: 6 to 8 servings

THANKSGIVING CORN PUDDING

1   (10 ounce) package frozen corn
1   cup half and half
3   eggs
2   tablespoons butter
2   tablespoons all-purpose flour
1   tablespoon sugar
1   teaspoon salt
    Dash of white pepper

Place corn and half and half in blender container; blend briefly to just mix corn and liquid. Add eggs, butter, flour, sugar and seasonings; blend thoroughly. Pour corn mixture into buttered 1-quart baking dish placed in pan filled with water to 1-inch depth. Bake at 350 degrees for 1 hour or until knife tip inserted near center comes out clean. If doubling or tripling recipe, increase baking time by about 20 minutes.

Yield: 3 or 4 servings

EGGPLANT SOUFFLÉ

2   medium eggplants, peeled and sliced
    Cold water
    Salt
1   cup diced onion
3   tablespoons butter
3   eggs, separated
1   tablespoon sugar
½   teaspoon black pepper
1½   cups (6 ounces) grated sharp cheese
½   cup buttered cracker crumbs

Soak eggplant in cold salted water for 30 minutes; drain. Cook in small amount of water until soft. Drain and mash. Sauté onion in butter. Beat egg whites until stiff and set aside. Beat egg yolks and add with onion, sugar, pepper and cheese to eggplant. Fold in egg whites. Spoon mixture into buttered 2-quart casserole. Sprinkle with crumbs. Place casserole in pan filled with water to 1-inch depth. Bake at 350 degrees for about 45 minutes.

Yield: 8 to 10 servings

FRIED EGGPLANT

1	medium eggplant, peeled, sliced and cut in strips
	Salt
1	egg
½	cup milk
	All-purpose flour
	Vegetable oil for deep frying
¼	cup grated Parmesan cheese

Sprinkle all sides of eggplant pieces with salt. Place in colander and let drain for 30 minutes. Blend egg and milk. Place flour in plastic bag. Dip eggplant pieces in egg mixture, then add to flour and shake to cover thoroughly. Deep fry in oil until golden brown. Remove and drain. Sprinkle with cheese.

Yield: 4 to 6 servings

GREEN BEAN CASSEROLE

1	teaspoon bacon fat
½	cup vinegar
½	cup sugar
½	cup firmly-packed brown sugar
1	(16 ounce) can green beans
1	(8 ounce) can shelley beans
1	onion, sliced

Combine bacon fat, vinegar and sugar in saucepan; simmer for a few minutes until sugar is dissolved. Drain beans, reserving liquid, and place in 1½-quart casserole. Pour sugar mixture over beans and top with onion slices. Bake at 300 degrees for 3 hours, adding reserved bean liquid as needed to keep beans covered.

Yield: 4 to 6 servings

BALSAMIC GREEN BEANS

3	tablespoons butter
1	tablespoon balsamic vinegar
	Salt and freshly ground pepper to taste
1½	pounds green beans, trimmed
	Boiling water

Combine butter, vinegar and seasonings in heavy skillet. Cook over medium heat, stirring constantly, for about 4 minutes or until mixture begins to brown. Remove from heat and set aside. Blanch beans in boiling water in large pot for about 5 minutes or until crisp-tender. Drain in colander. Place in serving dish and spoon sauce over beans.

Yield: 6 servings

BLEU CHEESE AND WALNUT GREEN BEANS

1	pound green beans, cut in thirds
4	slices bacon
1	(4 ounce) package bleu cheese, crumbled
1½	cups walnut halves
	Black pepper to taste

Steam beans until tender. Sauté bacon until crisp in large skillet; remove and drain on paper towel. Add beans to bacon grease in skillet and cook for 2 minutes, tossing gently. Stir in cheese and toss until melted and beans are coated. Add walnut halves. Cut each bacon slice in 4 pieces and add to beans. Season with pepper; do not add salt.

Yield: 4 or 5 servings

DILL BEAN CASSEROLE

2	(16 ounce) cans whole green beans
¼	cup bacon fat
1¼	teaspoons dill seed
5	tablespoons butter
5	tablespoons flour
2½	cups bean liquid
3	tablespoons grated onion
1	teaspoon cracked pepper
2½	teaspoons seasoning salt
	Hot pepper sauce to taste
	Cracker crumbs

Combine beans, bacon fat and dill seed in saucepan; cook for 45 minutes. Let beans cool in liquid. Drain, reserving liquid; place beans in buttered 2-quart casserole. Melt butter in saucepan. Blend in flour. Add bean liquid (add milk if bean liquid does not measure 2½ cups), onion and seasoning. Cook until sauce begins to thicken. Pour sauce over beans and sprinkle with crumbs. Bake at 350 degrees for 30 minutes.

Bean casserole may be assembled a day before serving. Store in refrigerator. Allow slightly longer baking time for cold ingredients.

Yield: 8 servings

GREEN BEAN AND CORN CASSEROLE

2	(16 ounce) cans seasoned French style green beans
1	(12 ounce) can shoepeg corn
1	(8 ounce) can water chestnuts, sliced
	Butter
1	(8 ounce) carton sour cream
1	(10¾ ounce) can cream of celery soup, undiluted
3	tablespoons mayonnaise
⅓	cup chopped onion (or less, to taste)
1½	cups (6 ounces) grated cheese
½	cup plus 2 tablespoons margarine, melted
30 to 36	round butter crackers, crushed

Drain vegetables in colander. Mix well and place in buttered 2-quart casserole. Dot with butter. Combine sour cream, soup, mayonnaise and onion; blend thoroughly and spread over vegetables. Sprinkle with cheese. Mix margarine and crackers; sprinkle on sauce layer. Bake at 350 degrees for 40 minutes.

Yield: 8 to 10 servings

STEAMED HORSEY BEANS

1	pound small whole green beans
¾	cup mayonnaise
¼	cup butter, melted
1½	teaspoons minced onion
1	tablespoon horseradish
1	teaspoon wine vinegar
¼	teaspoon salt
⅛	teaspoon black pepper
¼	teaspoon dry mustard

Steam beans until tender. Combine mayonnaise, butter, onion, horseradish, vinegar and seasonings in glass jar. Place in container of hot water and let stand until warm. Pour sauce over beans.

Sauce may also be used with broccoli or as a vegetable dip. It may be prepared a day in advance, then warmed just before using.

Yield: 3 or 4 servings

MARINATED BEAN BUNDLES

2	(16 ounce) cans whole green beans, drained
1	cup Italian salad dressing
6	slices bacon, cut in halves

Combine beans and dressing, tossing gently. Chill, covered, overnight. Drain beans and arrange in bunches of 10 to 12. Wrap a ½ bacon slice around each bundle and secure with wooden pick. Place on broiler pan; broil about 5 inches from heat source for about 7 minutes or until bacon is cooked.

Yield: 6 servings

QUICK MIXED GREENS

1	small head cabbage, chopped
1	cup cubed ham
1	teaspoon bacon drippings
1	small onion, chopped
	Water
1	(15 ounce) can turnip greens, drained
1	(15 ounce) can collard greens, drained
	Salt to taste
	Black pepper to taste

Combine cabbage, ham, bacon drippings and onion in saucepan with water to cover; cook until tender. Add greens to cabbage mixture and season with salt and pepper. Simmer for 10 minutes. Serve with cornbread.

Yield: 10 to 12 servings

OKRA FRITTERS

1	cup steamed sliced okra
1	egg, beaten
¼	cup diced onion
¾ to 1	cup self-rising cornmeal
½	teaspoon sugar
½	teaspoon salt
⅛	teaspoon black pepper
	Vegetable oil

Combine okra, egg and onion. Gradually add cornmeal until mixture is batter consistency. Season with sugar, salt and pepper. Deep fry in oil until golden brown. Serve hot with ketchup, tomato sauce or melted cheese.

Yield: 2 servings

Vegetables & Side Dishes

VIDALIA HONEY BAKED ONIONS

4	large Vidalia onions
1½	cups tomato juice
1½	cups water
2	tablespoons melted butter
2	tablespoons honey

Peel and trim onions; cut each in half. Place in buttered baking dish with cut surface up. Combine tomato juice, water, butter and honey; pour over onions. Bake at 325 degrees for 1 hour or until onions are soft.

Yield: 6 to 8 servings

VIDALIA ONION AND RICE CASSEROLE

½	cup regular rice, uncooked
1	cup water
7	medium-sized Vidalia onions, sliced
¼	cup butter
1	teaspoon salt
1	cup (4 ounces) grated Swiss cheese
⅔	cup half and half or evaporated milk

Prepare rice according to package directions, using 1 cup water. Sauté onions in butter until transluscent. Combine rice, onions, salt, cheese and milk. Spread mixture in buttered 13x9x3-inch baking dish. Bake at 325 degrees for 1 hour.

Yield: 6 to 8 servings

SAVORY STUFFED ONIONS

4	large Vidalia or other onions
1	(3 ounce) package cream cheese, softened
¼	cup shredded Cheddar cheese
3	slices bacon, cooked and crumbled
¼	cup chives
¼	cup sliced fresh mushrooms
½	teaspoon salt
¼	teaspoon black pepper
½	teaspoon garlic salt
2	drops red pepper sauce
¼	cup whipping cream
20	cooked shrimp
	Chopped parsley

Peel onions. Wrap each in damp paper towel and microwave at full power for about 10 minutes or until tender. (Or steam onions according to preferred method.) Cut slice from top of each onion and remove pulp, leaving 3 outer layers of onion to form a bowl. Place in 1-quart casserole and set aside. Combine cheese, bacon, chives, mushrooms, salt, pepper, garlic salt, pepper sauce and cream. Spoon mixture into onion bowls. Microwave at full power for 2 to 3 minutes or until thoroughly heated. Garnish each onion with 5 shrimp around top edge and sprinkle center with parsley.

Yield: 4 servings

CASHEW PEAS

½ pound fresh snow pea pods, strings removed
1 tablespoon water
1 (10 ounce) package frozen English peas
2 cloves garlic, minced
1 cup cashews
2 tablespoons chopped green onion
½ cup slivered red bell pepper
¼ cup butter
¼ cup chopped parsley
¼ teaspoon freshly ground black pepper

Cook pea pods in water in microwave at high setting for 2 minutes. Separately cook English peas at high setting for 2 minutes. Combine pods and peas; set aside. Sauté garlic, cashews, onion and pepper in butter for 1 to 2 minutes. Add pea mixture, parsley and black pepper; mix well and serve immediately.

Yield: 5 or 6 servings

DEVILED PEAS

3 tablespoons butter
3 tablespoons all-purpose flour
1½ cups milk
¼ teaspoon salt
¼ teaspoon white pepper
1 (16 ounce) can English peas, drained
1 green bell pepper, diced
1 cup chopped celery
1 (4 ounce) jar pimientos, drained
1 (4 ounce) can chopped mushrooms, drained
½ cup chili sauce
1 tablespoon Worcestershire sauce
1 (10½ ounce) can tomato soup, undiluted
1 cup (4 ounces) grated New York sharp cheese
6 hard-cooked eggs, sliced
½ cup breadcrumbs
¼ cup butter, cut in small pieces

Melt butter in saucepan over low heat. Add flour and stir briskly until lightly browned. Gradually add milk, stirring constantly, and cook until thickened. Season with salt and pepper. Combine vegetables. Mix white sauce, chili sauce, Worcerstershire sauce and tomato soup together; blend thoroughly. Stir in cheese. Place vegetables in buttered 2½-quart casserole. Pour sauce over vegetables and top with egg slices. Sprinkle with breadcrumbs and butter. Bake, uncovered, at 350 degrees for 30 minutes.

Yield: 12 to 14 servings

Vegetables & Side Dishes

Baked Red Potatoes

1	cup hot water
2½	chicken bouillon cubes, crushed
2	tablespoons instant minced onion
1	teaspoon minced garlic
¼	cup olive oil
2	tablespoons white vinegar
2	teaspoons crushed tarragon
¼	teaspoon black pepper
2	pounds small red potatoes, unpeeled and quartered
	Lettuce leaves (optional)

Combine water, bouillon, onion and garlic; let stand for 10 minutes. Add oil, vinegar and seasonings to bouillon mixture. Place potatoes in shallow 3-quart casserole. Pour dressing over potatoes, tossing to coat thoroughly. Bake, uncovered, at 350 degrees for 35 to 40 minutes or until potatoes are tender; stir occasionally. Serve at room temperature on lettuce leaves.

Yield: 6 servings

Cheesy New Potatoes

12	medium new potatoes, unpeeled and cubed
	Water
	Salt to taste
	Black pepper to taste
16	slices bacon, cooked and crumbled
½	cup melted butter
1	(5 ounce) jar old English processed cheese spread

Cook potatoes in boiling water until just tender. Drain well, season to taste and place half of potatoes in buttered 2-quart casserole. Sprinkle half of bacon on potatoes, pour half of butter over bacon and top with half of cheese; repeat layers. Bake at 350 degrees for 20 to 30 minutes or until cheese is bubbly.

Yield: 8 servings

POTATOES PARMESAN

2	tablespoons butter
2	medium potatoes, unpeeled, cut in ¼-inch slices
⅓	cup chopped onion
1	clove garlic, minced
¼	teaspoon salt
⅛	teaspoon pepper
¼	cup grated Parmesan cheese
	Paprika
	Chopped parsley

Melt butter in shallow 9-inch microwave-proof dish in microwave. Add potatoes, onion and garlic, tossing to coat with butter. Microwave, loosely covered with plastic wrap, at full power for 5 minutes. Stir in seasonings and microwave at full power for 3 minutes. Lightly stir in cheese, sprinkle with paprika and microwave, uncovered, at full power for 3 minutes. Let stand 2 minutes.

Yield: 2 or 3 servings

GOLDEN CRUSTED POTATOES

3	cups mashed potatoes (stiff, not creamy)
1½	cups creamed cottage cheese
½	cup sour cream
1	tablespoon minced green onion
¼	teaspoon white pepper
¼	teaspoon nutmeg
¼	cup melted butter

Combine potatoes, cottage cheese, sour cream, onion and seasoning; check seasoning and add salt if necessary. Spoon mixture into buttered shallow 1½-quart casserole. Drizzle butter over potato mixture. Bake at 350 degrees for 20 to 25 minutes or until bubbly and golden crusted.

Yield: 6 servings

CREAMY STUFFED POTATOES

3	(8 ounce) baking potatoes
½	cup buttermilk salad dressing
⅓	cup (1⅓ ounces) shredded Cheddar cheese
⅓	cup chopped chives
2	tablespoons butter
⅛	teaspoon salt
⅛	teaspoon white pepper

Bake potatoes until tender. Cut in halves lengthwise, scoop out pulp and place in bowl, reserving shells. Mix pulp, salad dressing, cheese, chives, butter and seasonings together; blend well. Spoon potato mixture into shells. Bake at 300 degrees for 10 minutes or until thoroughly heated.

Yield: 6 servings

Vegetables & Side Dishes

SPINACH AND ARTICHOKE CASSEROLE

1	(14 ounce) can artichoke hearts, drained
1	(8 ounce) package cream cheese
½	cup butter or margarine
3	(10 ounce) packages frozen chopped spinach, cooked and drained
1	clove garlic, minced
½	cup seasoned breadcrumbs

Place artichoke hearts in buttered 2-quart casserole. Combine cream cheese and butter in double boiler over hot water; mix until cream cheese is melted and blended with butter. Add spinach to cheese mixture. Stir in garlic. Pour spinach mixture over artichoke hearts. Bake at 350 degrees for 30 minutes. Sprinkle with breadcrumbs and bake for 10 minutes.

Yield: 8 to 10 servings

SPINACH CASSEROLE

2	(10 ounce) packages frozen chopped spinach, cooked and drained
2	tablespoons all-purpose flour
4	eggs, beaten
1½	cups (12 ounces) cottage cheese
1	cup (4 ounces) Cheddar cheese, melted
½	teaspoon salt
6	tablespoons margarine, melted

In sequence listed, combine spinach, flour, eggs, cottage cheese, Cheddar cheese, salt and margarine. Pour mixture into buttered 8-inch square baking dish. Bake at 400 degrees for 30 minutes.

Yield: 6 to 8 servings

BAKED SPINACH AND TOMATOES

2	(10 ounce) packages frozen chopped spinach, cooked and drained
1	tablespoon lemon juice
¼	cup sour cream
¼	pound mushrooms, chopped
2	tablespoons butter or margarine
5 to 6	tablespoons grated Cheddar cheese
2	large tomatoes, cut in ¼-inch slices
1	teaspoon salt
	Dash of black pepper
3	thin slices mozzarella cheese

Sprinkle spinach with lemon juice. Stir in sour cream. Sauté mushrooms in butter for 5 minutes or until softened; fold into spinach. Spoon half of spinach mixture into a buttered 1½-quart casserole. Sprinkle lightly with Cheddar cheese, add layer of tomato slices, season with half of salt and pepper and sprinkle with cheese; repeat layers. Top with mozzarella slices to cover. Bake at 375 degrees for 30 minutes or until bubbly and golden brown.

Yield: 4 to 6 servings

Among the Lilies

GRATED SWEET POTATO SOUFFLÉ

4	medium-sized sweet potatoes
¾	cup milk
2	cups sugar
1	(16 ounce) can crushed pineapple
1	cup raisins
1	cup chopped nuts
6	tablespoons butter, melted
1	teaspoon vanilla

Grate sweet potatoes into milk in mixing bowl. Add sugar, pineapple, raisins, nuts, butter and vanilla; mix thoroughly. Pour mixture into buttered shallow 2-quart casserole. Bake at 300 degrees for 45 minutes, stirring once or twice.

Soufflé is very sweet; decrease sugar amount if desired.

Yield: 8 servings

MEXICAN SQUASH

1	pound yellow crook neck squash, unpeeled and thinly sliced
	Water
1	medium-sized onion, thinly sliced
2	tablespoons butter or margarine
1½	green chilies (canned), finely chopped
½	teaspoon salt
1	teaspoon black pepper
1	egg, well beaten
¾	cup evaporated milk
½	cup (2 ounces) grated sharp cheese
	Paprika

Cook squash in small amount of water until nearly done. Drain and mash squash. Sauté onion in butter. Add onion with butter, chilies, salt and pepper to squash. Blend egg with milk; add to squash mixture. Pour into greased 1-quart casserole. Bake at 350 degrees for 30 to 35 minutes, sprinkling with cheese and paprika 10 minutes before completion of baking time.

Yield: 3 or 4 servings

SQUASH CASSEROLE WITH ALMONDS

2	pounds squash, sliced
¼	cup butter
¼	cup evaporated milk
1	small onion, chopped
	Salt to taste
	Black pepper to taste
2	eggs, beaten
2	cups (8 ounces) grated Cheddar cheese
1	cup (4 ounces) slivered almonds
10	buttery round crackers, crushed
1	tablespoon melted butter

Steam squash for 8 to 9 minutes or until tender; drain. Add butter, milk, onion, salt and pepper to squash. Blend in eggs. Combine cheese and almonds. Spoon layer of squash mixture into 1½-quart casserole, then layer of cheese mixture; repeat layers until both mixtures are used. Toss crackers in butter; sprinkle on layered squash and cheese mixtures. Bake at 350 degrees for 30 minutes.

Yield: 4 to 6 servings

BAKED TOMATOES

6	(¾ inch) slices tomatoes
	Salt to taste
	Black pepper to taste
6	thin slices onion
6	rounded teaspoons brown sugar
6	drops Worcestershire sauce
6	pinches dill weed
6	pinches oregano
6	teaspoons dry breadcrumbs
6	teaspoons grated Parmesan cheese

Arrange tomato slices in lightly greased baking pan. In sequence listed, layer ingredients on each slice. Bake at 350 degrees for 30 minutes.

Yield: 6 servings

BAKED TOMATO SURPRISE

1	(28 ounce) can tomatoes, drained
5	slices bread, crumbled
½	small onion, chopped
¼	cup sugar
¼	teaspoon salt
¼	teaspoon red pepper
½	cup butter, melted, divided

Combine tomatoes, breadcrumbs, onion, sugar, seasonings and ¼ cup butter. Pour into buttered 1½-quart casserole. Pour ¼ cup butter over tomato mixture. Bake at 350 degrees for 30 to 40 minutes.

Yield: 6 servings

FRESH HERBAL TOMATOES

6	ripe tomatoes, cut in halves
	Salt to taste
	Black pepper to taste
2	cloves garlic, crushed
3	tablespoons minced shallots
3	tablespoons minced fresh basil
2	tablespoons minced parsley
⅛	teaspoon thyme
⅛	teaspoon black pepper
¼	cup olive oil
½	cup fine dry breadcrumbs

Press tomatoes to remove seeds. Season with salt and pepper. Place cut side up in oiled baking pan. Combine garlic, shallots, seasonings, oil and breadcrumbs. Divide mixture equally among tomato halves, pressing slightly into tomatoes. Bake at 400 degrees for 15 minutes.

Yield: 12 servings

BAKED ZUCCHINI

4	medium zucchini, cut in halves lengthwise
	Seasoned salt
1	(8 ounce) carton sour cream
	Garlic powder
1	cup (4 ounces) shredded Cheddar cheese

Place zucchini halves in buttered 13x9x3-inch baking dish. Sprinkle with seasoned salt. Spread 2 tablespoons sour cream on each zucchini half. Sprinkle with garlic powder and top with cheese. Bake at 325 degrees for 35 to 40 minutes.

Yield: 8 servings

BAKED STUFFED ZUCCHINI

4	medium zucchini, cut in halves lengthwise
½	pound ground pork
½	cup chopped onion
¼	cup olive oil
½	teaspoon chopped garlic
1	egg, beaten
½	cup grated Parmesan cheese
½	cup breadcrumbs
1	teaspoon salt
¼	teaspoon black pepper
½	teaspoon oregano
1½	(8 ounce) cans tomato sauce
2	cups (8 ounces) grated mozzarella cheese

Scoop pulp from zucchini; reserve shells and chop pulp. Sauté meat and onion in oil. Stir in zucchini pulp and garlic. Drain excess grease. Combine meat mixture, egg, Parmesan cheese, breadcrumbs, salt, pepper and oregano. Spoon stuffing into zucchini shells and arrange in buttered 13x9x2-inch baking dish. Pour tomato sauce over stuffed shells. Bake, covered, at 350 degrees for 30 minutes. Sprinkle cheese over shells and sauce. Bake, uncovered, for 20 minutes.

Yield: 8 servings

170

Zucchini Casserole

1   pound zucchini, unpeeled and cubed
½   cup diced carrots
½   cup diced onion
2   cups (8 ounces) grated sharp cheese, divided
3   eggs, beaten
½   cup sour cream
1   envelope cream of chicken soup mix
¼   teaspoon salt
⅛   teaspoon black pepper
¼   teaspoon dry mustard
1   cup crushed cheese wafers or cheese curls

Steam zucchini, carrots and onion until tender; mash but do not puree. Combine vegetables with 1 cup cheese, eggs, sour cream, soup mix and seasonings. Spoon mixture into buttered shallow 1½-quart casserole. Sprinkle with 1 cup cheese; top with cheese crumbs. Bake at 325 degrees for 45 to 50 minutes or until center is firm.

Yield: 6 servings

Zucchini and Squash Provençal

2   cups sliced zucchini
1   medium-sized onion, sliced
½   cup instant rice, uncooked
3   tablespoons margarine, divided
2   cups sliced yellow squash
2   (16 ounce) cans stewed tomatoes
½   teaspoon black pepper
¾   teaspoon garlic salt
2   cups (8 ounces) shredded mozzarella cheese
2   tablespoons grated Parmesan cheese

Place zucchini in bottom of buttered 13x9x2-inch baking dish. Layer onion over squash. Sprinkle rice on onion. Dot rice with 1 tablespoon margarine. Layer yellow squash over rice. Slightly drain tomatoes, reserving ¼ cup juice; add tomatoes, juice and seasonings to squash. Dot tomato layer with 2 tablespoons margarine. Bake, tightly covered with aluminum foil, at 350 degrees for 50 minutes. Remove foil, sprinkle with cheeses and bake for 5 to 10 minutes or until cheese is melted.

Yield: 6 to 8 servings

Swiss Vegetable Medley

1	(16 ounce) package frozen broccoli, carrots and cauliflower, thawed and drained
1	(10¾ ounce) can mushroom soup, undiluted
⅓	cup sour cream
1	cup (4 ounces) shredded Swiss cheese, divided
¼	teaspoon black pepper
1	(3 ounce) can French fried onions, divided

Combine vegetables, soup, sour cream, ½ cup cheese, pepper and half of onions. Pour into buttered 1-quart casserole. Bake, uncovered, at 350 degrees for 30 minutes. Sprinkle with remaining cheese and onions; bake, uncovered, for 5 minutes.

Yield: 6 servings

Vegetable Jubilee

2	cups carrots cut in 3x¼-inch strips
2 to 3	cups fresh green beans cut in halves
1	(16 ounce) can yellow wax beans, drained
	Water
2	medium-sized onions, thinly sliced
½	pound mushrooms, sliced
½	cup butter
½	teaspoon salt
¼	teaspoon white pepper
½	teaspoon garlic salt
½	teaspoon rosemary or savory
1	cup chicken broth
2	tablespoons water
1	tablespoon cornstarch

Cook vegetables separately. Simmer carrots in water until crisp-tender, drain, rinse with cold water to halt cooking and drain again. Steam green beans for about 8 minutes or until crisp-tender. Heat yellow beans thoroughly. Sauté onions and mushrooms in butter in large skillet until onions are transluscent and tender. Add cooked vegetables and season with salt, pepper, garlic salt and rosemary or savory. Combine broth, water and cornstarch in small saucepan. Bring to a boil, reduce heat and simmer for 2 to 3 minutes. Pour over vegetables and toss lightly. Transfer vegetables and sauce to 2½-quart casserole. Bake at 350 degrees for 20 minutes. Vegetables may be prepared in advance, stored in refrigerator and reheated at 350 degrees for 30 minutes.

Yield: 12 servings

Vegetables & Side Dishes

GREEN VEGETABLES WITH HERB BUTTER

1¼   pounds broccoli flowerets
½   pound green beans, trimmed
     Boiling water
     Salt
½   pound snow peas, strings removed
¼   cup plus 2 tablespoons unsalted butter
1½   tablespoons mixed chopped parsley, thyme and rosemary
     Freshly ground black pepper

Blanch broccoli and green beans in boiling salted water for about 3 minutes or until crisp-tender. Use slotted spoon to remove vegetables from water, rinse under cold water and drain. Add snow peas to boiling water and blanch for 15 to 20 seconds. Drain, rinse under cold water and drain again. Melt butter in heavy skillet over medium heat. Add vegetables and heat thoroughly. Remove from heat, add herbs, salt and pepper and toss gently.

Yield: 4 servings

FETTUCINI ALFREDO

1   (8 ounce) package fettucini or medium egg noodles
¼   cup butter, melted
¼   cup grated Parmesan cheese
2   tablespoons half and half
¼   teaspoon salt
⅛   teaspoon black pepper

Prepare pasta according to package directions; drain in collander and keep hot. In warm serving dish, combine butter, cheese, half and half and seasonings. Toss hot pasta with cheese mixture, mixing to coat thoroughly. Serve immediately with additional cheese.

Yield: 2 servings

MACARONI AND CHEESE CASSEROLE

1   cup elbow macaroni
½   cup margarine
10   eggs
6   cups (24 ounces) shredded mild Cheddar cheese
4   cups whole milk

Prepare macaroni according to package directions, cooking just until tender. Drain. Add margarine and stir until melted. Beat eggs until fluffy. Place cheese in buttered 3-quart shallow casserole. Pour eggs over cheese. Add macaroni and stir carefully until cheese is partially melted. Add milk and stir. Bake at 375 degrees for 45 minutes or until firm and browned.

Yield: 15 to 20 servings

JAMAICA RICE AND PEAS

1	cup red peas
	Salt
3	cups water
1	medium-sized onion, chopped
½	sweet bell pepper, chopped
1 or 2	tomatoes, chopped
2	tablespoons bacon fat or oil
½	cup chopped beef or crumbled bacon
1	coconut
2	cups regular rice, uncooked

Cook peas in salted water until tender. Sauté vegetables and meat in fat or oil until browned. Grate coconut and make 1 cup milk from coconut pulp. Add rice, coconut milk and meat mixture to peas. Cook until rice is done, stirring constantly.

Yield: 4 to 6 servings

RICE CASSEROLE

1	(8 ounce) carton sour cream
1	(10¾ ounce) can cream of celery soup, undiluted
1	(4 ounce) can green chilies
1	cup cooked rice
3	cups (12 ounces) grated extra sharp Cheddar cheese

Blend sour cream and soup. Drain chilies, reserving juice. Chop chilies. Add chili juice to soup mixture. Layer rice, chilies, cheese and sauce in buttered 2-quart casserole. Bake at 325 degrees until bubbly and cheese is melted.

Yield: 4 to 6 servings

CHINESE FRIED RICE

6	slices bacon
1	egg, beaten
2	tablespoons butter
⅓	cup chopped green onion with tops
½	cup thinly sliced cabbage
1	carrot, sliced and quartered
½	pound mushrooms, thinly sliced
⅛	pound snow peas
2 to 3	cups cooked rice
	Vegetable oil
1	teaspoon Worcestershire sauce
1	tablespoon soy sauce
1	tablespoon oyster sauce
2	drops hot sauce
	Cooked shrimp (optional)
	Cooked pork cubes (optional)

Cook bacon in large skillet until crisp. Remove, cool and crumble bacon; reserve 3 tablespoons bacon fat in skillet. In separate skillet, scramble egg in butter; set aside. Sauté vegetables, 1 at a time, in bacon fat; remove and set aside. Sauté rice in bacon fat until browned; add oil if necessary to prevent sticking. Add vegetables and crumbled bacon to rice. Stir in egg. Season with sauces. Serve immediately.
Shrimp or pork may be added to rice; heat thoroughly.

Yield: 4 servings

LUAU RICE

¼	cup chopped green onion
1	clove garlic, crushed
1	tablespoon vegetable oil
1	tablespoon butter
1	teaspoon curry powder
1	cup long-grain rice, uncooked
1	cup pineapple juice
1½	cups water
1	teaspoon salt
1	(8 ounce) can sliced water chestnuts
½	cup raisins

Sauté onion and garlic in mixture of oil and butter until onion is transluscent. Add curry powder and cook for 2 minutes over medium heat, stirring constantly. Stir in rice, pineapple juice, water and salt; simmer for 20 minutes. Add water chestnuts and raisins; cook for 5 to 10 minutes or until water is evaporated.

Yield: 6 to 8 servings

SPANISH RICE

2	cups regular rice, uncooked
1	tablespoon vegetable shortening
¼	cup minced onion
½	cup minced celery
1	(16 ounce) can whole tomatoes or (8 ounce) can tomato sauce
	Salt to taste
	Black pepper to taste

Sauté rice in shortening in large skillet until browned; remove and set aside. Sauté onion and celery for a few minutes. Stir in rice and tomatoes, adding water if necessary. Cook until rice is tender, fluffy and somewhat dry. Season to taste.

Yield: 6 to 8 servings

APPLE AND CHEESE CASSEROLE

½	cup margarine, softened
1	(8 ounce) package processed cheese spread, softened
1	cup sugar
¾	cup all-purpose flour
2	(20 ounce) cans sliced pie apples

Using electric mixer, cream margarine and cheese until smooth. Add sugar and flour; blend well. Place undrained apples in buttered 2-quart casserole. Spread cheese mixture over apples. Bake at 350 degrees for 30 minutes or until lightly browned.

Yield: 8 servings

CURRIED FRUIT BAKE

1 (16 ounce) can peach halves
1 (16 ounce) can pineapple chunks
1 (16 ounce) can pear halves
2 bananas, sliced
1 (6 ounce) jar maraschino cherries
⅓ cup butter
¾ cup firmly-packed light brown sugar
1 teaspoon curry powder
1 teaspoon fresh lemon extract

Assemble 1 or 2 days before serving. Drain canned fruit and place on paper towels to dry. Layer fruit in buttered 1½-quart casserole. Combine butter, sugar and curry; heat until butter is melted and sugar is dissolved. Pour syrup over fruit. Bake, uncovered, at 350 degrees for 1 hour. Store in refrigerator. About 30 minutes before serving, reheat casserole at 350 degrees for 30 minutes. Serve warm. Sprinkle with lemon extract and ignite. (Extract must be fresh in order to flame.)

Yield: 12 to 16 servings

CRANBERRY APPLE BAKE

1¼ cups sugar
2 cups fresh cranberries
3 cups chopped apples
½ cup butter
½ cup firmly-packed brown sugar
½ cup quick-cooking oats, uncooked
1 cup chopped nuts

Combine sugar, cranberries and apples; pour into buttered 9-inch square baking dish. Mix butter, brown sugar, oats and nuts together until crumbly. Sprinkle over fruit mixture. Bake at 350 degrees for 1 hour.

Yield: 9 servings

PINEAPPLE TROPICAL CASSEROLE

4	eggs
1	cup sugar
½	cup margarine, softened
2	(20 ounce) cans crushed pineapple, undrained
5	slices white bread, crusts removed
¼	cup toasted coconut
¼	cup toasted slivered almonds, crushed

Using electric mixer, combine eggs, sugar and margarine, beating well. Stir in pineapple. Crumble bread into buttered 9-inch square baking dish. Pour pineapple mixture over bread. Bake at 325 degrees for 45 minutes, sprinkling with coconut and almonds 5 minutes before completion of baking time.

Yield: 8 to 10 servings

CHEESY PINEAPPLE CASSEROLE

1	(20 ounce) can pineapple chunks or tidbits, drained and juice reserved
½	cup sugar
3	tablespoons all-purpose flour
1	cup (4 ounces) shredded sharp cheese
¼	cup melted butter
½	cup buttery cracker crumbs

Combine 3 tablespoons pineapple juice, sugar and flour. Add pineapple and cheese, mixing thoroughly. Spoon mixture into buttered 1-quart casserole. Mix butter and crumbs well; sprinkle over pineapple mixture. Bake at 350 degrees for 20 to 30 minutes or until crumbs are lightly browned.

Yield: 4 servings

LESSED IS THE

NATION WHOSE

GOD IS THE LORD, THE PEOPLE

WHOM HE HAS CHOSEN FOR

HIS OWN INHERITANCE.

Psalm 33:12

AUSTRALIAN BOILED FRUIT CAKE

1 cup sugar
1 (12 ounce) package mixed dried fruit or
   3 cups raisins, currants or finely
   chopped candied peel
1 cup vegetable shortening or margarine
¾ cup water
1 teaspoon baking soda
1 teaspoon apple pie spice
2 eggs, beaten
   Few drops vanilla
   Few drops lemon flavoring
   Few drops almond flavoring
1¼ cups self-rising flour
1 cup all-purpose flour

Combine sugar, fruit, shortening or margarine, water, baking soda and apple pie spice in saucepan; bring to a boil and softly boil for 10 minutes. Cool. Combine eggs and extracts; add to cooled fruit mixture. Sift flours together and fold into fruit mixture. Pour batter into greased and floured 8- or 9-inch round or square baking pan. Bake at 325 degrees for 50 to 60 minutes or until wooden pick inserted near center comes out clean.

Yield: 12 to 16 servings

HUMMINGBIRD CAKE

CAKE

3 cups all-purpose flour
2 cups sugar
1 teaspoon baking soda
1 teaspoon salt
1 teaspoon cinnamon
3 eggs, beaten
1 cup vegetable oil
1½ teaspoons vanilla
1 teaspoon butter flavoring
1 (8½ ounce) can crushed pineapple,
   undrained
2 cups chopped bananas
1½ cups chopped pecans, divided

CREAM CHEESE FROSTING

1 (8 ounce) package cream cheese,
   softened
½ cup butter, softened
1 (16 ounce) package powdered sugar
1 teaspoon black walnut flavoring

Combine dry ingredients in large mixing bowl. Add eggs and oil; stir until dry ingredients are moistened but do not beat. Stir in vanilla, butter flavoring, fruit and 1 cup pecans. Spoon batter into greased and floured 10-inch tube pan. Bake at 350 degrees for 1 hour and 10 minutes. Cool completely in pan. Prepare frosting by creaming cheese and butter together until smooth. Add powdered sugar and black walnut flavoring; beat until light and fluffy. Frost top and sides of cake; sprinkle with ½ cup pecans. Chill for 24 hours to blend and intensify flavors before serving.

Yield: 16 servings

HARVEST APPLE CAKE

CAKE

3	cups all-purpose flour
2	cups sugar
1	teaspoon baking soda
1	teaspoon salt
1	teaspoon cinnamon
1½	cups vegetable oil
3	eggs
1	teaspoon vanilla
3	cups chopped apples
1	cup chopped nuts

GLAZE

¾	cup firmly-packed brown sugar
¼	cup plus 1 tablespoon lemon juice

Sift dry ingredients together into large mixing bowl. Add oil, eggs and vanilla; mix well by hand (not spoon). Add apples and nuts and mix thoroughly. Spoon batter into greased 10-inch tube pan. Do not preheat oven. Bake at 350 degrees; do not open oven door for 1 hour. Cake should be crusty on top and separate from pan sides. Continue baking for 10 minutes if necessary. Cool in pan for 15 minutes. Place on serving plate and drizzle with glaze, prepared by blending brown sugar and lemon juice. Store in cool place. Cake flavor improves on second day.

Yield: 16 servings

CARROT CAKE

CAKE

2	cups sugar
2	cups all-purpose flour
2	teaspoons baking soda
1	teaspoon salt
1	cup vegetable oil
4	eggs
3	cups grated carrots
2	teaspoons cinnamon

FROSTING

1	(8 ounce) package cream cheese, softened
½	cup butter or margarine, softened
1	(16 ounce) package powdered sugar
1	teaspoon vanilla
1	cup chopped nuts

Sift dry ingredients together into large mixing bowl. Add oil, mixing thoroughly. Add eggs, beating well. Stir in carrots and cinnamon. Pour batter into two 9-inch round baking pans. Bake at 350 degrees for 35 minutes. Cake is very moist; let stand overnight, uncovered. Prepare frosting by blending cream cheese and margarine until smooth. Add sugar and beat well. Add vanilla and nuts. Spread on cooled cake.

Yield: 12 servings

WHITE FRUIT CAKE

4	cups cake flour, divided
2	teaspoons baking powder
1	(16 ounce) package candied cherries, chopped
1	(16 ounce) package candied pineapple, chopped
1	cup golden raisins or chopped dates
4	cups pecans, chopped
1	cup margarine, softened
2	cups sugar
6	eggs, divided
1	cup milk, divided
1	tablespoon vanilla

Preheat oven to 300 degrees. Sift 3 cups flour and baking powder together; set aside. Combine remaining 1 cup flour with fruit and pecans; set aside. Cream margarine and sugar until smooth. In sequence, add 2 eggs, 1 cup flour-baking powder mixture and ⅓ cup milk to creamed mixture, beating after each addition; repeat twice with remaining ingredients. Blend in vanilla. Add batter to fruit mixture and stir until thoroughly blended. Prepare 10-inch tube pan by greasing bottom and sides, lining with waxed paper, greasing paper and dusting with flour. Spoon batter into pan. Bake at 300 degrees for 1 hour; reduce temperature to 250 degrees and bake for 1 hour and 45 minutes, checking often to avoid overbaking.

Yield: 16 to 20 servings

DOUBLE CHOCOLATE MOUSSE CAKE

CAKE

2	(8 ounce) packages semi-sweet chocolate squares
2	cups butter or margarine
1	cup sugar
1	cup half and half
1	tablespoon vanilla flavoring
½	teaspoon salt
8	eggs, lightly beaten
1	cup whipping cream

CHOCOLATE GLAZE

1	(6 ounce) package semi-sweet chocolate chips
2	tablespoons butter or margarine
3	tablespoons milk
2	tablespoons light corn syrup

Preheat oven to 350 degrees. Combine chocolate, butter or margarine, sugar, half and half, vanilla and salt in saucepan. Cook over low heat, stirring constantly, until chocolate is melted and mixture is smooth. Beat chocolate mixture into eggs in large bowl. Pour batter into greased 10x3-inch springform pan. Bake at 350 degrees for 45 minutes or until wooden pick inserted 2 inches from edge comes out clean. Cool in pan on wire rack; remove cooled cake, wrap in plastic wrap and chill for at least 6 hours. Prepare glaze by melting chocolate chips with margarine in saucepan, blending until smooth. Remove from heat and beat in milk and syrup. Spread warm glaze over top and on sides of chilled cake. Whip cream until stiff peaks form. Pipe whipped cream around edges of cake. Chill if not serving immediately. May be garnished with candied violets.

Yield: 16 servings

CHOCOLATE MINT MOUSSE CAKE

CAKE

1	(18½ ounce) package butter recipe chocolate cake mix

FILLING

1	(12 ounce) package semi-sweet chocolate chips
⅓	cup boiling water
1	tablespoon hot strong coffee
8	eggs, separated
¼	cup plus 2 tablespoons creme de menthe syrup
1	cup butter, softened
¼	teaspoon cream of tartar
¼	cup sugar

GARNISH

1	cup whipping cream, whipped and sweetened to taste
	Chocolate shavings or miniature chocolate mint candies

Prepare cake mix according to package directions. Bake half of batter in 8- or 9-inch round baking pan; remaining batter may be used for another cake layer or cupcakes. Cool cake in pan for 5 minutes, remove and complete cooling on wire rack. Return cake layer to baking pan and freeze while preparing mousse. Combine chocolate chips, hot water and coffee in top of double boiler; place over simmering water and stir until chocolate is melted and blended. Add egg yolks and creme de menthe; blend thoroughly. Add butter, ½ cup at a time, and beat well. In separate bowl, use clean dry beaters to whip egg white with cream of tartar until soft peaks form. Gradually add sugar, continuing to beat until stiff, shiny peaks form. Fold about ¼ of egg whites into chocolate mixture, then fold in remaining egg whites. Slice frozen cake layer into 3 layers. Place 1 layer in bottom of 9-inch spring-form pan (cake should be about ¼-inch smaller than pan). Pour 2 to 3 cups mousse mixture over layer, cover with second cake layer, add mousse to flow down sides of cake layers, top with third cake layer and cover with remaining mousse. Chill for 8 hours or overnight before serving. Mousse cake may be frozen. Before serving, remove springform pan, place on serving plate, garnish around edges and center with whipped cream and sprinkle with chocolate.

Yield: 12 to 16 servings

FUDGE CAKE

CAKE

1	cup butter, softened
2	cups sugar
4	eggs
1½	cups sifted all-purpose flour
½	cup plus 1 tablespoon cocoa
1	cup chopped pecans
2	tablespoons vanilla

FROSTING

½	cup butter
2	(1 ounce) squares bitter chocolate
1	egg
1	(16 ounce) package powdered sugar, divided
	Pinch of salt
1	tablespoon lemon juice
2	tablespoons vanilla flavoring

Cream butter and sugar until smooth. Add eggs, 1 at a time, beating well after each addition. Sift flour and cocoa together; add with pecans and vanilla to creamed mixture. Spoon thick batter into waxed paper-lined 13x9x2-inch baking pan. Bake at 350 degrees for 25 minutes; do not overbake. Let cool in pan for 5 minutes; sprinkle with powdered sugar before inverting on serving platter or board. Prepare frosting by melting butter with chocolate; blend well and let cool. Beat egg into cooled chocolate mixture. Mix 1 cup powdered sugar with salt; stir into chocolate mixture and add remaining sugar. Add lemon juice and vanilla and beat well. Spread frosting on warm cake.

Yield: 12 to 16 servings

COLA CAKE

CAKE

2	cups all-purpose flour
2	cups sugar
2	tablespoons cocoa
1	teaspoon baking soda
1	teaspoon salt
1	cup butter or margarine
1	cup cola-flavored carbonated soft drink
½	cup buttermilk
2	eggs, beaten
1	teaspoon vanilla
1½	cups miniature marshmallows

FROSTING

½	cup butter or margarine
2	tablespoons cocoa
¼	cup plus 2 tablespoons cola-flavored carbonated soft drink
1	(16 ounce) package powdered sugar
1	teaspoon vanilla flavoring
1	cup chopped nuts

Combine flour, sugar, cocoa, baking soda and salt in mixing bowl. Combine butter and cola in saucepan; bring to a boil and add to dry ingredients. Add buttermilk, eggs, vanilla and marshmallows; mix well to form thin batter with marshmallows floating at surface. Pour into greased and floured 13x9x2-inch baking pan. Bake at 350 degrees for 45 to 60 minutes. Prepare frosting by combining butter, cocoa and cola in saucepan; bring to a boil. Pour mixture into powdered sugar in bowl and mix well. Add vanilla and nuts. Spread over hot cake.

Yield: 12 to 16 servings

White Chocolate Cake

Cake

⅓	pound white chocolate
½	cup water
1	cup butter, softened
2	cups sugar, divided
4	eggs, separated
1	teaspoon vanilla
2½	cups sifted cake flour
1½	teaspoons baking powder
½	teaspoon salt
1	cup buttermilk
1	cup chopped nuts
1	(7 ounce) package flaked coconut

Frosting

1	(8 ounce) package cream cheese, softened
½	cup butter, softened
1	(16 ounce) package powdered sugar
1	teaspoon vanilla

Melt chocolate with water in top of double boiler over simmering water; set aside to cool. Cream butter and 1½ cups sugar until light and fluffy. Add egg yolks, 1 at a time, beating well after each addition. Stir in vanilla. Sift flour, baking powder and salt together. Combine dry ingredients, chocolate mixture, creamed mixture and buttermilk; stir in nuts and coconut. Beat egg whites, gradually adding ½ cup sugar, until moist peaks form; fold into batter. Spread batter in 3 greased and floured 9-inch round baking pans. Bake at 350 degrees for 30 to 35 minutes. Cool before frosting. Prepare frosting by blending cream cheese, butter, powdered sugar and vanilla together; beat until smooth. Spread frosting on layers, stack and frost sides and top of cake.

Yield: 16 servings

Mississippi Mud Cake

1	cup butter
½	cup cocoa
2	cups sugar
4	eggs, beaten
1½	cups all-purpose flour
	Pinch of salt
1	teaspoon vanilla
1½	cups chopped pecans
1	(10 ounce) package miniature marshmallows

Frosting

¼	cup butter
⅓	cup cocoa
1	(16 ounce) package powdered sugar
½	cup milk
½	teaspoon vanilla flavoring

Melt butter with cocoa in large saucepan. Add sugar, eggs, flour, salt and vanilla; mix well. Stir in pecans. Pour batter into greased and floured 13x9x3-inch baking pan. Bake at 350 degrees until wooden pick inserted near center comes out clean. Sprinkle marshmallows on top of hot cake and cover with aluminum foil. Allow cake to cool before frosting. Prepare frosting by melting butter with cocoa in saucepan. Add powdered sugar, milk and vanilla; beat until smooth. Spread on cooled cake in pan.

Yield: 16 to 20 servings

COCONUT MOUND CAKE

CAKE

1	(18½ ounce) package Swiss chocolate or devil's food cake mix

FILLING

1	cup sugar
½	cup butter or margarine
1	cup evaporated milk
24	large marshmallows
1	(14 ounce) package finely shredded coconut

FROSTING

1	(16 ounce) package powdered sugar
½	cup cocoa
¼	cup plus 2 tablespoons butter or margarine, softened
⅓	cup evaporated milk

Prepare cake mix according to package directions. Bake in 2 greased and floured 8- or 9-inch round baking pans. Cool in pans for 5 minutes, remove and complete cooling on wire racks. Split layers to form 4 layers. Prepare filling by combining sugar, butter and milk in saucepan. Bring to a boil and cook for 2 minutes. Remove from heat, add marshmallows and coconut and stir well. Spread filling between cake layers. Prepare frosting by sifting powdered sugar and cocoa together. Blend in butter and milk. Spread frosting on top and sides of assembled cake.

Yield: 16 servings

COCONUT POUND CAKE

CAKE

1½	cups vegetable shortening
2½	cups sugar
5	eggs
3	cups all-purpose flour
1	teaspoon baking powder
¼	teaspoon salt
1	cup milk
1	(3½ ounce) can flaked coconut
2	teaspoons coconut flavoring

GLAZE

2	tablespoons margarine, softened
1¼	cups sugar
3	tablespoons light corn syrup
¾	cup buttermilk
1	(3½ ounce) can flaked coconut

Cream shortening with sugar until smooth. Add eggs, 1 at a time, beating well after each addition. Blend flour, baking powder and salt. Add dry ingredients, milk, coconut and flavoring to creamed mixture. Pour batter into greased and floured 10-inch tube pan. Bake at 300 degrees for 1 hour and 25 minutes. Prepare glaze by combining margarine, sugar, syrup and buttermilk in saucepan; bring to a boil over low heat. Stir in coconut. Pour half of glaze on hot cake in pan and let stand 5 minutes. Invert on serving plate and spread remaining glaze on top and sides of cake.

Yield: 12 to 16 servings

FRESH COCONUT LAYER CAKE

CAKE

1	cup margarine, softened
2	cups sugar
4	eggs
3	cups all-purpose flour
2½	teaspoons baking powder
½	teaspoon salt
1	cup milk
1	teaspoon almond flavoring
1	teaspoon vanilla flavoring

FILLING

½	cup all-purpose flour
1	cup sugar
¼	teaspoon salt
¼	cup water
1¼	cups orange juice
¼	cup lemon juice
4	egg yolks, well beaten

FROSTING

1½	cups sugar
½	teaspoon cream of tartar
⅛	teaspoon salt
½	cup hot water
4	egg whites
½	teaspoon almond flavoring
½	teaspoon coconut flavoring
½	cup finely grated coconut

Cream margarine until smooth. Gradually add sugar, beating until light and fluffy. Add eggs, 1 at a time, beating well after each addition. Combine flour, baking powder and salt. Alternately add dry ingredients and milk to creamed mixture, beginning and ending with dry ingredients. Stir in flavorings. Pour batter into 3 greased and floured 9-inch round baking pans. Bake at 375 degrees for 20 to 25 minutes or until wooden pick inserted near center comes out clean. Cool cakes in pan for 10 minutes, remove and cool on wire rack. Prepare filling by combining flour, sugar, salt and water in heavy saucepan. Stir in fruit juices. Cook over medium heat, stirring constantly, until mixture is thickened and bubbly. Gradually add about ¼ of hot mixture to egg yolks; add egg yolk mixture to hot mixture, stirring constantly. Bring to a boil and cook for 1 to 2 minutes, stirring constantly. Remove from heat and cool completely. Filling will be thick. Prepare frosting by combining sugar, cream of tartar, salt and hot water in heavy saucepan. Cook over medium heat, stirring constantly, until clear. Cook without stirring until syrup registers 240 degrees on candy thermometer (soft ball stage). Beat egg whites until soft peaks form; continue beating, gradually adding syrup. Add flavorings, beating until stiff peaks form and frosting is thick enough to spread. Spread cooled filling between cool cake layers. Frost top and sides of assembled cake; sprinkle with coconut.

Yield: 12 to 16 servings

GINGERBREAD

BREAD

1	cup butter, softened
1	cup firmly-packed dark brown sugar
2	eggs, beaten
⅓	cup light corn syrup
⅓	cup molasses
2½	cups all-purpose flour
2	teaspoons ginger
2	teaspoons ground coriander seed
½	teaspoon cinnamon
½	teaspoon nutmeg
½	teaspoon ground cloves
1⅓	cups golden raisins
	Boiling water
1	tablespoon all-purpose flour
1	teaspoon baking powder
⅓	cup chopped candied ginger
	Grated peel of 1 lemon
	Grated peel of 2 oranges
1¼	cups milk
2	teaspoons baking soda

LEMON SAUCE

	Juice of 2 lemons
1¼	cups water, divided
½	cup sugar
2	tablespoons cornstarch
2	tablespoons butter
	Grated peel of 1 lemon
	Dash of salt

Cream butter with sugar until smooth. Add eggs, syrup and molasses; beat until smooth. Sift flour and spices together; add to molasses mixture and mix well to form stiff batter. Soak raisins in boiling water to cover. Drain, pat dry and dust with 1 tablespoon flour and baking powder. Add raisins, candied ginger and fruit peel to batter. Warm milk slightly. Add soda and stir to dissolve. Add milk to batter and mix thoroughly. Spread batter in greased and floured 13x9x2-inch baking pan. Bake at 325 degrees for 1 to 1½ hours, checking during last 30 minutes of baking time. Cool. Prepare lemon sauce by combining lemon juice, ¾ cup water and sugar in saucepan; bring to a boil. Dissolve cornstarch in ½ cup water and add to lemon mixture; cook until thickened. Remove from heat. Stir in butter, grated peel and salt. Serve warm over gingerbread squares.

Yield: 12 to 16 servings

HAZELNUT CAKE

½	cup butter (or ¼ cup butter and ¼ cup margarine)
⅔	cup sugar
2 or 3	eggs, lightly beaten
1	cup all-purpose flour
1½	teaspoons baking powder
	Pinch of salt
½	cup finely ground hazelnuts
½	cup milk

Melt butter in saucepan. Add sugar and eggs to butter; mix well with wire whisk. Combine flour, baking powder, salt and hazelnuts. Alternately add dry ingredients and milk to egg mixture, blending thoroughly. Pour batter into greased 9-inch square baking pan. Bake at 350 degrees for 30 to 35 minutes. Serve plain or with chocolate frosting.

Yield: 9 servings

Desserts

OATMEAL CAKE

CAKE

1¼	cups boiling water
1	cup quick-cooking oatmeal
½	cup margarine
1	cup sugar
1	cup firmly-packed brown sugar
2	eggs, beaten
1⅓	cups all-purpose flour
2	teaspoons baking soda
½	teaspoon salt
½ to 1	teaspoon cinnamon
½ to 1	teaspoon nutmeg

BROILED FROSTING

¼	cup margarine
2	tablespoons cream or milk
½	cup firmly-packed brown sugar
½	cup chopped nuts
1	cup shredded coconut (optional)

Combine boiling water, oatmeal and margarine in saucepan; let stand, covered, for 20 minutes. Using electric mixer, beat sugars and eggs thoroughly. Sift flour, soda, salt and spices together. Add dry ingredients and oatmeal mixture to egg mixture, beating on low speed until well mixed. Pour batter in greased 13x9x2-inch baking pan, two 9x5x3-inch loaf pans or 10-inch tube pan. Bake at 350 degrees for 35 minutes or until done. Cool cake in pan. Prepare frosting by combining margarine, cream or milk and brown sugar in saucepan; bring to a boil. Remove from heat and stir in nuts and coconut. Spread frosting on cake. Broil until frosting is bubbly and toasted.

Yield: 16 servings

HAWAIIAN CAKE

CAKE

1	cup butter, softened
2	cups sugar
5	eggs
1	teaspoon baking powder
¾	teaspoon baking soda
1	cup milk
1	(3½ ounce) can flaked coconut
1	cup pecans, chopped
1	(14 ounce) package graham cracker crumbs

PINEAPPLE FROSTING

¾	cup butter, melted
1	(20 ounce) can crushed pineapple, well drained
1	(16 ounce) package powdered sugar

Cream butter with sugar until light and fluffy. Add eggs, 1 at a time, beating well after each addition. Blend in baking powder and soda. Gradually add milk, beating thoroughly. Stir in coconut and pecans. Gradually add crumbs and beat until well mixed. Pour batter into three greased and floured 9-inch round baking pans. Bake at 350 degrees for 35 to 40 minutes. Cool in pans for 5 minutes, remove and complete cooling on wire racks. Prepare frosting by mixing butter and pineapple. Gradually beat in sugar. Use frosting to assemble cake layers and spread on top and sides of cake.

Yield: 12 to 16 servings

189

PEACH POUND CAKE

1	cup butter, softened
3	cups sugar
6	eggs
2	cups chopped, peeled fresh peaches
1	cup whipping cream
3	cups all-purpose flour
½	teaspoon baking powder
1	tablespoon vanilla
½	teaspoon almond flavoring

Cream butter with sugar until smooth. Add eggs, 1 at a time, beating well after each addition. Combine peaches and cream. Mix flour with baking powder. Alternately add dry ingredients and peach mixture to creamed mixture, beginning and ending with dry ingredients. Stir in flavorings. Pour batter into greased and floured 10-inch tube pan. Do not preheat oven. Bake at 400 degrees for 10 minutes, then reduce oven temperature to 325 degrees and bake for 1 hour; turn cake around, and bake for 20 more minutes.

Yield: 12 to 16 servings

NANCY'S POUND CAKE

1	cup Land O'Lakes® butter, softened
½	cup vegetable shortening
3	cups sugar
1½	teaspoons vanilla
½	teaspoon almond flavoring
5	eggs
3½	cups sifted all-purpose flour
½	teaspoon baking powder
1	cup milk

Using electric mixer, cream margarine and shortening with sugar for 15 to 20 minutes or until light and fluffy. Add flavorings and mix well. Add eggs, 1 at a time, beating well after each addition. Combine flour and baking powder. Alternately add dry ingredients and milk to creamed mixture, beginning and ending with dry ingredients. Pour batter into 10-inch tube pan, prepared by greasing bottom and tube and dusting bottom with flour. Bake at 290 degrees for 1½ hours.

For chocolate pound cake, use 3 cups flour and ½ cup cocoa.

Yield: 16 servings

SOUR CREAM POUND CAKE

CAKE

1	cup butter, softened
3	cups sugar
6	eggs, separated
1	teaspoon vanilla
1	teaspoon lemon flavoring
3	cups all-purpose flour
¼	teaspoon baking soda
⅛	teaspoon salt
1	(8 ounce) carton sour cream

LEMON GLAZE

1¾	cups powdered sugar
	Juice of 1 lemon

Cream butter with sugar until smooth. Add egg yolks, 1 at a time, beating well after each addition. Stir in flavoring. Sift flour, soda and salt together. Alternately add dry ingredients and sour cream to creamed mixture, beating thoroughly. Beat egg whites and fold into batter. Pour batter into greased 10-inch tube pan. Bake at 300 degrees for 1½ hours. Prepare glaze by mixing powdered sugar and lemon juice, beating until smooth. Pour glaze over hot cake.

Yield: 16 servings

POPPY SEED SOUR CREAM CAKE

CAKE

1	cup butter, softened
3	cups sugar
6	eggs
1	(8 ounce) carton sour cream
3	cups all-purpose flour
¼	teaspoon baking soda
2	teaspoons lemon flavoring
1	teaspoon vanilla
1	teaspoon orange flavoring
1	teaspoon butternut flavoring
1	teaspoon coconut flavoring
1	teaspoon almond flavoring
¼	cup poppy seed

ORANGE GLAZE

1½	cups powdered sugar
½	cup orange juice
1	teaspoon vanilla
1	teaspoon almond flavoring
1	teaspoon butter flavoring

Cream butter with sugar until smooth. Add eggs, 1 at a time, beating well after each addition. Add sour cream and mix thoroughly. Add flour and soda, blending well. Stir in flavorings and poppy seed. Spread batter in greased and floured 10-inch smooth or fluted tube pan. Bake at 350 degrees for 1 hour or until wooden pick inserted halfway between edge and center comes out clean. Prepare glaze by mixing powdered sugar, orange juice and flavorings, beating until smooth. Pour glaze over warm cake.

Yield: 16 servings

SUGAR PLUM CAKE

CAKE

1½	cups sugar
2	cups cake flour
2	teaspoons baking powder
1	teaspoon baking soda
2	teaspoons cinnamon
1¼	teaspoon allspice
1	teaspoon nutmeg
1	teaspoon ground cloves
¾	cup vegetable oil
1	cup buttermilk
3	eggs
1	teaspoon vanilla flavoring
1	cup chopped prunes
1	cup chopped pecans

MAPLE GLAZE

1	teaspoon baking soda
1	cup buttermilk
2	cups sugar
¼	cup plus 1 tablespoon butter
2	teaspoons maple syrup

HARD SAUCE

2 to 5	tablespoons butter, softened
1	cup sifted powdered sugar
¼	teaspoon salt
1	teaspoon vanilla flavoring
¼	cup whipping cream

Combine dry ingredients in mixing bowl. Add oil and buttermilk, mixing well. Add eggs, 1 at a time, beating well after each addition. Blend in vanilla. Stir in prunes and nuts, mixing thoroughly. Spread batter in greased and floured 10-inch tube pan or two 8-inch square baking pans. Bake at 325 degrees for 1 hour for tube pan and 40 minutes for square pans. Prepare glaze by dissolving soda in buttermilk. Combine buttermilk, sugar, butter and syrup in saucepan; gradually bring to a boil, stirring occasionally, and cook for 30 minutes. Pour hot glaze over hot cake in pan, piercing to allow glaze to soak into cake. Serve cake with hard sauce. Prepare sauce by creaming butter until soft. Gradually add sugar and blend well. Add salt and vanilla. Blend in cream, beating until smooth. Chill thoroughly.

Yield: 16 servings

10TH STREET POUND CAKE

1	cup butter or margarine, softened
¼	cup vegetable oil
3	cups sugar
6	eggs
1	teaspoon vanilla
1	teaspoon almond or lemon flavoring
3	cups self-rising flour
1	cup milk

Combine all ingredients in electric mixer bowl. Beat for 6 minutes. Pour batter into greased and floured 10-inch tube pan. Bake at 350 degrees for 1 hour or until wooden pick inserted between edge and center comes out clean.

Yield: 16 servings

CHOCOLATE CHEESECAKE WITH COCONUT PECAN TOPPING

CRUST
- 3 cups graham cracker crumbs
- 2 (1 ounce) squares semi-sweet chocolate, grated
- ¾ cup butter, melted
- 3 tablespoons sugar

FILLING
- 3 eggs
- 1 cup sugar
- 3 (8 ounce) packages cream cheese, softened
- 12 (1 ounce) squares semi-sweet chocolate
- ¾ cup butter
- 1 (8 ounce) carton sour cream
- 1 teaspoon vanilla

COCONUT PECAN TOPPING
- ¼ cup butter
- ¼ cup firmly-packed brown sugar
- ⅔ cup half and half or evaporated milk
- 4 egg yolks or 2 whole eggs
- 1 teaspoon vanilla
- 1 cup chopped pecans
- 1 cup flaked coconut

Prepare crust by combining crumbs, chocolate, butter and sugar, mixing well. Press crumbs into two 8½-inch springform pans and set aside. Beat eggs with sugar until thickened. Add cream cheese and whip until smooth. Melt chocolate with butter in top of double boiler, mixing thoroughly. Add sour cream and vanilla to chocolate, then blend with cream cheese mixture. Divide batter equally between 2 crusts. Bake at 325 degrees for 2 hours. Cool in pans. Remove from pans and chill. Prepare filling by combining butter, brown sugar, half and half or milk and eggs in heavy saucepan. Cook over low heat, stirring constantly, until thickened. Remove from heat and stir in vanilla, pecans and coconut. Cool. Spread topping on top of chilled cheesecake.

Yield: 16 to 24 servings

PRALINE PECAN CHEESECAKE

CRUST

1	cup graham cracker crumbs
¼	cup butter, melted

FILLING

3	(8 ounce) packages cream cheese, softened
1¼	cups firmly-packed brown sugar
3	eggs
1	cup chopped pecans
2	tablespoons all-purpose flour
1½	teaspoons vanilla

TOPPING

½	cup firmly-packed brown sugar
¼	cup butter
	Pecan halves

Prepare crust by combining crumbs and butter, mixing well. Press crumbs into buttered 9-inch springform pan. Chill for 1 hour. Combine cream cheese and brown sugar. Add eggs, 1 at a time, beating after each addition. Stir in pecans, flour and vanilla; mix thoroughly. Pour filling into prepared pan. Bake at 350 degrees for 50 to 55 minutes. Cool. Prepare topping by blending brown sugar and butter in saucepan; cook over low heat for about 5 minutes or until smooth and thickened. Pour topping over cooled cheesecake, spreading evenly to cover top. Garnish with pecan halves. Remove springform pan sides. Store in refrigerator.

Yield: 12 servings

COCONUT CREAM CHEESECAKE

CRUST

⅔	cup all-purpose flour
1	tablespoon sugar
¼	cup plus 1 tablespoon cold butter, cut in pieces

FILLING

3	(8 ounce) packages cream cheese, softened
1½	cups sugar
4	eggs, at room temperature
2	egg yolks, at room temperature
2	cups flaked coconut
1	cup whipping cream
1	teaspoon fresh lemon juice
½	teaspoon vanilla
½	teaspoon almond flavoring
	Toasted coconut (optional)

Prepare crust, combining flour and sugar in mixing bowl. Using pastry blender or knives, cut butter into flour mixture until it resembles coarse meal. Shape into a ball, enclose in plastic wrap and chill for 15 minutes. Press dough into 10-inch springform pan. Bake at 325 degrees for 15 to 20 minutes or just until golden brown. Cool slightly. Reduce oven temperature to 300 degrees. Beat cream cheese with sugar until smooth. Add eggs and yolks, 1 at a time, beating well after each addition. Stir in coconut, cream, lemon juice and flavorings, mixing thoroughly. Pour batter into baked crust. Bake for 1 hour and 10 minutes or until edges are firm. Cool in pan completely. Remove springform. Chill, covered, for 4 hours before serving. Sprinkle with coconut. Cheesecake may be frozen.

Yield: 12 servings

PUMPKIN CHEESECAKE

CRUST
¾ cup graham cracker crumbs
½ cup finely chopped pecans
¼ cup sugar
¼ cup firmly-packed light brown sugar
¼ cup unsalted butter, melted and cooled
1 teaspoon ground cinnamon

FILLING
1½ cups solid pack pumpkin (not pie filling)
3 large eggs
½ cup firmly-packed brown sugar
½ teaspoon salt
1½ teaspoons ground cinnamon
1½ teaspoons ground nutmeg
½ teaspoon ground ginger
3 (8 ounce) packages cream cheese, softened
¾ cup sugar
2 tablespoons whipping cream
1 tablespoon cornstarch
1 teaspoon vanilla
1 teaspoon rum extract
2 teaspoons water

TOPPING
1 (16 ounce) carton sour cream
2 tablespoons sugar
1 teaspoon rum extract
2 teaspoons water
16 pecan halves for garnish

Prepare crust by combining crumbs, pecans and sugars. Stir in butter. Press crumb mixture in bottom and ½-inch up sides of buttered 9-inch springform pan.

Chill for 1 hour. Preheat oven to 350 degrees. Whisk together pumpkin, eggs, brown sugar, salt and spices. Using electric mixer, beat cheese and sugar until smooth. Add cream, cornstarch, flavorings and pumpkin mixture, beating until filling is smooth. Pour into prepared pan. Bake for 50 to 55 minutes or until center is just firm. Cool in pan on rack for 5 minutes. Prepare topping by whisking sour cream, sugar, rum extract and water together. Spread on cheesecake and bake for 5 minutes. Cool cheesecake on wire rack, then chill, covered, overnight. Remove springform pan sides. Garnish with pecans arranged in ring on outer edge of top of cheesecake.

Yield: 12 to 16 servings

New York Cheesecake

2	(8 ounce) packages cream cheese, softened
2	cups (16 ounces) creamy cottage cheese
1½	cups sugar
4	eggs, lightly beaten
3	tablespoons cornstarch
3	tablespoons all-purpose flour
1½	teaspoons lemon juice
1	teaspoon grated lemon peel
1	teaspoon vanilla
½	cup melted butter
1	(16 ounce) carton sour cream

Using electric mixer, beat cream cheese and cottage cheese at high speed. Gradually add sugar, then eggs, beating well. Add cornstarch, flour, lemon juice, peel and vanilla; beat at low speed until well blended. Add butter and sour cream; beat just until smooth. Pour batter into greased 9-inch springform pan. Bake at 325 degrees for 1 hour and 10 minutes; turn oven off and let cheesecake remain in oven for 2 hours (or longer); do not open oven door or cake will fall or bubble. Remove from oven and let stand for 2 hours (or longer). Chill for 3 hours. To remove from pan, run spatula along sides and release clasp. Place on serving plate, leaving pan bottom under cake. Cheesecake may be frozen.

Yield: 16 to 20 servings

Flaky Pie Crust

3	cups all-purpose flour
	Dash of salt
1¼	cups vegetable shortening
1	egg
1	tablespoon vinegar
¼	cup plus 1 tablespoon water

Combine flour and salt; cut shortening into dry ingredients. Beat egg, vinegar and water together; add to flour mixture and blend thoroughly. Chill dough for 15 minutes before using. Divide dough into 4 or 5 portions. Roll to circle shape, place in pie plate and prick bottom with fork tines. For pastry shell, bake at 475 degrees for about 10 minutes. Dough may be stored in refrigerator for 3 days or may be frozen.

Yield: 4 or 5 shells

Basic Pie Crust

⅔	cup vegetable shortening
2	cups all-purpose flour
½	teaspoon salt
	Ice water

Cut ⅓ cup shortening into flour mixed with salt, working until texture is consistency of cornmeal. Cut in remaining ⅓ cup until particles are size of small peas. Add just enough ice water to hold dough together. Chill thoroughly. Roll dough quickly and lightly. Use as directed in pie recipes.

Yield: 2 shells

PAPER BAG APPLE PIE WITH PRALINE SAUCE

PIE

6 to 7	cups sliced peeled apples
1	cup sugar, divided
½	cup plus 2 tablespoons all-purpose flour, divided
½	teaspoon nutmeg
1	unbaked 9-inch pastry shell
2	tablespoons lemon juice
½	cup butter or margarine, softened

PRALINE SAUCE

1	cup light corn syrup
½	cup sugar
⅓	cup butter or margarine
1	egg, beaten
1	tablespoon vanilla
1	cup chopped pecans

Combine apples, ½ cup sugar and 2 tablespoons flour; add nutmeg and toss to mix thoroughly. Place apples in pastry shell and sprinkle with lemon juice. Combine ½ cup sugar with ½ cup flour; cut in butter to form crumbs and sprinkle over apples. Place pie in large, heavy paper bag; fold open end twice to enclose and secure with paper clips. Place on baking sheet. Bake at 425 degrees for 1 hour. Serve warm with scoop of ice cream and Praline Sauce. Prepare sauce by combining syrup, sugar, butter or margarine in heavy saucepan; mix well. Bring to a boil over medium heat, stirring constantly; boil for 2 minutes without stirring. Remove from heat and stir in vanilla and pecans.

Yield: 6 to 8 servings

CHOCOLATE ANGEL PIE

MERINGUE SHELL

2	egg whites
⅛	teaspoon salt
⅛	teaspoon cream of tartar
½	cup sifted sugar
½	cup finely chopped pecans
½	teaspoon vanilla

FILLING

1	(4 ounce) package German sweet chocolate
3	tablespoons water
1	teaspoon vanilla
1	cup whipping cream, whipped

Using electric mixer, beat egg whites with salt and cream of tartar until soft peaks form. Gradually add sugar, beating until stiff. Fold in pecans and vanilla. Spread mixture in lightly-greased 8-inch pie pan, shaping to make a shell and forming sides ½-inch higher than edge of pan. Bake at 300 degrees for 50 to 55 minutes. Cool. Prepare filling by placing chocolate and water in saucepan over low heat; stir until chocolate is melted. Cool until thickened. Stir in vanilla. Fold chocolate mixture into whipped cream. Spoon into meringue shell. Chill for 2 hours (or longer) before serving.

Yield: 6 to 8 servings

MICK'S CHOCOLATE PIE

CRUST

1   (8 ounce) package chocolate wafers, crushed

3   tablespoons melted butter

FILLING

1¼   cups sugar

¾   cup plus 2 tablespoons all-purpose flour

⅛   teaspoon salt

½   cup cocoa

4   cups milk

4   egg yolks, beaten

1¼   cups semi-sweet chocolate chips

½   teaspoon vanilla

¼   cup butter

Combine crushed wafers and melted butter. Press mixture in bottom and along sides of 9-inch pie pan. For filling, combine sugar, flour, salt and cocoa in top of double boiler. Gradually add milk, blending well. Cook over boiling water, stirring constantly, until milk is scalded. Stir 1 cup milk mixture into egg yolks, then add egg yolk mixture to remaining milk mixture. Cook until thickened. Remove from heat and stir in chocolate chips, vanilla and butter. Pour mixture into prepared shell. Chill for 24 hours. Servings may be garnished with whipped cream, chocolate shavings and chocolate wafer crumbs.

Yield: 6 to 8 servings

CHOCOLATE CHIP PIE

½   cup butter, melted and cooled

¾   cup sugar

4   eggs

¾   cup light corn syrup

½   teaspoon vanilla

½   (6 ounce) package semi-sweet chocolate chips

½   cup chopped pecans

1   unbaked 9-inch pastry shell
   Whipped cream

Combine butter and sugar, mixing thoroughly. Add eggs, syrup and vanilla; use electric mixer at medium speed to beat well. Stir in chocolate chips and pecans. Pour mixture into pastry shell. Bake at 350 degrees for 45 minutes. Serve warm with whipped cream.

Yield: 6 to 8 servings

TOASTED COCONUT PIE

3   eggs, beaten

1½   cups sugar

½   cup melted butter

1⅓   tablespoons lemon juice

1   teaspoon vanilla

1   (3½ ounce) can flaked coconut

1   unbaked 9-inch pastry shell

Combine eggs, sugar, butter, lemon juice and vanilla; mix well. Stir in coconut. Pour filling into pastry shell. Bake at 350 for 40 to 45 minutes. Cool before serving.

Yield: 6 to 8 servings

COUNTRY PLACE'S CHOCOLATE TOFFEE PIE

CRUST
1	(8 ounce) package chocolate wafer cookies, ground
½	cup butter, melted

FILLING
29	(1 ounce) squares semi-sweet chocolate
⅔	cup hot coffee
4	eggs, separated
3	tablespoons sugar
1⅓	cups whipping cream
½	cup chopped (½-inch chunks) chocolate-covered toffee bars
½	cup caramel sauce

GARNISH
4	cups whipped cream
2	cups caramel sauce
2	cups crushed chocolate-covered toffee bars

Combine cookie crumbs and butter. Press mixture in bottom and along sides of 10-inch pie pan. Bake at 350 degrees for 8 minutes. Set aside to cool. Prepare filling by melting chocolate and coffee together in top of double boiler, whisking until smooth. Remove from heat. Beat egg yolks; add ½ cup chocolate liquid and beat until smooth; pour yolk mixture into remaining chocolate liquid and mix until smooth. In separate bowl, beat egg whites until foamy. Gradually add sugar, whipping until stiff. Fold egg whites into chocolate mixture. Cool to room temperature. Whip cream until peaks form; fold into chocolate mixture. Sprinkle candy pieces in cooled crust. Spread caramel sauce evenly over candy. Pour chocolate filling on caramel layer. Chill for 8 hours. To serve pie, cut into 8 pieces. Top each with whipped cream, caramel sauce and crushed candy.

Yield: 8 servings

COCONUT PIE

2	cups sugar
1	teaspoon cornstarch
1	teaspoon vanilla
6	eggs, beaten
½	cup margarine, melted
2	cups grated coconut
1	(12 ounce) can evaporated milk
2	unbaked 9-inch pastry shells

Combine sugar and cornstarch. Add vanilla, eggs, margarine, coconut and milk; beat well. Pour filling into pastry shells. Bake at 350 degrees for 45 minutes to 1 hour.

Yield: 12 servings

MERINGUE LEMON PIE

MERINGUE SHELL

4	egg whites
¼	teaspoon cream of tartar
1	cup sugar

FILLING

4	egg yolks
½	cup sugar
	Juice and grated peel of 1 large lemon
1	cup whipping cream
2	tablespoons powdered sugar

TOPPING

1	cup whipping cream
2	tablespoons powdered sugar
¼	teaspoon vanilla

Beat egg whites until soft peaks form. Gradually add cream of tartar and sugar; beat until glossy. Spread mixture in buttered 10-inch pie pan, shaping to form shell and extending along sides. Bake at 275 degrees for 1 hour; turn oven off, open oven door slightly and leave shell in oven for 1 hour. For filling, beat egg yolks in top of double boiler over gently boiling water for about 5 minutes or until thickened. Add sugar, lemon juice and peel; cook, stirring frequently, until very thick. Set aside to cool. Whip cream with powdered sugar and fold into cooled lemon mixture. Spoon mixture into meringue shell. Chill, covered for 24 hours. Prepare whipped topping 4 hours before serving. Whip cream with sugar and vanilla. Spread over filling. Chill until served.
To make miniature meringues, shape filling into about 50 1-inch shells on buttered baking sheet. Bake at 225 degrees for 1 hour; turn oven off, open oven door slightly and let shells dry for 30 minutes.

Yield: 8 servings

PECAN PIE

1	cup sugar
1	cup light corn syrup
⅓	cup butter
4	eggs, beaten
1	teaspoon vanilla
¼	teaspoon salt
1	unbaked 9-inch pastry shell
1¼	cups pecan halves

Combine sugar, corn syrup and butter in saucepan; cook until sugar is dissolved. Cool slightly. Add eggs, vanilla and salt, mixing well. Pour filling into pastry shell. Arrange pecan halves on filling. Bake at 325 degrees for 50 to 55 minutes.

Yield: 8 servings

BUTTERMILK PECAN PIE

½   cup butter
2   cups sugar
2   teaspoons vanilla
3   eggs
3   tablespoons all-purpose flour
¼   teaspoon salt
1   cup buttermilk
½   cup chopped pecans
1   unbaked 9-inch pastry shell

Cream butter with sugar, adding sugar ½ cup at a time. Blend in vanilla. Add eggs, 1 at a time, beating well after each addition. Combine flour and salt; add gradually to creamed mixture. Add buttermilk and mix well. Sprinkle pecans in bottom of pastry shell. Pour filling over pecans. bake at 300 degrees for 1½ hours. Serve at room temperature.

This pie was a family recipe often prepared by a career Navy chef for dignitaries including President Harry Truman. During his military career, the chef declined to share the recipe but after retirement, permitted its publication in a Navy newspaper.

Yield: 6 servings

PEACH CREAM TART

CRUST

1¼   cups all-purpose flour
½   cup butter, softened
2   tablespoons sour cream

FILLING

7   medium-ripe but firm peaches, peeled and cut in thick slices
3   egg yolks
½   cup sour cream
¾   cup firmly-packed brown sugar
¼   cup all-purpose flour

Combine flour and butter in food processor, then add sour cream. Process to form dough. With lightly-floured hands, press dough on bottom and along sides of ungreased 9-inch round baking pan with removable bottom or round baking dish. Bake at 375 degrees for about 15 minutes or until firm but not browned. Cool. Prepare filling by arranging peach slices in circles on crust, overlapping if necessary. Combine egg yolks, sour cream, brown sugar and flour; beat until smooth. Pour mixture over peaches. Bake at 350 degrees for about 1 hour or until firm and pale golden, covering with loose aluminum foil tent to prevent overbrowning. Cool on wire rack. Remove sides of pan.

Apples may be substituted for peaches. Tart may be glazed with melted apricot or peach preserves mixed with small amount of lemon juice.

Yield: 8 servings

PINEAPPLE CHEESE TART

CRUST

2	cups unsifted all-purpose flour
½	teaspoon baking powder
¼	teaspoon salt
⅔	cup butter
⅓	cup sugar
2	egg yolks
2	tablespoons whipping cream
½	teaspoon grated lemon peel

FILLING

¼	cup butter, softened
⅔	cup sugar
2	(8 ounce) packages cream cheese, softened
1	egg yolk
¼	cup whipping cream
1	(8 ounce) can crushed pineapple, drained
½	cup chopped dates
1	teaspoon grated lemon peel
	Powdered sugar

Sift flour, baking powder and salt together into large bowl. Cut in butter until mixture resembles coarse crumbs. Add sugar, egg yolks, cream and lemon peel; mix just until pastry holds together. Knead on lightly-floured surface for about 2 minutes or until smooth. Chill for 30 minutes. Prepare filling by combining butter, sugar and cream cheese; beat until blended. Add egg yolk and cream; beat until smooth. Stir in pineapple, dates and lemon peel; set aside. Press ¾ of chilled dough in bottom of lightly-greased 10-inch springform pan. Bake at 350 degrees for 12 minutes. Cool. Pour filling over cooled crust. Roll and cut remaining dough into 10-inch strips and arrange on filling in lattice pattern. Bake at 350 degrees for 40 minutes. Cool for 10 minutes. Sprinkle with powdered sugar before serving.

Yield: 12 servings

FRESH FRUIT TART

1	(16 ounce) package frozen cookie dough
1	(8 ounce) package cream cheese, softened
1	teaspoon vanilla
½	cup sugar
	Strawberry slices
	Kiwi slices
	Peach slices
	Mandarin orange sections
	Banana slices
	Raspberries
	Blueberries
¼	cup apricot preserves
1	tablespoon water

Cut cookie dough into ⅛-inch slices. Place on greased pizza pan or tart pan, arranging slices about ¼ inch from edge of pan and overlapping if necessary. Bake at 350 degrees for 10 minutes or until golden brown. Cool thoroughly. Combine cream cheese, vanilla and sugar, beating until smooth. Spread evenly over crust. Arrange fruit in rings on cheese layer. Combine preserves and water; brush on fruit. Chill well.

Yield: 8 to 10 servings

Desserts

APPLE STRUDEL

1	cup soft white breadcrumbs
1	cup ground walnuts
1	tablespoon butter
8	medium cooking apples, peeled, quartered and thinly sliced
1	cup golden raisins
1	tablespoon grated lemon peel
1	tablespoon lemon juice
1	cup sugar
1	teaspoon cinnamon
16	strudel or filo leaves
¾	cup unsalted butter, melted
	Powdered sugar

Combine breadcrumbs, walnuts and 1 tablespoon butter in skillet over medium heat; cook, stirring frequently, for 5 minutes or until breadcrumbs are golden brown; remove from heat. Combine fruit, lemon peel and juice, sugar and cinnamon in large bowl. Place 4 filo leaves on a towel; top with 4 leaves, overlapping, to form 18-inch square. Brush dough with melted butter. Sprinkle half of crumb mixture over buttered leaves. Spoon half of apple mixture evenly along one side of dough 2 inches from edge. Using towel, lift dough over filling, folding adjacent sides toward center to enclose filling, then rolling, jelly roll fashion, to form 15x3-inch roll. Place seam side down on 15x10x1-inch jelly roll pan. Repeat with remaining ingredients. Bake at 400 degrees for 35 minutes, brushing several times with melted butter. Cool on pan for 15 minutes. Sprinkle with powdered sugar.

Yield: 16 servings

CALYPSO PIE

PIE

20	cream filled chocolate sandwich cookies, crushed
¼	cup margarine, melted
½	gallon vanilla or other flavor ice cream, softened

SAUCE

¼	cup butter
1½	(1 ounce) squares unsweetened baking chocolate
⅔	cup sugar
⅛	teaspoon salt
⅔	cup evaporated milk
1	teaspoon vanilla

Combine cookie crumbs and margarine; press mixture into greased 13x9x2-inch baking pan or 10-inch round quiche dish. Spread ice cream in crust. Freeze until firm. Prepare sauce by melting butter in saucepan over medium heat. Add chocolate and stir until melted. Add sugar and continue cooking. Blend in milk and salt; cook, stirring often, for 4 to 5 minutes or until mixture is thickened. Remove from heat and stir in vanilla. Cool for 45 minutes. Pour sauce over ice cream. Refreeze. Let stand at room temperature for a few minutes before cutting. Pie may be garnished with whipped cream, cherries and nuts.

Yield: 12 servings

CHEESECAKE COOKIES

CRUST

⅓	cup firmly-packed brown sugar
1	cup all-purpose flour
½	cup chopped walnuts
⅓	cup butter, melted

FILLING

1	(8 ounce) package cream cheese, softened
¼	cup sugar
1	egg
1	tablespoon lemon juice
2	tablespoons half and half
1	tablespoon vanilla

Combine brown sugar, flour and walnuts. Stir in butter. Reserving 1 cup for topping, press remaining walnut mixture in bottom of 8-inch square baking pan. Bake at 350 degrees for 12 to 15 minutes. Prepare filling by beating cream cheese with sugar until smooth. Add egg, lemon juice, half and half and vanilla; beat well. Pour filling over partially baked crust. Spread reserved topping over filling. Bake at 350 degrees for 25 minutes. Chill overnight before cutting and serving.

Yield: 16 to 20

CHERRY COCONUT BARS

CRUST

1	cup sifted all-purpose flour
½	cup butter (not margarine), softened
3	tablespoons powdered sugar

FILLING

2	eggs, lightly beaten
1	cup sugar
¼	cup all-purpose flour
½	teaspoon baking powder
¼	teaspoon salt
1	teaspoon vanilla
½	cup flaked coconut
½	cup chopped maraschino cherries, drained

Blend flour, butter and sugar with fork or pastry blender. Press dough evenly in bottom of 10x6x1½-inch baking pan. Bake at 350 degrees for about 20 minutes or until lightly browned. Prepare filling by combining eggs, sugar, flour, baking powder, salt, vanilla, coconut and cherries, stirring to mix well. Spread filling over partially baked crust. Bake at 350 degrees for 25 minutes. Cool before cutting into bars.

Yield: 15 to 20

Black and White Bars

Cake

1	cup margarine, softened
2	cups sugar
4	eggs
1½	teaspoons vanilla
2	cups sifted all-purpose flour
½	teaspoon salt
1	cup chopped pecans or nuts
2	(1 ounce) squares unsweetened baking chocolate

Frosting

1	(16 ounce) package powdered sugar
½	cup margarine, softened
¼	cup plus 2 tablespoons cocoa
4 to 5	tablespoons coffee liquid
1	tablespoon almond flavoring

Cream margarine with sugar until smooth; add eggs and vanilla. Stir in flour, salt and nuts. Divide batter in 2 portions. Add chocolate to half of batter and spread in greased 13x9x2-inch baking pan. Spoon remaining batter over chocolate layer. Bake at 350 degrees for 35 to 40 minutes. Prepare frosting by creaming margarine with powdered sugar until smooth. Add cocoa, coffee and flavoring, blending well. Spread frosting on cooled bars.

Yield: 24 to 30

Easy Bake Brownies

1	cup butter, melted
¼	cup cocoa
2	cups sugar
2	eggs
1	teaspoon vanilla
⅛	teaspoon salt
1½	cups all-purpose flour
1	cup broken pecans

Combine ingredients in order listed, stirring with wooden spoon until blended. Spread batter in greased and floured 13x9x2-inch baking pan. Bake at 350 degrees for 30 minutes; do not overbake. Serve with vanilla ice cream and Rich and Easy Chocolate Topping (page 221).

Yield: 12 to 15

Chocolate-Coconut Pecan Bars

½	cup butter
1½	cups graham cracker crumbs
1	(13 ounce) can sweetened condensed milk
1	(6 ounce) package semi-sweet chocolate chips
1	cup chopped pecans
1	(7 ounce) package flaked coconut

Place butter in 13x9x2-inch baking pan; melt in oven at 350 degrees. Press crumbs firmly in butter in bottom of pan. Slowly pour milk evenly over crumb layer. Sprinkle chips, pecans and coconut evenly over milk layer. Bake at 350 degrees for 18 to 20 minutes or until coconut is browned. Chill before cutting into 1½-inch squares. Store in refrigerator.

Yield: 48

CHOCO-CHEWY BUTTERSCOTCH SQUARES

1	cup margarine, softened
1	(16 ounce) package brown sugar
2	eggs
1	tablespoon vanilla
2	cups all-purpose flour
1	teaspoon baking powder
½	teaspoon salt
½	cup chopped nuts
1	(12 ounce) package semi-sweet chocolate chips
1	(13 ounce) can sweetened condensed milk
1	tablespoon margarine

Using electric mixer, cream 1 cup margarine with brown sugar until smooth. Beat in eggs. Sift flour, baking powder and salt together; add to creamed mixture and beat thoroughly. Spread half of dough in greased 15x10x1-inch jelly roll pan. In top of double boiler over simmering water, combine chocolate chips, milk and 1 tablespoon margarine; stir until chips are melted and mixture is smooth. Pour over dough layer in pan; top with remaining dough. Use knife to marble chocolate through dough. Bake at 350 degrees for 30 minutes.

Yield: 36

TOFFEE BARS

CRUST

½	cup butter, softened
1	cup all-purpose flour
½	cup firmly-packed brown sugar

FILLING

2	eggs, beaten
1	cup firmly-packed brown sugar
½	teaspoon vanilla
2	tablespoons all-purpose flour
1	teaspoon baking powder
	Pinch of salt
1	cup shredded coconut
1	cup chopped walnuts or pecans
	Powdered sugar

Cream butter, flour and brown sugar together until smooth. Press dough in bottom of greased 8- or 9-inch square baking pan. Bake at 350 degrees for 10 minutes. Set aside to cool. Prepare filling by combining eggs, brown sugar, vanilla, flour, baking powder and salt; beat thoroughly. Stir in coconut and nuts. Spread filling on partially baked crust. Bake at 350 degrees for 25 minutes. Cut into squares and dust with powdered sugar.

Yield: 30 to 36

WHITE CHOCOLATE CHUNK MACADAMIA COOKIES

1¼   cups all-purpose flour
½   teaspoon baking soda
½   teaspoon salt
½   cup butter or margarine, softened
¼   cup sugar
½   cup firmly-packed brown sugar
1   egg
1   teaspoon vanilla
1   tablespoon water
1   (6 ounce) white chocolate or Swiss confectionery bar, coarsely chopped
1   (7 ounce) jar macadamia nuts, coarsely chopped

Combine flour, baking soda and salt in large electric mixer bowl. Add butter or margarine, sugar, egg, vanilla and water. Using electric mixer at low speed, beat until blended. Stir in chocolate and nuts. Drop level tablespoonfuls of dough about 2 inches apart on ungreased baking sheets; flatten with spatula to form 2-inch circles. Bake at 375 degrees for 10 to 15 minutes or until lightly browned. Cool cookies on wire rack. Store in tightly-covered container.

Yield: 2½ dozen

CHOCOLATE CHIPPERS

1   cup vegetable shortening
1½   cups firmly-packed brown sugar
2   eggs
1   teaspoon vanilla
2½   cups all-purpose flour
1   teaspoon baking soda
1   teaspoon salt
1   (6 ounce) package semi-sweet chocolate chips
4   cups chopped walnuts

Cream shortening with brown sugar until smooth. Add eggs and vanilla; blend thoroughly. Combine flour, soda and salt; add to creamed mixture and mix well. Stir in chocolate chips and nuts. Drop level tablespoonfuls of dough on ungreased baking sheets. Bake at 350 degrees for 10 minutes. Cool cookies on wire rack.

Yield: 5 dozen

CHOCOLATE MINT SNOWFLAKE COOKIES

1½   **cups all-purpose flour**
1½   **teaspoons baking powder**
¼   **teaspoon salt**
1   **(10 ounce) package mint-flavored**
    semisweet chocolate chips, divided
½   **cup plus 2 tablespoons butter, softened**
1   **cup sugar**
1½   **teaspoons vanilla extract**
2   **eggs**
    Powdered sugar

Combine flour, baking powder and salt; set aside. Melt 1 cup mint chocolate chips in top of double boiler over simmering water, stirring until smooth. Cream butter and sugar together until smooth. Add melted chocolate and vanilla. Beat in eggs. Gradually add dry ingredients, mixing thoroughly. Stir in remaining chips. Wrap dough in plastic wrap and freeze until firm. Preheat oven to 350 degrees. Shape dough into 1-inch balls and dust with powdered sugar. Place on ungreased baking sheet. Bake for 10 to 12 minutes or until tops appear cracked. Cool on baking sheets for 5 minutes, then transfer to wire racks.

Yield: 3 dozen

CHOCOLATE-TIPPED BUTTER COOKIES

1   **cup butter or margarine, softened**
½   **cup sifted powdered sugar**
1   **teaspoon vanilla extract**
2   **cups all-purpose flour**
1   **(6 ounce) package semisweet chocolate**
    chips
1   **tablespoon vegetable shortening**
½   **cup finely chopped pecans**

Cream butter and sugar together until light and fluffy. Stir in vanilla. Gradually add flour and mix well. Shape dough into 2½x½-inch sticks. Place on ungreased baking sheet. Using fork tines, flatten ¾ of each cookie lengthwise to ¼-inch thickness. Bake at 350 degrees for 12 to 14 minutes. Cool on wire rack. Combine chocolate chips and shortening in top of double boiler. Bring water to a boil, then reduce heat to low and cook until chocolate is melted, stirring occasionally. Remove from heat, leaving chocolate mixture over hot water. Dip unflattened tips of cookies in chocolate, coating both sides; roll tips in chopped pecans. Cool on wire racks until chocolate is firm. Layer cookies between wax paper sheets in airtight container and store in cool place.

Yield: 4 dozen

Desserts

$250 Chocolate Chip Cookies

2   cups butter, softened
2   cups sugar
2   cups firmly-packed brown sugar
4   eggs
2   teaspoons vanilla
5   cups oatmeal
4   cups all-purpose flour
2   teaspoons baking powder
2   teaspoons baking soda
1   teaspoon salt
2   (12 ounce) packages semi-sweet chocolate chips
1   (8 ounce) chocolate bar, grated
3   cups chopped nuts

Cream butter with sugar. Add eggs and vanilla; mix well. Grind oatmeal in food processor. Combine oatmeal, flour, baking powder, soda and salt; add to creamed mixture. Stir in chocolate chips, grated chocolate and nuts. Roll dough into 1-inch balls and place 2 inches apart on ungreased baking sheet. Bake at 375 degrees for 6 minutes. Cool cookies on wire rack.

Yield: 10 to 12 dozen

Gingersnaps

1½   cups vegetable shortening
2   cups sugar
2   eggs
½   cup molasses
4   cups bread flour
2   teaspoons baking soda
1   teaspoon salt
2   teaspoons ginger
2   teaspoons cinnamon
2   teaspoons ground cloves
  Sugar

Cream shortening with sugar until smooth. Add eggs and molasses; beat thoroughly. Combine flour, baking soda, salt and spices; add to creamed mixture and mix well. Roll dough into 1-inch balls, dip in sugar and place 2 inches apart on ungreased baking sheet. Bake at 350 degrees for 8 to 10 minutes. Cool cookies on wire rack.

Yield: 5 to 6 dozen

LEMON TASSIES

½ cup butter, softened
1 (3 ounce) package cream cheese, softened
1¼ cups all-purpose flour
3 tablespoons fresh lemon juice
3 tablespoons butter, melted
2 eggs
⅔ cup sugar
Whipped cream for garnish

Using electric mixer, cream butter and cream cheese until light and fluffy. Add flour and blend until crumbly. Shape dough into a ball. Preheat oven to 350 degrees. Prepare 1¾-inch muffin pan cups with vegetable cooking spray. Press 1 tablespoon dough into each muffin cup. Combine lemon juice, butter, eggs and sugar; mix thoroughly. Divide filling evenly among dough-lined muffin cups. Bake for 40 to 45 minutes. Remove from pan while slightly warm and cool on wire racks. Garnish with whipped cream.

Yield: 20

PECAN CRISPIES

1 cup butter (or ½ cup butter or margarine and ½ cup vegetable shortening)
2½ cups firmly-packed brown sugar
2 eggs, beaten
2½ cups all-purpose flour
½ teaspoon baking soda
¼ teaspoon salt
1 cup pecans, chopped

Cream butter with sugar until smooth. Add eggs and beat well. Sift flour, soda and salt together; add to creamed mixture and blend thoroughly. Stir in pecans. Drop level tablespoonfuls of dough about 2 inches apart on greased baking sheet. Bake at 350 degrees for 12 to 15 minutes. Cool cookies on wire rack.

Yield: 5 to 6 dozen

Desserts

RASPBERRY SWIRL COOKIES

½	cup butter or margarine, softened
1	cup sugar
1	egg
1	teaspoon vanilla extract
2	cups all-purpose flour
1	teaspoon baking powder
¼	teaspoon salt
½	cup seedless raspberry jam
½	cup flaked coconut
¼	cup finely chopped walnuts

Using electric mixer, cream butter until smooth. Gradually add sugar, beating at medium speed. Add egg and vanilla; beat well. Combine flour, baking powder and salt; add to creamed mixture and beat thoroughly. Shape dough into a ball, wrap in plastic wrap and chill for just 2 hours. Combine jam, coconut and walnuts; set aside. On lightly-floured wax paper, roll dough to form a 12x9-inch rectangle. Spread raspberry filling evenly on dough, leaving ¼-inch margin along edges. Carefully roll dough, jelly roll fashion, starting at a long end and peeling wax paper from dough as it rolls up. Pinch side seam to seal, leaving ends open. Wrap in plastic wrap and chill for 1 hour or until firm. Remove plastic wrap and cut roll into ¼-inch slices. Place 2 inches apart on greased baking sheets. Bake at 375 degrees for 8 to 10 minutes or just until cookies brown around edges. Cool on wire racks.

Yield: 3½ dozen

OLD FASHIONED TEA CAKES

1	cup butter, softened
2	cups sugar
2	eggs
4	cups sifted all-purpose flour
1⅓	tablespoons baking powder
1	teaspoon salt
1	teaspoon vanilla
1	teaspoon lemon flavoring

Cream butter until smooth. Gradually add sugar, beating until light and fluffy. Add eggs and beat thoroughly. Sift flour, baking powder and salt together 3 times; gradually add to creamed mixture and mix well. Stir in flavoring. Chill dough. On lightly-floured surface, roll dough to ⅛-inch thickness, cut with cookie cutters and place on baking sheet. Bake at 400 degrees for 6 to 10 minutes or until lightly browned.

Yield: 5 to 6 dozen

LOTTIE MOON'S TEA CAKES

This tea cake recipe was used by Lottie Moon as she entertained Chinese children with stories about Jesus. The recipe was published in 1872 and last used in 1912.

Three teacups of dry sugar, one of butter, one of sour milk, three pints of flour, three eggs, well beaten, half a teaspoonful of soda, flavor to taste. Roll thin, cut with cookie cutter and bake in a quick oven.

SATIN CHOCOLATE FUDGE

4½   cups sugar
1   (12 ounce) can evaporated milk
¼   cup plus 2 tablespoons butter or margarine
3   (6 ounce) packages semi-sweet chocolate chips
1   (16 ounce) jar marshmallow creme
2   cups broken nuts

Combine sugar, milk and butter or margarine in saucepan; bring to a boil and cook for 6 minutes. Combine chocolate chips, marshmallow cream and nuts in a large bowl. Pour syrup over mixture in bowl and mix thoroughly. Drop by teaspoonfuls on waxed paper. Cool until firm.

Yield: 100

PEANUT BRITTLE

3   cups sugar
1½   cups water
1   cup light corn syrup
3   cups raw peanuts
¼   cup margarine
1   teaspoon vanilla
2   teaspoons baking soda

Combine sugar, water and corn syrup in saucepan; cook, stirring frequently, over medium heat for 30 to 40 minutes or until mixture spins a thread or reaches hard crack register on candy thermometer. Add peanuts and stir until golden brown. Stir in margarine and vanilla; mix well. Add soda and continue to stir until puffy. Pour candy onto greased baking sheets. Cool until firm. Break into pieces.

Yield: 3 pounds

TEXAS PRALINES

3   cups sugar
1   cup buttermilk
1   teaspoon baking soda
1   teaspoon vanilla
1   tablespoon butter or margarine
2 to 2½   cups pecan halves

Combine sugar, buttermilk, soda and vanilla in heavy pan. Cook, stirring constantly, over medium heat until syrup registers 234 degrees on candy thermometer (soft ball stage). Remove from heat. Stir in butter and beat for 2 to 3 minutes or just until mixture begins to thicken. Stir in pecans. Working quickly, drop tablespoonfuls of mixture onto lightly buttered waxed paper. Cool until firm.

Yield: 3 dozen

CHOCOLATE MOUSSE

2   (4 ounce) bars German sweet chocolate
6   eggs, separated
1   cup whipping cream

Shave a small amount of chocolate to use as garnish for individual servings of mousse. Melt remaining chocolate in double boiler over simmering water. Combine melted chocolate with egg yolks, beating with spoon or electric mixer. Using mixer, beat egg whites until stiff. Pour chocolate mixture into egg whites, mixing thoroughly. Spoon into dessert glasses and chill overnight. Whip cream; add dollops to mousse servings and sprinkle with chocolate.

Yield: 6 to 8 servings

Mousse de Coco (Coconut Mousse)

Mousse

2 tablespoons unflavored gelatin
⅓ cup water
6 egg whites
¼ cup plus 2 tablespoons sugar
¾ cup plus 2 tablespoons coconut milk
½ coconut, grated

Baba de Moca (Coconut Syrup)

1⅓ cups sugar
2½ cups water
2 teaspoons butter
6 egg yolks
¾ cup plus 2 tablespoons coconut milk
4 drops vanilla flavoring

Soften gelatin in water; set aside. Beat egg whites, gradually add sugar, coconut milk, gelatin liquid and coconut. Pour into moistened and lightly-oiled mold. Chill until firm. Prepare syrup by combining sugar and water in saucepan. Bring to a boil and cook to thin syrup consistency. Cool. Stir in butter. Strain egg yolks, add to syrup and mix thoroughly. Add coconut milk and vanilla. Mix well and cook to thick syrup consistency. If mixture curdles, strain, blend and reheat. Pour syrup over unmolded mousse.
If using cream of coconut for coconut milk, omit sugar.

Yield: 6 to 8 servings

Chocolate Trifle

1 (18½ ounce) package chocolate cake mix
1 teaspoon instant coffee granules
2 tablespoons warm water
1 (6 ounce) package instant chocolate pudding mix
3 cups milk
3 chocolate-coated toffee candy bars, crushed
1 (9 ounce) container frozen whipped topping, thawed
¼ cup chopped walnuts

Prepare cake mix according to package directions, baking in 13x9x2-inch baking pan. Cool in pan. Remove half of cake and freeze to use later for another trifle. Dissolve coffee in warm water; add to pudding mix with milk and beat well. Let stand until partially firm. Crumble half of cake into 2-quart glass serving bowl, pour half of pudding mixture over cake, sprinkle with half of crushed candy and spread with half of topping; repeat sequence. Garnish with chopped nuts. Chill before serving.

Yield: 8 to 10 servings

Among the Lilies

RASPBERRY BOMBE

MOLD

- 1 (16 ounce) package frozen unsweetened sliced peaches, thawed and drained
- 1 (8 ounce) carton sour cream
- ½ cup grenadine
- ½ gallon vanilla ice cream, softened
  Fresh raspberries for garnish
  Mint sprigs for garnish

SAUCE

- 2 (10 ounce) packages frozen raspberries in syrup, thawed and undrained
- 1 cup light corn syrup
- 2 tablespoons frozen orange juice concentrate, undiluted
- ¼ teaspoon orange extract

Place peaches in food processor bowl; process until smooth. Add sour cream and grenadine and process until well blended. Combine peach mixture and ice cream in large mixing bowl. Using electric mixer, beat at low speed until thoroughly blended. Pour into 11-cup mold prepared with vegetable cooking spray. Freeze, covered, for 8 hours or until firm. Two hours before serving, use tip of knife to loosen edges of ice cream from mold. Invert on chilled serving plate. Wrap a warm towel around mold for 30 seconds, remove towel and, holding mold and plate together, gently shake and lift off mold. Immediately return bombe to freezer. Prepare sauce by placing raspberries in food processor bowl; process for 1 minute or until raspberries are pureed. Strain and discard seeds. Add corn syrup, orange juice concentrate and orange extract to pulp. To serve bombe, cut into slices and top each with ⅓ cup sauce.

Yield: 12 servings

BURNT CREAM

CREAM

- 2 cups whipping cream
- 4 egg yolks
- ½ cup sugar
- 1 tablespoon vanilla

TOPPING

- ¼ cup sugar
- 1 teaspoon brown sugar

Heat cream in saucepan over low heat just until bubbles foam at edge. Combine egg yolks and sugar; beat for about 3 minutes or until thickened. Gradually add warm cream to egg yolk mixture, beating well. Stir in vanilla. Pour into 6 custard cups, place in shallow baking pan with water to ½-inch depth. Bake at 350 degrees for 25 minutes or until firm. Chill for about 2 hours. Prepare topping by combining sugars; sprinkle 2 teaspoons of mixture on each custard. Place on top shelf and broil until topping is medium brown. Chill before serving.

Yield: 6 servings

BREAD PUDDING WITH LEMON SAUCE

PUDDING

3	cups cubed day-old bread or dinner rolls
3	cups hot milk
3	eggs, separated
¾	cup plus 2 tablespoons sugar, divided
1	teaspoon vanilla
¼	teaspoon cardamom
¼	cup thinly sliced pecans

LEMON SAUCE

1	cup sugar
2	cups water, divided
¼	cup lemon juice
2	tablespoons cornstarch
¼	teaspoon salt
¼	cup butter
2	teaspoons grated lemon peel

Place bread cubes in bowl. Pour milk over bread and let stand for 10 minutes. Mix egg yolks, ½ cup sugar, vanilla and cardamom together. Lightly fold egg mixture into bread mixture; do not overmix. Beat egg whites, gradually adding 6 tablespoons sugar and beating until whites are very stiff. Fold egg whites into bread mixture. Pour into greased 13x9x2-inch baking dish. Sprinkle with nuts. Place dish in larger pan with water to ½-inch depth. Bake at 350 degrees for 30 to 40 minutes. Prepare sauce by combining sugar, 1½ cups water and lemon juice in saucepan. Bring to a boil. Dissolve cornstarch and salt in ½ cup water, add to lemon mixture and cook until thickened. Stir in butter and lemon peel. Serve over individual portions of pudding.

Yield: 10 to 12 servings

THAI BIKO

3	cups sweet rice (available in oriental food market)
4½	cups water
2	(14 ounce) cans coconut milk
1½	cups firmly-packed dark brown sugar
1	teaspoon ground ginger (optional) Juice and minced peel of 1 lemon or lime

Cook rice in water in rice cooker or heavy saucepan until tender. In separate pan, bring coconut milk to a boil and cook, stirring constantly, until volume is reduced by two-thirds. Add brown sugar, ginger, fruit juice and peel; cook over medium heat, stirring constantly, for about 10 minutes or until consistency of syrup. Add rice and mix well. Serve cooled but not chilled with fresh fruit.

Yield: 10 servings

DATE PUDDING

1½	cups firmly-packed light brown sugar, divided
1	cup water
1	tablespoon butter
1	cup all-purpose flour
2	teaspoons baking powder
¼	teaspoon salt
½	cup milk
½	cup walnut pieces
1	cup chopped dates
1	(9 ounce) carton frozen whipped topping, thawed

Combine 1 cup brown sugar and water in small saucepan; cook over medium heat, stirring often, until sugar is dissolved; simmer for 3 minutes. Remove from heat, stir in butter and pour into greased 13x9x3-inch baking dish. Sift flour, baking powder and salt together. Add milk and ½ cup brown sugar, stirring until smooth. Fold in dates and walnuts. Pour batter over syrup in pan. Bake at 350 degrees for 35 to 40 minutes. Cool to room temperature. Alternately layer pudding and whipped topping in large serving bowl, using rounded teaspoonfuls of pudding and ending with whipped topping. Chill for 1 hour before serving.

Yield: 8 servings

PAVLOVA

6	egg whites, at room temperature
1¾	cups plus 2 tablespoons sugar
2	tablespoons white wine vinegar
	Whipped cream
	Strawberries, kiwi or passionfruit slices for garnish

Smoothly line pizza pan or baking sheet with aluminum foil. Preheat oven to 250 degrees. Beat egg whites until fluffy. Gradually add 1½ cups sugar, beating until thick and sugar is dissolved. Add ¼ cup plus 2 tablespoons sugar and beat for 3 to 4 minutes. Add vinegar and beat thoroughly. Using spatula, spread egg white mixture onto foil and smooth into circular shape 1½ to 2 inches high; pat to remove air bubbles. Bake for 1½ hours. Cool. Invert on serving platter. Spread with whipped cream and decorate with fruit.

Yield: 6 to 8 servings

HEAVENLY TRIFLE

1	angel food cake, cut in cubes
½	cup canned peach slices, drained
1	(8 ounce) can mandarin oranges, drained
1	(22 ounce) can cherry pie filling
2	bananas, sliced
1	cup blueberries
1	(5 ⅝ ounce) package vanilla instant pudding mix
1	cup sliced strawberries
1	(12 ounce) carton frozen whipped topping, thawed

Place ⅓ of cake cubes in bottom of very large glass serving bowl. In sequence, layer ½ of peaches, ½ of oranges, cherry pie filling, remaining peaches, remaining oranges, ⅓ of cake cubes, bananas, blueberries, pudding, remaining cake cubes and strawberries. Spread whipped topping over strawberries.

Yield: 16 servings

SOUTH GEORGIA PEACH ICE CREAM

4	eggs
2½	cups sugar, divided
	Pinch of salt
2	teaspoons almond flavoring
4	cups hot (not boiling) milk
4	cups mashed ripe peaches
	Juice of ½ lemon
2	cups whipping cream

Beat eggs. Gradually add 1 cup sugar, beating well. Blend in salt and flavoring. Pour egg mixture into hot milk in top of double boiler. Cook over low heat, stirring, until custard is thickened. Set aside to cool. Combine peaches and 1½ cups sugar (adjust sugar amount if peaches are very sweet). Stir in lemon juice. Add peaches to cooled custard. Add cream, stirring to blend thoroughly. Pour mixture into ice cream freezer and process according to freezer directions.

Yield: 3 quarts

PINEAPPLE MINT SHERBET

½   gallon vanilla ice cream
½   gallon pineapple sherbet
1   (12 ounce) carton frozen whipped topping, thawed
½   cup plus 2 tablespooons creme de menthe syrup
      Toasted coconut
      Chopped pecans
      Mint sprigs

Combine ice cream, sherbet, topping and syrup; blend until smooth. Freeze until firm. Using scoop, shape into balls and roll in coconut or pecans. Place on baking sheet and freeze. Garnish individual servings with mint sprig.

Yield: 36 2-inch balls

BUTTER PECAN ICE CREAM

2   cups pecans, coarsely chopped
3   tablespoons butter
4   eggs
2   cups sugar
½   teaspoon salt
5   cups milk, heated
1⅔   tablespoons vanilla
4   cups whipping cream, icy cold

Sauté pecans in butter. Set aside to cool. Beat eggs and sugar well. Add salt. Stir egg mixture into hot milk in saucepan. Simmer, stirring constantly, until thickened. Pour mixture into ice cream churn. Add vanilla and whipping cream. Churn for 25 minutes. Add pecans to ice cream in churn. Continue churning until firm. Place churn in freezer for 2 to 3 hours before serving to improve texture of ice cream.

Yield: 3 quarts

Desserts

PUMPKIN ICE

1 (16 ounce) can plain pumpkin
½ cup firmly-packed brown sugar
Dash of salt
¼ teaspoon cinnamon
¼ teaspoon nutmeg
¼ teaspoon ginger
1 quart vanilla ice cream, softened
1 (9 inch) gingersnap crust

Combine pumpkin, brown sugar, salt and spices; beat well. Add to ice cream and blend thoroughly. Spread ice cream in crust. Freeze until firm.

Yield: 6 servings

FRESH PEACH DELIGHT

CRUST
1 cup all-purpose flour
½ cup melted margarine
1 tablespoon sugar
½ cup chopped nuts

FILLING
1 cup powdered sugar
1 (8 ounce) package cream cheese, softened
1 cup whipped topping

TOPPING
3 large peaches, sliced
1 teaspoon lemon juice
1 cup sugar
1 cup water
¼ cup self-rising flour
¼ cup peach gelatin

Combine flour, margarine, sugar and nuts, mixing well. Spread mixture in 13x9x2-inch baking dish to form crust. Bake at 350 degrees until lightly browned. Set aside to cool. Prepare filling by mixing powdered sugar and cream cheese together, beating until fluffy. Add whipped topping. Spread filling on cooled crust. Prepare topping by sprinkling peaches with lemon juice; set aside. Combine sugar, water, flour and gelatin in saucepan; cook until thickened. Stir in peaches. Cool peach mixture before spreading on cream filling.

Yield: 12 to 16 servings

PEACH COBBLER

1	stick prepared pie crust pastry
7	large Georgia peaches, peeled and sliced
⅓	cup sugar
½	lemon
1	tablespoon all-purpose flour
1	tablespoon cornstarch
⅓	cup water
1	tablespoon butter
3	tablespoons brown sugar

Reserving 1 tablespoon pastry, prepare crust mix according to package directions and roll into rectangle shape; set aside. Place peaches in 2½-quart casserole. Sprinkle with sugar. Cut 3 thin slices from lemon and arrange on peaches; squeeze juice from remaining lemon portion over peaches. Combine flour, cornstarch and water; pour over peaches. Cut pastry in 1-inch strips and arrange on peaches in lattice pattern. Place thin slices of butter on pastry. Using fork, mix reserved pastry with brown sugar until crumbly; sprinkle over pastry on peaches. Bake at 375 degrees for 45 minutes.

Yield: 8 servings

STRAWBERRIES DIPPED IN WHITE CHOCOLATE

2	pints fresh strawberries
1	(6 ounce) package white chocolate or white-chocolate-flavored baking bar, grated

Blot strawberries on paper towels to remove all moisture; chocolate will not stick to wet berries. Melt chocolate in top of double boiler over simmering hot water, stirring until smooth. Grasp each berry by stem and dip into melted chocolate. Place on wire rack sprayed with vegetable cooking spray. Chill until firm. Serve dipped berries within 8 hours.
Semi-sweet chocolate may be substituted for white chocolate or a combination of white and dark chocolate may be used. For large parties, increase strawberry and chocolate amounts, melt chocolate and place in chafing dish to allow guests to dip own berries.

Yield: 3 to 4 dozen

PRALINE SAUCE

1	cup light corn syrup
½	cup sugar
⅓	cup butter or margarine
1	egg, beaten
1	tablespoon vanilla
1	cup chopped pecans

Combine syrup, sugar, butter or margarine in heavy saucepan; mix well. Bring to a boil over medium heat, stirring constantly; boil for 2 minutes without stirring. Remove from heat and stir in vanilla and pecans. Serve warm or at room temperature over ice cream.

Yield: 2 cups

RICH AND EASY CHOCOLATE TOPPING

⅓	cup cocoa
1	cup sugar
¾	cup evaporated milk
¼	cup butter or margarine
⅛	teaspoon salt
½	teaspoon vanilla

Combine cocoa and sugar in small saucepan; blend in milk. Add butter and salt. Cook, stirring constantly, until mixture begins to boil. Remove from heat and stir in vanilla. Serve warm over Easy Bake Brownies, ice cream or other desserts.

Yield: 2 cups

HOT FUDGE SAUCE

¼	cup light corn syrup
1	(5 ounce) can evaporated milk
	Dash of salt
1	(6 ounce) package semi-sweet chocolate chips
1	teaspoon vanilla

Combine syrup, milk and salt in microwave-safe bowl; microwave just until ready to boil. Stir in chocolate chips and whisk until blended. Add vanilla and blend. Serve over ice cream or other desserts.

Yield: 1½ cups

HE STEADFAST OF MIND

THOU WILT KEEP IN PERFECT

PEACE, BECAUSE HE TRUSTS IN THEE.

Isaiah 26:3

Among the Lilies

ACKNOWLEDGEMENTS

We gratefully acknowledge our indebtedness to our pastor and friend, Dr. Charles Frazier Stanley, who continually feeds us spiritually from the abundant overflow of his prayerful walk with our Lord. This commitment to prayer and teaching Truth from the living Word has greatly enriched and benefited the lives of all the First Baptist family.

We are also indebted to him for his skilled photography which so enhances each section. We are grateful to serve with an under-shepherd whose vision encompasses the whole world.

Women in Missions

The cookbook committee wishes to thank the numerous testers, proof-readers, typists and advisors who made special contributions with their time and talents. You thought you were doing it for us, but you were doing it for Him.

Julie Arnold	Laurie Crowell	Bobbie Shellnut
Karen Bryan	Vernetti Currin	Andrea Shupert
Carolyn Butler	Kristi Grace	Margie Sidey
Gloria Cagle	Jere Leavell	Barbara Sixsmith
Gwen Cobb	Robb McClure	Carol Williams
Diane Collier	Barbara Mitchell	Martha Williams
Carol Cottrell	Dennis Mock	Bee Wolter
Ann Crosby	Pat Mock	

Acknowledgements

We also want to thank the many people who shared their favorite recipes.

KeLinde Abolarin
Sara Adkerson Alcides
Jacqueline Alford
Laurie Alford
Jean Allgood
Don Almand
Ron Amerson
Patricia Anderson
Marilyn Andrews
Pat Arnold
Clarita F. Asibal
Ruth Askew
Mary Lynn Atherton
Roberta Attaway
Cathy Bailey
Farieda Barghout
Bob Barnard
Jane Barnard
Casey Barr
Jane Bateman
Larry Bateman
Melody Baumgardner
Jerry Beal
Shelby Beal
Charlene S. Bell
Robert E. Bell
Barbara Bennett
Bob Bennett
Frank Bennett
Ruth Bennett
Carmen Blackburn
Norma Blake
Eiizabeth Boggs
Joe Boggs
Beth Bond
Gina Booth
Elizabeth Bottoms

Linda Boyd
Julie Braddy
Bill Brannon
John Brannon
Herb Braselton
Leslie Brautigam
Sandra Breaden
Diane Brennan
John Brennan
Danny Brett
Ben Brewer
Larry Brewer
Sheila J. Brooks
Betty C. Brown
Diana Brown
Jerry C. Brown
Don Brundage
Kathy Brundage
Karen Bryan
Betty Bryant
Bob Bryant
Millie Bryant
Wylene Buchanan
Gerry Bullard
Joyce Burklin
Blondine Burrell
Earl Bush
Bob Butler
Carolyn Butler
Sandra Byars
Bernice Byrd
Bill Byrd
Carolyn L. Cameron
Jenni Camp
Sara Inez Campbell
Bernadine Cantrell
Carolyn Carter

Anne Chalvet
Christy Chamblee
David Chamblee
Julia Chamblee
Rebecca Lynn Chandler
Maurice Chron
Susan Clamon
Karen Clarke
Martha Clem
Bob Cobb
Gwen Cobb
Joe Cobb
Rick Cobb
Ruth Cobb
Kimberly Collins
Jane M. Cook
Evelyn Cooper
Kathy Corley
Cheryl Cottingham
Opal Cotton
Carol Cottrell
Stan Cottrell
Ruth Cox
Charlotte C. Cozens
Bobby Cranford
Ann Crosby
Lanier Crowe
Dick Csehy
Sherri Csehy
Terry Currin
Vernetti Currin
Betty Dasher
E. Guy Dasher
Kathy David
Gail Davidson
Ethel L. Davis
Beverly Day

Robert Deadwyler
Bob Dean
Paul Diamond
Ed Dilbeck
Eva Dilbeck
Margaret Dobbs
Virginia Downes
Beverly L. Dreier
John D. Dreier
Joyce Duckett
Chick Durrett-Smith
Carol Dyer
Nancy Dyer
Terrell Dyes
Betsy Eager
Angie Elkins
Michelle Ellinas
M. A. Ellis
Donna G. Epp
Marvin Epp
Ethel Evans
Bill Evert
Mary Martha Farneman
Mary Dee Farrow
Judy Fenlason
Beverly Fetner
Vicki B. Finney
Alma D. Fischman
Joan Fisher
Ruth Fisher
Mrs. Harold Foster
Hortense Fowler
Kay Fox
Melinda Fox
Andrew Frahler
Claire Frahler
June Franklin

Among the Lilies

Margaret Friesen
Bill Frisby
Lisa Frisby
Charles Germany
Sandra Germany
Sherry Gettmann
Exie Gibbs
Martha Jeane Giglio
Liza Gilbert
Sue Gilmore
Kathleen Gladfelter
Helen Gleason
Janet Glover
Gary Golden
Helen Granette
Mary Nell Graves
Betty C. Green
Mary Ann Green
Ted Hagstrom
Barbara Hall
Rebecca Stanley Hall
Sheila J. Hall
Doris Hallmon
Starla Halvorson
Harry H. Hamilton
David S. Hansen
Jack Hardy
Anne Harper
Betty Harper
Barbara Harris
Margaret Harrison
Rhonda Hatley
Ethel Mae Havird
Anne Hayes
Margaret Hewitt
Mary Alice Hill
Gwen Hixon
Rufus Hixon
Charlaine Holcombe
Lucy Holliday

Rea Holliday
Ralph Hollingsworth
Ruby Hollingsworth
Cleo Holme
Suzanne Hoover
Jan Horne
Don Keith Howard
Hugh Howard
Libby Howard
Caryl A. Huffstetler
Cleo R. Hulme
Janice Anne Hurd
Sandy Hutchinson
Martha Inman
Brenda Jackson
Carter L. Jacoby
Bill James
Kelly Jenkins
Noel Jenkins
Lois Jenks
Ann Johnson
Nelladine Johnson
Phyllis Johnson
Sandra Johnson
Sandy Johnson
Evie Jones
Martha Jones
Robert H. Jones
Lane Jordan
Peter Kakadelis
Tom Kakadelis
Cindy Kaye
Gene Ketchem
Irene Kiblinger
John Kieffer
Becky Kimsey
Jackie Kimsey
Faye B. Kinard
Judy B. Kitchens
Billy Kite

Josh Kite
Joe Kordys
June Kordys
Jeanine Kott
Pamela Jo Kuester
Debbie Ladd
Margie Land
Joy Lanford
Connie LeHeup
Mary C. Lemon
Eleanor Lewis
Randy Lewis
Dorothy Little
Lossie Lively
Mariella P. Long
Al Lubbers
Alice Lubbers
Susan Ludwick
Elizabeth C. Lundy
Vicki Mabry
Connie Mackey
Marie Maddox
Irene Manacop
Lois Martin
Norma Martin
Ray Martin
Virginia Martin
June Matthie
Alicia McCall
Celeste McCall
Ron McCall
Perry McCarty
Lillian McCaughan
Jane McCauley
Jan McCollum
Margie McCollum
Annelle McCool
A. Milton McCool
Sue McCombs
Regina McGrow

Lauren Reed McGuire
Mary McKinley
Amy McNair
Jackie Meeks
Cham Meredith
Era Middleton
Marjorie R. Mills
Barbara Mitchell
Pat Mock
Angelon B. Montgomery
Laurie Moore
Penny Moore
Jackie Morgan
Jeanette Morgan
Shelby Mosier
Linda Muma
Hilda E. Muncy
Sonia Murphy
Anne Myers
Una Myers
Dennis Namirr
George O. Neal
Dudley Nesmith
Susan Newby
Mrs. Flynt Nobles
Dorothy North
Bonnie Nutt
Warren Nutt
Ed Nutting
Forrest Nutting
Sandra Oakley
Douglas Olive
Nathan Olive
George O'Neal
Diane Osborne
Jeff Osborne
Lucille Ostrom
Dale H. Pace
Karen Sue Parman
Gail Parsons

Acknowledgements

Jane Hamilton Patton
Leslie Patton
Carole Pearson
Lorraine Pederson
Mannie Lou Peppers
Diane Perdue
Rebecca Pilgrim
Alice Pitchford
Betsy Pittman
Rosemary Poole
Judy Pocoroba
Donna Powell
Fred Powell
Charles Preston
Evelyn Price
Frances Price
Keith Price
Pattie Prichard
Gwyneth Puckett
Hazel Puckett
Ronnie Puckett
Sidney Puckett
Randy Purcell
Sandra Purdom
Betty Queen
Barbara Quigley
Donna Rasmussen
Dot Rast
Eileen Rawlin
Jackie Reed
Violet E. Reimann
Loraine Rhea
Nancy Rhea
Pat Rhea
Stacey Rider
Patty Rigdon
Joanne Roberson
Judy Rodgers
Karen Rogeberg
Dorothy Ross

Barbara Royster
Kay H. Ruck
Myrtle Salters
Gerrie Saxon
Nancy Schaefer
Ann Schonberg
Carole Schroeder
Lawson Schroeder
Barbara Seithel
Sherry Shedd
Penny Sheppard
Minda Shimamura
Edith F. Shipley
V. Jay Shropshire
Andy Sixsmith
Barbara Sixsmith
Faye Sklar
Inez Smeeks
Diane Smith
Harriett Smith
Isabelle C. Smith
Joy Smith
Keith Smith
Linda Smith
Rick Smith
Stephen Smith
Susan B. Smith
Wendy Smith
Gene Smoak
Susan Smoak
Claire Snyder
Bonnie Solid
Edith Spears
Anna Stanley
Dr. Charles Stanley
Nancy Steinman
June B. Stevens
Catherine Stevenson
Hugh Stevenson
Mary Jane Stewart

Dottie Stiles
Jack Stiles
Gladys Stowers
John Stratton
Cindy Strickland
Gayle Strickland
Shirley Strickland
Marcia Stuber
Paul Stuber
Janice Sweat
Helen Tatum
Linda Taylor
Lynn Taylor
Marion Thornton
Alice Todoruk
Anne Trippe
Eddie Tucker
Vickie Tucker
Carolyn Tumlin
Peggy Turner
Scott Turner
Susan Turner
Cheryl Turnipseed
Kathy Umberger
Martha Underwood
Vernon Underwood
Ellen Varnum
Leanna Vaughn
Jerry Verkatesh
Mary Ann Vinson
Helen Wade
Polly Walden
Paul Walker
Sandra Walker
Audrey B. Walsh
Kathleen C. Walton
Lynn A. Warren
Bill Webb
Cheryl Webb
Peggy Webb

Lee Webster
Lewis Weeks
Louise Weimer
Linda S. Weiss
Bob Weldon
Liz Welsh
Patricia Werst
Frances M. White
James White
Linda White
Trudy Cathy White
Yvonne White
Al Whittinghill
Mary M. Whittinghill
Carol Williams
Dwight L. Williams
Roger Williams
Sandy Williams
Ginny Williamson
Connie Elaine Wills
Cathy Wilson
Lois M. Wilson
E.L. Wingard
Tom Woodward
Wanda Wray
Gloria Wurst
Rosemary Youmans
Angie Young
Connie Younger
Lisa Younger

Index

Index

Index

Index

Index